ALL THAT'S LEFT BEHIND

ALL THAT'S LEFT BEHIND

CaraMia Alberga

NEW DEGREE PRESS

COPYRIGHT © 2021 CARAMIA ALBERGA

ALL THAT'S LEFT BEHIND

ISBN

978-1-63676-477-1 *Paperback*
978-1-63730-378-8 *Kindle Ebook*
978-1-63730-377-1 *Digital Ebook*

To my forever sister.

CONTENTS

"Grief, I've learned, is really just love. It's all the love you want to give, but cannot. All that unspent love gathers up in the corners of your eyes, the lump in your throat, and in that hollow part of your chest. Grief is just love with no place to go."

—JAMIE ANDERSON

PREFACE

Dear Readers,

2020 was a significant year. During that time, I gained an understanding of grief and loss that I never had before. Through the COVID-19 outbreak, I could see loss all around me, in how many lives it touched and the kinds of losses we experienced. I saw peers drop out of college, friends lose their jobs, families lose their connection, and millions of people lose their lives.

Yet, despite the horrendous events around us, life went on.

We were expected to take care of our families, go to work and school, hop out of bed every day and perform business-as-usual, all while trying to quiet the anxious beating of our hearts. All of a sudden, and all at once, millions of people understood what it meant to have interrupted grief.

Interrupted grief is something I recognized a year prior to the pandemic. That's the year my sister died. Just as suddenly and unexpectedly as she passed, I went back to my normal life. I did not give myself a single day away from school or work to grieve. Looking back, that was the worst thing I could have done. The single loss soon brought a wave of others. Like dominoes, the pillars of my life fell one after another. My family, identity, routine, and health all suffered. These were the disenfranchised losses—the ones I didn't know I should grieve. I felt isolated, running from the memories I tried to avoid and pain I refused to acknowledge. Soon my emotional isolation became physical, as lockdown and quarantine ensued.

The time in lockdown provided an unexpected blessing. It forced me to sit with my grief and acknowledge it. Confined by four walls with nowhere to run, I slowly found my way to acceptance and hope. As I witnessed so many people suffering, I felt a responsibility to use my experiences to help others struggling with grief. I knew what it meant to experience loss while feeling separate from the rest of the world. I knew the damage complicated grief could cause, and its inevitability when losses, big or small, are ignored.

I learned this not only through my experiences, but also through the experiences of others and my studies in psychology. During that time, I gained an abundance of information on theories, tools, and processes related to both grief and resilience. I saw my life reflected in textbooks, and for me, to acknowledge and understand is to begin the healing process. However, scientific articles only go so far to explain a process that doesn't obey the laws of time, logic, or reason. Thus, I struggled to find a vehicle to show these concepts. Until I remembered my great love of literature. Growing up reading Frances Hodgson Burnett and Katherine Paterson, I found no better understanding of the world around me than through the eyes of *The Secret Garden's* beloved heroine Mary Lennox, or *Bridge to Terabithia's* Jesse Aarons. So, I built my protagonist Emma, a twenty-year-old girl burdened by losses that seemed too overwhelming to bear.

Emma's story represents those who are enveloped in grief and follows a journey of transformation as she grows stronger through connection and acceptance of life's uncontrollable nature. Through her, I show the many layers of grief. Thus, I seek to dispel the misconception that the only loss worth grieving is the loss of a person—loss is much more complex than that.

Grief is a lifelong process, and this is the story of Emma finding the beginning of hers. Like many others, Emma learned to fear the journey of grieving. The inner turmoil of avoiding the inevitable permeated all aspects of her life. What she had yet to realize, however, is that grieving is an act of love.

With that, I offer Emma's story to anyone who has experienced a loss of any kind. This is for anyone in the grieving process, or for those who want to help someone through their grief. Emma has taught me so much about appreciating life's uncontrollable moments. I hope others may find comfort and solace when relating to a shared experience. So that in their grief, nobody ever feels left behind.

Yours truly,
CaraMia Alberga

PROLOGUE

On a cold winter day in December, two letters rested side by side on a mahogany desk. One held a question, the other, an answer. A single blue paper sat on the left side. The letter softened at the edges where hands had gripped the paper. Ink blotched where teardrops had landed. The letter on the right was crisp and white as snow. Layered in a pile, the white pages rested in a thick stack, waiting to be encased in an envelope. The words bled with fresh ink, which had been penned over and over again in search of the combination that would make them easier to hear. But the truth was never easy.

It took me a long time to write these words, and this may not be easy to read. I understand the ache in your heart more than you know, and I hope this story brings you comfort. I have asked all the same questions that burden you; maybe this will give you some answers. Most of all, I want you to know that you are not alone in your grief. The journey forward was a long one for all of us. Mine started at a cemetery in the woods one year ago on a blustery day, not unlike the one during which I currently write. I only ask that you read with an open heart and remember the strength that I know already exists within you.

PART ONE

ONE

On December twelfth, I became an only child. Now I stood in the dense snow, shivering while it soaked through my stockings and black formal shoes. As the cold seeped up my ankles, a chill shot through my body. I hugged myself tighter and curled my shoulders to shield myself from the stinging wind. Snowflakes fell from the milky sky to form a blanket on top of the sprawling pine tree forest. Small ice crystals swirled between the trees, carried by howling winds that collided in a small clearing.

A group of twenty people dressed in black scattered across the white plain like an unkindness of ravens that flocked among the icy shroud. Some held umbrellas, grasping at their handles as the merciless gale tugged them. Mama and I stood at the center of the clearing, near the edge of a gaping hole in the ground. The wind picked up, and the force of it drew the air out of my lungs. I looked around. Did anyone else struggle to breathe? The others stood farther away, covered by a veil of falling snow that only revealed their dark figures. I tried to recall their identities, but I had met most of them only once as a young child, over fifteen years ago. After today, I doubted we would meet again. I only recognized Mama, Nana, and Uncle Al's family.

Uncle Al stood a pace behind Mama and me, his broad frame as still and unwavering as the tall pine trees that surrounded us. Snow landed on his black, swooping hair and on the shoulders of his fine wool coat. Compared to Mama's ashen face, his glowing olive complexion made him appear a decade younger than her, despite being five years older. Only the speckles of gray along his chin and brow gave any hints to the age gap between them. He focused past our small circle and out into the stark white horizon. His eyes reflected our surroundings with a distinct shade of forest green that he had inherited from Nana.

Nana stood near Uncle Al's side, her small, frail body childlike in comparison. She wore a solemn expression that twisted her round face. Uncle Al held her wool-clad arm at the elbow, ensuring she would not wander away. She peered up at him, her attention shifting between the snow pooling around her feet and his face. He didn't turn to meet her gaze.

Meanwhile, Uncle Al's wife, Aunt Maeve, hunched over her phone, mumbling about poor reception, while my four dark-haired cousins bickered among themselves. In their boredom, the younger two colluded against their elder siblings by launching snowballs, prompting a harsh scolding.

I turned forward and fastened my scarf around my neck and mouth to contain the violent chattering of my teeth. Numbness crept up my legs, and the wind squeezed my lungs. Was I the only one affected by the storm? Mild impatience played beneath stoic faces, but the guests remained out of obligation or perhaps even intrigue. I had more reason than anyone to be here, but I couldn't stand against the blustering storm for much longer. Could no one else feel it? Every limb, muscle, and finger shook with such ferocity that I could only stay upright by leaning against Mama's shoulder. Maybe the cold was within me, something inching its way toward my heart. What would happen when it reached its target? Would it envelop me like a poison? Or would it callous around my heart and simply stop it from beating?

Mama grabbed my wrist after failing to pry my rigid fist. She leaned over and whispered, "The funeral director should be here soon." She wore a tired expression. The darkness under her puffy brown eyes was exaggerated by the black wool she wore and the hollowness of her high cheekbones. As her eyes watered, the permanent crease between her brows deepened. Her thin lips spread a tight line that dared to betray her resolve with the smallest quiver. Then she scooted closer and tilted the umbrella to shield me from the wind. As I continued to shiver, Mama pulled on my scarf, tightening it around my neck until its wool fibers scratched my skin. Mama's overbearing nature didn't bother me as much now. I couldn't imagine the past few weeks without her.

Headlights shone through the trees, followed by the low rumble of a large truck. Slowing to a crawl, the truck approached our group while maneuvering between tombstones and statues. More than one person exhaled a breath of relief as the truck halted and parked in-line with the carved plot. The funeral director emerged wearing a suit and black overcoat, followed by a middle-aged man wearing a yellow construction vest. The men moved quickly to the back of the truck. The vested man opened the back doors and pulled out a thick set of chains. He strained to climb up the truck and attach the chains to the pulley device protruding from the back.

Feet shuffled, and people mumbled, but everything was drowned out by the cacophony of mechanical beeping and clanking of chains as the casket raised above the back of the truck. I winced as the noise bombarded my eardrums. Mama and I took a few steps back as the dark oak casket approached the rectangular opening. Then, the vested man maneuvered the casket above the hole like a puzzle piece. For a moment, it hovered over the earth. The clearing filled with silence.

I held my breath and listened as my heart beat in my ears, like steps chasing down pavement. The casket shook as the loud beeping resumed. At a crawling pace, it lowered into the hole. I froze and then turned to Mama, whose shoulders shuttered as she wept. I grabbed onto Mama's arm with both hands. I wanted to shake her from her inconsolable, howling cries. I couldn't even find the words to protest. This is a horrible mistake, I wanted to say. My breaths grew quick and shallow as the casket began to disappear beneath the white blanket. Somebody had this all wrong. I couldn't make the pieces of information fit together, the reality I knew was stubborn, and remained intractable. My name was Emma Leone, I was twenty years old. I went to college, I lived with Mama and Nana in the outskirts of Chicago, I had hopes and dreams, I had a sister—

A sickening feeling overtook me. My reality crumbled, as if the ground dissolved beneath my feet. This couldn't be happening. Panicked thoughts spilled out into a quiet murmur, drowned out by Mama's violent sobbing.

"Someone has to do something. This is wrong. My sister is supposed to be in Texas. She has to be there in Texas with her dog and her boyfriend. She can't be dead. This is all wrong. This can't be true." My whispered words tumbled out, too quiet to be heard. I wanted to scream, to yell the words at the vested man and at Mama, but I couldn't.

Because it wasn't a lie.

My sister lay in that casket at only twenty-seven years old. The ceremony was closed casket so people couldn't see the marks on her body sustained from the injuries and autopsy. Since I never saw my sister in that casket, I hoped it was empty, and Grace was away somewhere in Texas floating through life as she always had.

I held on to that hope with every breath, until the wooden frame collided with the ground somewhere deep in the earth, and a final thud resounded beneath our feet. Then I realized it was not a mistake. Among the ice-covered trees and blistering wind, surrounded by strangers and the punishing sound of grinding chains, this was it.

This was how we said goodbye?

Tears escaped as I realized the vested man would not halt and apologize. I wished he would say, "Sorry, it appears we've got the wrong family. You can all go home, folks."

It wasn't a practical joke. I wasn't in a play, acting out someone's life. This was my life now. And I couldn't help but think that something had gone terribly wrong.

• • •

We returned to the funeral home parlor for a brief reception that slowly wound down to a close. Mama and I stood near the door as we waited for the guests to trickle out. I wanted nothing more than to go home and curl up in my pajamas, but I needed to hold myself together for a while longer. At least I didn't have to make conversation with the guests like Mama did. She thanked our distant family members as they left, accepting their condolences on behalf of us both. Some looked over her shoulder to where I stayed a few paces behind her. They shifted their gazes back and forth, contemplating if they should say something to me as well. I felt their eyes peer at me as they perused my burning face for a beat too long.

I dreaded that moment as I bolstered myself with a forced smile. I knew they judged how well I held together, how close I was to breaking, if it would be safer to ignore me. A few offered sympathetic smiles, but no one said anything. What was there to say? I was relieved they didn't ask. I was used to being put together and in control. I didn't need a spotlight as my life fell apart.

The small, dimly lit room began to empty as most guests offered Mama a hug or a handshake, leaving without lingering. Except for one man who approached Mama and stayed talking with her for a quarter of an hour. He spoke in a low voice, but I had heard enough of the conversation to learn they were cousins. Like most of the people here, I had never met him before.

"I wish I had kept in touch more often, maybe there's something I could've done. I—I just can't believe it," he said.

Mama patted his arm. "There's nothing anyone could have done, Carlo."

His shoulders slumped while Mama offered reassurances, as she had done for the guests all evening. Between comforting the guests and fielding questions, I wondered how she remained calm and collected. From the moment I stepped foot in the funeral home parlor, every muscle in my body tensed, my breaths became shallow, and I told myself: Hang on for five more minutes…and now five more.

"I still remember when Grace was this big." Carlo motioned his arms as if cradling a baby. "She was so small, but still had all that red hair." He gave a flicker of a smile before shaking his head.

Mama smiled at the memory, but her eyes filled with tears. She cleared her throat before changing the subject. "I can't believe it's been over ten years since we've seen each other."

He stood up straighter, seeming to snap out of his grief. "Yes, it's been too long. And I'm sorry to see you under these terrible circumstances. Please let me know if you or your family need anything," he said, nodding toward me.

I looked down—unable to tolerate any more sympathy. I could deal with empty condolences. But this man was kind, and his watering eyes brought tears to my own. His kindness reminded me that all the people here didn't just gather for an ostentatious display of family obligation. Something terrible had happened, and it happened to my sister. That's why I froze there, standing in my black, itchy wool dress with soaking wet shoes, holding back tears in a strange place filled with strange people who stared at me like a zoo animal and patted me like a child. At least with this man I wouldn't have to fear him asking the dreaded question—he was far too polite.

The dreaded question, just two words: "What happened?" Mostly everyone uttered the words like a reflex—they couldn't help it. People are curious by nature, and when you say that someone has passed away, they would always have to ask, as if knowing the cause would somehow make it okay.

A few days before the funeral, Mama and I had rehearsed our story of how we were going to answer, but I always hoped I wouldn't have to repeat it. For Mama, it was inevitable. It started with at least five phone calls a day. Mama told the immediate family first, and once Aunt Maeve knew, it was only a matter of time before everyone else found out, too.

Eventually, Mama had enough. She stopped answering the phone calls, but then the constant ringing became unbearable. When the phone rang a sixth time, she leaped off the couch and ripped the phone cord right out of the wall, and stood there, staring at it, as if it had shocked her. We prepared stories to tell family, friends, and strangers—such as the blond woman who now strode toward us in tall, stiletto heels.

A cool draft blew in as Carlo gave Mama a hug, said his goodbyes, and walked out the door. I steeled myself as the woman approached to take his place. With her towering height and fair hair, she could only be related to us through marriage. She placed her hand on Mama's shoulder, and her hot pink nails grazed Mama's black, faded cardigan.

Mama straightened at the contact and turned her head up to meet the blond woman's heavily lined eyes.

"Gina, I'm so sorry, honey. I can't imagine what you're going through. It was all so sudden, too." The woman shook her head in disbelief. "I never heard what happened." The sentence hung in the air while I hoped for someone to intervene. To my disappointment, the only person within hearing range was Aunt Maeve, and I knew she had been waiting all day for someone to ask us that question.

Aunt Maeve's head turned, attention piqued, and she walked toward us, dragging her four children along. Thus far, she had refrained from asking us herself, but she didn't pass up the opportunity to hear Mama's answer. She greeted the blond woman with a smile and a one-armed hug. It made sense they were friends. They shared a need for answers to questions that didn't concern them. Standing side by side, they waited for Mama's answer as if Aunt Maeve had been a part of the conversation the entire time.

"It was an accident," Mama replied to the growing crowd. She looked away for a lingering moment and sighed. "We don't have any details, really. We received a call from a hospital in Texas a little over two weeks ago. So, we packed an overnight bag and raced down there, not knowing exactly what to expect when we arrived. By the time we reached the hospital, she was gone."

She looked between Aunt Maeve and the woman, furrowing her brows in a sorrowful expression, but her eyes betrayed the display. They held no emotion, only the redness of exhaustion. The real sorrow came later. It wasn't pretty. It wasn't polished. And it didn't belong in this place or to any of these people.

How odd, that life after loss so closely resembled the theater, as you're forced to act out every moment of a life that couldn't be yours, just to please onlookers consumed by the story. Add some sadness to this scene, but not so much that they become uncomfortable. You're tired, your feet hurt, and your head pounds, but the show goes on. So get up there, and whatever you do, don't let them see you cry. The last thing we need is poor reviews. Mama understood this. Her performance was impeccable.

The woman nodded in understanding and quickly removed her talon from Mama's shoulder as if the misfortune was contagious. She opened her mouth as if more questions were poised on her tongue, ready to jump out.

Isabella, my nine-year-old cousin, interjected with a fit of squeals as her younger brother pulled on her hair. I exhaled a relieved breath as the two chased each other around Aunt Maeve's legs, saving Mama and me from further questions.

"Would you two cut that out?" Aunt Maeve said.

Sofia, my eldest cousin who looked like the dark-haired version of her mother, pulled them apart, holding a shirt collar in each hand.

Isabella began to cry and reached for her older brother, Marco.

I knew Marco better than the rest of my cousins. Being closest in age, we stuck with each other at family functions, but Mama and I hadn't attended one in years. In that time, he had grown to tower over me, allowing him to look over my head and avoid my eyes. I thought it was odd that he hadn't said a single word to me thus far. But as he ignored Isabella tugging at the bottom of his shirt, I remembered I didn't know him anymore. When we were younger, he had comforted his younger siblings when Aunt Maeve and Sofia scolded them, but he wasn't the person I had known, and I wasn't the person who had known him.

Aunt Maeve rolled her eyes at her children's tantrum. "Has anyone seen Al?"

"I think he's over there, talking to my husband and Rosetta," the blond woman said. She pointed to Uncle Al, Nana, and another man chatting across the room.

"Come on, kids." Aunt Maeve grabbed Isabella's hand, moving in Uncle Al's direction. "I'll have him look after these two for a while." She motioned her head for the blond woman to follow her, and they walked away.

After they left, I held on to the moment of quiet. The respite didn't last long as another guest approached us. The remaining few took their turn to shake Mama's hand or offer a quick hug on the way out. The funeral home emptied, aside from Nana, Uncle Al, and his family.

It was over. Finally. Mama sighed and turned to me. "Let's go home."

Mama didn't want a formal dinner afterward. She said it would be too much—the last thing she wanted was to deal with people and answer more questions. However, Nana insisted that we invite Uncle Al, who was her favorite child, and his family over for dinner. Having the family together for dinner was important to her, so Mama didn't argue.

Mama and I bundled up and left to heat the car for Nana, who waited inside.

"Mama, the car is this way," I pointed to a lot in the opposite direction Mama was facing.

"I have to find Al first. You can go start the car if you want," Mama said.

I couldn't force my footsteps to turn around. Instead, I followed Mama through the slippery parking lot. It felt just the same as when I was little and Mama had called me "little duckling" because wherever she went, I would follow three steps behind. I even refused to go to kindergarten because we would be apart. Mama tried everything. No one, not even Grace, could convince me to step outside the narrow path set by Mama's steps. The teacher threatened to hold me back for missing so much school. At her wit's end, Mama came home one day with a fluffy white kitten named Harry. The bundle of fur made everyone fall in love with his otherworldly blue eyes, silky soft fur, and rabbit-like hind legs. I began to follow the cat around instead of Mama, and I started going to school on my own, too. Mama had told me, "You just needed something to take care of. Once you're responsible for something, all other fear melts away, and the only thing that matters is protecting that fragile life." She admitted she was afraid of a lot of things until Grace was born, then she was only afraid of one thing.

I guess she had nothing left to fear now.

Uncle Al's outline appeared as he wiped snow from his windshield.

Mama called toward him as he opened the door of his sleek, black minivan. "Al, make sure you avoid the highway on the way to Mom's, or you'll be sitting in traffic for hours." She kept her tone light, but her lips formed a hard line, and her eyes locked on his.

Despite Nana's fragile state, Uncle Al hadn't spared a trip home in over five years. Mama wouldn't let him backtrack on his word this time.

If Mama's warning bothered him, he gave no sign other than a pause to conjure his charming smile. "Thanks, sis, but I know the way home."

She leveled his stare. "Right. Well, since you haven't visited in years, I thought maybe you forgot."

I was careful not to meet Uncle Al's eyes and focused on his polished, black shoes. The sudden need to be near Mama's side dissipated. I should have gone to start the car.

He evaluated us, and I knew he saw the cracks in my porcelain skin. I could fool them all from afar, but up close, my family would see the ragged lines where I had tried to glue myself back together in time for the funeral. I twisted my coat buttons and adjusted the scarf around my neck. Mama always told me, "If you stand still and hold their gaze, people will think you're confident even if you're not." Fiddling gave my apprehension away, but I needed to save my courage for the challenging family dinner ahead.

Uncle Al crossed his arms but said nothing.

"I'll see you back there then," Mama said.

"We'll be there around five. We're going to stop and check into our hotel and then change into something drier."

"Why don't you stay with us?" Mama asked. There's no way she wanted the entire Rizzo family to stay under our roof, but she was polite to a fault.

"Nah, that's all right. The last thing you need is this bunch crowding you." He thumbed toward the minivan where Aunt Maeve and my cousins waited. "I have some work waiting for me back at the office, so we have to head home by tomorrow afternoon, anyway."

Mama nodded, and Uncle Al gave a small wave before sliding in his car.

"I can't believe you invited them to stay," I said as we headed to warm up the car and retrieve Nana.

"I knew he'd never agree to it. He hasn't stayed at Nana's house since he was eighteen years old, and there would be no point in returning just for an inflatable mattress in the living room."

At his first chance, Uncle Al left home for a New York corporate finance job and only visited once a year to collect his Christmas checks from Nana. When Nana's money dwindled from mishandled accounts and growing medical bills, he stopped coming around. Of course, he only had himself to blame for the mishandled accounts since he oversaw Nana's finances at that time. Then, he stuck us with the financial responsibility, not unlike what my dad did to Mama, Grace, and me fifteen years ago. After all, Uncle Al and my dad were old college buddies. Both were finance majors, both had dreams of working in the big cities with shiny desks and six-figure salaries, and neither had it in them to stick around home for long.

I thought Uncle Al felt guilty about losing Nana's money. I couldn't imagine any other reason to avoid Nana. When I was younger, she always made tea in the morning and played classical music while she cleaned. Her bookshelf teemed with books, and her pantry spilled over with homemade tomato sauce and fruit preserves from her garden. She took the simple things in life and made them magical, though Uncle Al and Mama never appreciated that about her. It made their childhood difficult when she had her head in the clouds and left the responsibility of real life to everyone else. But for two sisters growing up on fairy tales and stories from the local library, Nana was a role model—a fairy godmother come to life. When Grace and I visited Nana's house, all our worries drifted away. But I eventually saw the problems with pretending. It would be all too easy to believe the stories you told yourself.

I remembered the stories Mama and I told each other on the way to the hospital. "She'll be fine, we'll just take her home and help her recover." Then there were the stories on the way home. "If only we had gotten there sooner, she would've been okay." I could lose myself in them, analyzing the endings over and over until I halfway convinced myself that Grace was still alive and well.

It happened to Nana, too. She had been calling me by my sister's name, talking to me as if Grace were still here. Except, she did so because she couldn't remember the truth. It started with the small details that slipped past her, a couple of years later it progressed to people, events, and names. We were careful not to leave her alone for long. Now she sat in the empty funeral home with the funeral director who had agreed to watch her while we retrieved the car.

After thanking the funeral director and wishing him a good-night, I took hold of Nana's hand and led her to where the car idled out front.

"Beautiful night, isn't it?" Nana's face lifted to the sky, streaked with orange and shedding a stream of snowflakes. Her eyes held a carefree innocence that I could no longer share with her.

"Yeah, it is," I said.

"What's wrong?"

I looked down. "Nothing, Nana." She couldn't always understand what was going on, but she always understood me and knew when I was upset.

"Come here." She pulled me into a hug, pausing in the middle of the parking lot. My arms wrapped around her thin frame, and I held on as if she were my last tether to the ground. A few tears escaped, freezing on my cheeks, and I swallowed the lump in my throat. I didn't want to worry Nana. I couldn't hide my feelings from her, but I couldn't explain them to her, either. It would be too distressing trying to tell her Grace died every time she forgot. But with Nana, I didn't need to explain. She pulled away and brushed snowflakes from my shoulder. "You won't be sad forever," Nana crooned. "It's freezing out here. Let's go to the car. What do you say, chickadee?"

I smiled. "Together is my favorite place to be." My heart warmed at our special phrase—something she only shared with me and Grace.

"That's right." She took my hand, and we made our way through the cold, icy storm.

TWO

The short December evening had faded into darkness by the time we returned home. The takeout containers covering the back seat made the car smell like an Italian restaurant. Mama pulled up to the curb in front of our ranch-style brick house. It looked like a gingerbread house in the winter with its bright red door, standing out from the gray, profiteer-built apartments and condos around it. Unique, twentieth-century houses previously lined the former suburb. One by one, they all became dilapidated, and developers turned them into affordable apartments as people spilled over from the booming metropolis.

Nana lived in this house for over fifty years. She said it told a history, just like her books, and it needed to be protected. Mama complained she went broke trying to keep the house standing, but Nana cared little for finances.

I hopped out of the car to help Nana from the passenger seat.

"Thank you, dear," Nana said. She emerged from her seat with a strained grunt. I grasped her arm and navigated us both down the walkway, aware of each crack and bump in the concrete that could cause her to stumble.

Mama hurried to the door, clouds of her breath trailing behind her. She fiddled with the lock, growing frustrated.

Original to the hundred-year-old house, the red door often stuck in the winter.

Mama rattled the doorknob and slammed the door with her side. She stumbled in as it gave way. I entered the house behind Nana and leaned against the door as I pushed it closed. I sighed, grateful to be engulfed by the welcoming smell of cinnamon and cloves.

I ran to my room and rid myself of my scratchy wool dress and drenched socks. My feet were blueish and wrinkled from where water had seeped into the holes of my worn, formal shoes. I put on warm slippers and jeans with a simple sweater. It wasn't the attire Nana approved of for dinner with guests. Though, she had stopped paying attention to her stringent rules a while ago. I still liked to follow them in case she noticed. Except for tonight.

Mama had the same idea, and we set the table while squeaking around the house in our matching bunny slippers. We wore them mostly because my cat, Harry, loved to pounce at our feet as we walked, and it was nice to feel normal for a moment before the others arrived.

Mama handed me silverware while I tucked forks and knives into delicately folded napkins.

"You know, Aunt Maeve is going to ask a lot of questions," Mama said.

I nodded. "I figured."

"I want you to be prepared. Not just for this dinner, but for after as well. You might have to answer questions for a long time."

"I don't think so. I'm pretty sure everyone we have ever known already called and talked to you last weekend."

Mama shook her head. "Not those kinds of questions. I'm talking about the kind that catch you off guard. Like what if someone comes up and asks you if you have any siblings? What would you say?"

I opened my mouth to speak, but nothing came out. Frustrated tears burned my eyes as I searched for an answer that made sense.

"That's why you have to be ready. We have to be strong now." Her voice softened. "People will ask how you're doing. Don't act too happy, just keep it polite. Tell people what they want to hear. Tell them that you're doing just fine."

I knew things were bad whenever Mama told me to be strong. She said it when we lost our old apartment and moved into Nana's seven years ago, then when Gramps died a few years later, and again when Nana became ill.

As always, I replied, "I'll try to be." But the thought of facing questions, going out into the world, and navigating conversations full of emotional landmines made me want to stay at home forever.

Mama gave me a quick hug. "That's my girl."

The doorbell rang, and I ran to hide our slippers in the back room. No way would I let Aunt Maeve catch us wearing them.

A chorus of cheery hellos echoed from the entrance, and I considered taking Harry and hiding in my room for the extent of dinner. Except then Mama would be on her own, and I couldn't leave her to fend for herself.

The nine of us settled around the crowded dining table. Cramped with extra chairs and place settings, the small room strained to accommodate our guests. Traditional decor accented the dining room with maroon velvet curtains draping across foggy windows and dark wood floors contrasting the crystal chandelier.

Nana and Gramps never owned many lavish things, but they treasured what they had. Nana used to keep the room spotless and the furniture gleaming, but now dust accumulated on the armoire and wooden chest. Until tonight, the dining room had gone unused for years. No one came over for dinner anymore.

"This smells great, let's dig in," said Uncle Al, motioning to the lasagna, sausage, and steaming garlic mashed potatoes that we had set out on Nana's fine china.

Aunt Maeve held up one of the remaining takeout containers as we passed the serving dishes around. "I see you made one of your secret recipes tonight," she said to Mama, followed by her braying laughter.

I stiffened at the obvious insult. Mama's cooking was just short of alchemy. After a long shift at work, she still managed to make something out of nothing, and she stretched it until her next paycheck. I wanted to say that to Aunt Maeve, not that she would understand. She hadn't worried about a paycheck since she married Uncle Al.

Mama handed me the serving plate, interrupting my thoughts. I scooped a piece of lasagna that oozed at the sides and made my stomach turn. Any other day, the smell alone would have made my mouth water, but I had lost my appetite. I passed the plate to my left to Isabella.

She mumbled a polite "Thank you," and kept her eyes trained on the table. I frowned at the girl and her curtain of black hair. Perhaps the funeral had upset her. Isabella seemed nothing like the others. Maybe Aunt Maeve hadn't finished molding her into the family's perfect image of identical looks and personalities. Instead, Isabella maintained an introverted and sensitive nature that reminded me of myself. Maybe I had a chance at getting along with someone in my dwindling family.

Loud voices clashed back and forth across the table, so I leaned over toward Isabella. "I have some cards in my room. We can play a game after dinner, if you would like."

The girl looked up and her gentle face transformed as she wrinkled her nose. She shook her head and looked away as if my offer was the last thing she wanted to do. I shouldn't be surprised. After all, she had her mother's attitude, without the stinging words. The exchange went unnoticed, and I slipped into the background of the table's loud conversation.

I shook with the sting of rejection, and the hole in my heart widened with a painful clench. Why did my cousin—no, this unfamiliar child—affect me so? My veins buzzed, making my heartbeat heavier and faster. Had I come down with an illness that caused a sudden attack of weakness and disorientation? No, the feeling wasn't new, having first appeared nine years ago in the wake of slammed doors and Grace's packed suitcases. If only it were an illness. If only it were something I could recover from. But it wouldn't be so simple. I was afflicted with loneliness. The kind that grew from missing someone who would never return. There could be no cure.

Like blood in water, signs of my distress leached out across the table and caught Aunt Maeve's attention. I looked down, but it was too late. Aunt Maeve inspected my tear-rimmed eyes and shaking hands.

She opened her mouth to say something when Mama interjected, "How is school going Marco?"

Surprised, the second eldest looked up and glanced at Aunt Maeve before responding. "Good. I decided on engineering for my major and I'm looking for some internships for next semester. I sent out applications last week, so fingers crossed." He chuckled before averting his eyes. Like his father, he carried himself with confident shoulders and a lifted chin, but something about Mama's kind gaze made him squirm.

Aunt Maeve patted Marco's arm. "Oh, he's just being modest. He's a shoo-in for those internships. You know, he made the dean's list last semester."

"Very impressive," Mama said.

I gave Mama a grateful look. The distraction had worked long enough for me to regain my composure.

Sofia, however, was not as appreciative. She rolled her eyes at the exchange and crossed her arms. I imagined she was tired of hearing Aunt Maeve praise her intelligent little brother. The last I had heard, Sofia had pursued a career in party planning. Though Aunt Maeve didn't like to brag about that. She had the highest hopes for Marco. Isabella preferred ballet over school, and the youngest, Enzo, clearly didn't have an inclination toward academics. He was a curly-haired boy with restless feet and a penchant for spills. He hadn't changed much since I last saw him as a toddler. Now seven years old, he still had too much energy to contain and bounced in his seat.

Aunt Maeve looked at me from across the table. "So, Emma, how is school going for you? You're still at community college, right?"

"I actually just finished my last semester there," I said, pretending to cut my food to avoid the gazes that turned my way.

Aunt Maeve raised her brows. "A semester early?"

"I took some classes over the summer, and a few transferred from high school." I had taken more than a few advanced placement classes in high school, and my school counselor thought I should apply to top colleges, but I disagreed. Aside from volunteering at a retirement home, I didn't have many extracurriculars for my résumé. Mama pushed me to apply in case I qualified for a scholarship, but then Nana received her diagnosis and I ended up at community college so I could help Mama take care of her. Now two weeks remained until the spring started, and this time I would be at a four-year university—if we could find a way to pay for it.

"What school are you transferring to?" Aunt Maeve asked.

"I'm not sure yet. I'm still waiting to hear back from a few." The truth was, in the weeks that we spent driving back and forth to Texas and arranging Grace's funeral, I had been too overwhelmed to decide on which school's offer to accept. Normal life continued without me as I contemplated my future, unable to envision myself at any of the schools for the next two years. The deadlines to claim my spot and accept scholarships passed, one by one, making the decisions for me. I eventually chose from the remaining few, but I wouldn't give Aunt Maeve the opportunity to compare my school to Marco's.

She leaned forward, resting her elbow on the table. "Why would you go back to school so soon? With everything going on, don't you think it would be too much for you to handle?"

I tried to make my voice firm. "I'm sure it will be fine." Eight pairs of eyes continued to stare at me. "I think it will be nice to go back. I'll have something to keep me busy and regain some sense of normalcy." I shoved a forkful of food in my mouth and struggled to swallow. The days of going to school and worrying about grades seemed like a different life. A sinking feeling formed in my stomach as I realized just how far away my normal had become. But I could get it back. I had to get it back.

Aunt Maeve turned to Mama, seeming to lose interest in our conversation. "Gina, dear, would you happen to have some wine?"

"I'm sure I could find something around here." Mama patted me on the knee before getting up from the table. Mama had bought a bottle before they came over for dinner, and I was grateful for her forethought; Aunt Maeve acted much more amicably when she had a glass of wine in front of her.

The sound of knives and forks scraping against plates filled the silence as the room grew quiet. Aunt Maeve took advantage of the opportunity. Her voice cut through the quiet. "Emma, I've been wanting to ask, how is your mom doing, really?" I blinked at her. Why would she ask a question like that? She lowered her voice, "Because if she isn't doing well, you know you could tell us." She would be the last person that I would tell. I wanted to cry, I wanted to scream, I wanted to tell the lot of them to get out and never come back.

But I didn't, because Mama had prepared me for this moment. I flashed her a polite smile and said, "Thank you so much for your concern, but my mom is strong and she's doing remarkably well given the circumstances. We're both doing just fine."

Aunt Maeve narrowed her eyes at me. She wouldn't relent until she discovered some details that satisfied her. In the same way some people search their whole lives for love and acceptance, Aunt Maeve searched for power. Apparently, her life hadn't been easy until she met Uncle Al. I would feel sorry for her if she was kinder. Instead, her misfortune had made her hard, cold, and desperate for something she could find only by putting others down. Mama and Uncle Al had been close once, but Aunt Maeve saw her as a threat to the sizable inheritance she expected. Then Nana became penniless apart from the house we lived in. Now I was the only threat left. Aunt Maeve wanted her children to be Nana's favorites, the center of attention with superior accomplishments. Much to her disappointment, that could never be the case. Nana and I had a special bond. Even now, after her dementia set in, we remained close. My cousins would never have the chance to know Nana as I did.

Now Nana's glossy eyes passed over the Rizzo children without recognition. They didn't seem to care.

Sofia hardly touched her food, instead texting under the table. Isabella occupied herself by repeatedly stabbing her lasagna. Enzo squealed as he smacked his hands in the sea of red sauce. Marco just looked bored.

Aunt Maeve scolded her youngest son as she wiped his hands and face. At least Enzo kept her busy. The boy shrieked at his mother's prodding.

Uncle Al's forehead formed a crease. His shoulders rose toward his neck like he was in pain, and he exhaled a sigh that came from his very depths.

Nana tilted her head and winced. She had become sensitive to loud noises.

Aunt Maeve gave up trying to wipe Enzo clean and tossed the napkin on the table. She perked up when Mama returned with the bottle and a few wine glasses. "Oh good, you can set that right here." She patted the table in front of her. Mama did as she was asked and returned to her seat. Aunt Maeve's cheeks reddened as she sipped her first glass. "Gina, I don't mean to pry, but I noticed that Victor isn't here. What's the deal with that? Haven't you contacted him?" she asked, an innocent expression playing on her angular features.

We had lost contact with my dad, Victor, after the divorce. I was only five when it happened, but Grace was twelve, old enough to remember and miss him.

"I've reached out to him," Mama's voice was measured, "but he's stuck somewhere on business. You know how he is." That was another story we had rehearsed. In truth, Mama had called and spoken to him for the first time in years. He was shocked by the news, but that shock turned to anger as he blamed Mama for what happened. He refused to come to the funeral, claiming he couldn't stand to be anywhere near Mama. I thought that was best. He hadn't been in touch since I was eleven years old, I saw no point in him coming around now.

Nana shook her head. "That Victor was always no good. I told you, Gina, you never should have married him." Mama shot a look at Nana, who munched on a breadstick.

Uncle Al cleared his throat and shifted in his seat. As far as we knew, he had also lost touch with his old college buddy, though there was no way to know for sure. Aunt Maeve emptied her wine glass and poured a refill.

"Don't you think you've had enough of that, honey?" Uncle Al said, nodding to the bottle in Maeve's hand. She rolled her eyes at him and scoffed.

Mama's phone rang from the kitchen. Rising from her seat, she excused herself to retrieve it. The walls were thin, and we could hear every word.

"Hello? Yes, this is she." She paused. "I see. Yes, of course, you can stop by tomorrow. Do you have my address on file? Great, see you then." Her footsteps approached the dining room, and everyone looked to their plates as if they hadn't been listening.

Except for Aunt Maeve. She inclined her head as Mama took her seat. "Was that about Grace?"

Mama's eyes were wide and unblinking, as if her mind were somewhere else. "Yes, that was the detective working on her case."

"What did the detective say?" Aunt Maeve asked.

"Maeve..." Uncle Al warned.

Mama put up a hand. "It's okay. He didn't say anything. He's coming over tomorrow to discuss her case."

Aunt Maeve wouldn't relent. "Well, what have you heard from the investigation so far?" she asked.

All eyes were on Mama. The silent room expected her response. Uncle Al wouldn't protest this time. After all, this was the reason they came.

The tip of Mama's nose and the apples of her cheeks bloomed red, the way it always did when she became furious or upset. I watched with the rest of them, unsure if her waning resolve would hold enough to prevent a full-blown scene.

"You know just as much as I do," she said.

Flustered by the speculative glances that turned our way, I shrank in my seat. Just as I decided the room had become too suffocating to bear, Mama stood.

"I'll be right back. I have to get the dessert," she said.

I quickly scooted out of my chair. "I'll help." We made our way to the kitchen and turned to each other. "Can you believe Aunt Maeve? I've never been more disgusted by her, and all the rest of them for that matter. They just sat there like they were watching some kind of circus show. Why did we invite them? We knew what would happen," I whispered.

"Because it's important to your grandma that we have the family here. I just need a minute," Mama said. She closed her eyes and leaned against the marble countertop, exhaling a sigh. Tears escaped and fell down her cheeks until the dam broke and she began to sob quietly. I jumped to action, gathering paper towels, and handed them to her. Mama blew her nose. "All I wanted was a nice, quiet dinner where people respected Grace's memory. And now it's all ruined," she said between stutters and cries.

Tears brimmed my eyes, but I refused to let a single one escape. "I can't wait until this is over, so we never have to talk to these people again."

I held it together for the both of us while Mama continued, "Let them say whatever they want, they have for years." She wiped at the mascara running down her face. "Let's go back, I don't want to leave Nana for too much longer."

Even in the midst of tragedy, I still couldn't count on my family to come together.

I took the dessert from the freezer and led Mama back to the table. We passed around lemon ice cups, which we had chosen because they needed to be eaten quickly before melting. We didn't need Aunt Maeve lingering over a dessert.

When I reached Nana, the unmistakable look of her belligerent confusion filled me with dread. Worry showed in her wide, green eyes as she twisted her frail frame in the chair, scanning the room with increased urgency. I tapped Mama's shoulder and inclined my head to Nana.

Mama took firm hold of her hand. "What's wrong, Mom?" she asked.

"When's Frank going to get here?" Nana asked, her voice high and thin from worry.

Mama squeezed Nana's hand and blinked rapidly, searching her empty plate for a reply. Frank, Nana's husband of fifty-four years, passed away when I was in high school. A couple years after we moved in with Nana and Gramps, he was diagnosed with cancer. In a blink, he was gone. In the past few months, Nana forgot all of it.

Marco and Sofia went wide-eyed. They didn't know Nana made comments like this daily. Mama updated Uncle Al on Nana's condition every once in a while, yet he didn't look concerned. And why would he be? Nana wasn't his responsibility to look after.

"He can't come today, Nana, he's still on that business trip," I said, trying to keep my voice even. At first, we had tried to tell her the truth, but she had become more upset than I had ever seen her. So, we told her a story instead. Because Gramps had taken many trips for his job as a business manager, the explanation appeased her.

Nana sank back in her chair, and we ate in silence for a few moments. Then Nana's brow twisted in confusion again. "And where's Grace? That girl is always out somewhere."

My spoon clattered onto my plate. Uncle Al erupted in a coughing fit and almost spat his coffee, and even Aunt Maeve looked shocked.

"I think we should get going before the roads get too icy," Uncle Al said. He regained his composure, a stone-like hardness covering his discomfort at Nana's forgetfulness.

We rose from the table, headed to the front room, then waited while Uncle Al and his family dressed in coats and scarves. Mama handed Aunt Maeve a grocery bag full of Sofia's leftovers and the half-empty wine bottle.

Aunt Maeve smiled. "Thanks for a lovely dinner, Gina, we must catch up again soon." Mama plastered on a smile that didn't reach her eyes. Looking around, Aunt Maeve asked, "Now where are my other children?"

A screeching cry echoed from down the hall, and I rushed to the sound, stopping short when I found Isabella and Enzo sitting on the floor of my room laughing in hysterics as they yanked on my cat's ears and tail.

"Stop that right now," I said, my voice shaking. I pulled my screeching cat from their tight grasp and held on to Harry as he shook with fear. I stared at the children as they glared at me for ruining their fun.

Mama reached the doorway and ushered the kids out of my room. I carried Harry with me, holding him tightly.

Uncle Al gave Mama and Nana a hug and promised to call, though I knew he wouldn't. Mama held open the door as they left, and a gust of cold air brushed my face. My cousins shuffled out the door. Only Marco said goodbye. He offered me a small smile, and I thought he almost looked sorry, though I felt sorrier for him. After all, he had to go home with that family.

"Hey kids, what movie do you want to go see?" said Aunt Maeve, halfway out the door. They didn't even wait to cross the threshold before erupting in a cacophonous debate. Nor did they look back as Mama shut the door behind them.

Nana wandered back to the living room while Mama and I stood in the entryway, both of us unwilling to move from the spot. My muscles turned to stone as the shock and exhaustion set in. We stayed standing like that for an indiscernible amount of time until Harry squirmed in my arms, and I set him down. Mama took a deep breath and headed to her room without a word.

I stumbled through the motions of brushing my teeth and getting ready to go to sleep. My head pounded and exhaustion weighed on my limbs. I barely had enough energy to change into my pajamas and crawl into bed. Darkness surrounded me as I tossed under my sheets. I had made it through the day, but what about tomorrow? The detective working on Grace's case would come soon. I wondered what he would say. Would he bring resolution, or would he bring us more pain? I closed my eyes, but sleep didn't come.

My thoughts ran rampant—a stampede of angry bulls trampling any hope for rest. My heart still raced to the thundering of charging hooves. Each step was an echo of Grace's eulogy. "Taken too young…Kind-hearted, treasured by those that knew her…A beloved daughter, friend, and sister."

I jumped from my bed, tiptoed down the hallway, and peered in Nana's cracked door. The whirring of Nana's nighttime breathing machine filled her room. I hadn't sneaked into her room since I was really little, around five years old. Not since Mama, Grace, and I stayed here for a few months just after my dad filed for divorce and we needed time to find an apartment we could afford.

I entered slowly, and two glowing eyes reflected the moonlight streaming through the window. Harry greeted me with a soft meow, and I patted him as he lay on the foot of the bed. I peeled back the covers on the left side and slid beneath, careful not to squeak the springs. Nana shifted beside me, though her full breathing mask and entwined tubes prevented her from moving too much. I settled a bit closer, closed my eyes, and waited for the steady inhale and exhale of the machine to lull me to sleep.

A wave of sorrow washed over me, and my entire body drowned.

I could feel it in my shaking fingers, in the tightening of my lungs, in the aching pressure behind my eyes. I tried to lie still. My teeth chattered as I restrained my sobs. As I pinned myself in place, a steady stream of tears flowed from the corners of my eyes, and I focused on my breath, slow and steady. Not loud enough to wake Nana, just enough air in and out to relieve the pressure suffocating my lungs. I dreaded the darkness as I wondered if sleep would ever come. When exhaustion won out, the moon hung high in the sky, and I succumbed to the numbness somewhere in between asleep and awake.

THREE

I woke up the next morning, disoriented by the stream of light that just touched the bed. What time is it? I reached for my alarm clock, knocking over a cup full of pens as I searched through squinted eyes. Nana gasped and her machine whooshed as it strained to give her more oxygen. Realizing where I was, I slid out of bed and waited for Nana to settle before making any movements.

Nana must have tossed the covers last night. I retrieved the pink and purple blanket from the floor and spread it over her curled-up body. I traced my fingers over the intricate knitted stitches, seeing Nana's fingers work through every loop. She made the blanket just over a year ago; it was the last one she finished before she forgot how to knit completely.

I opened the creaking door and tiptoed back into my room. The clock read *9:30 a.m.*, three and a half hours later than I typically woke up. Mama decided to sleep in as well. Her door remained shut across the hall. I looked around my room. Everything remained as I had left it, but somehow felt out of place. I reached over to my nightstand and grabbed a picture that framed me, Mama, Nana, and Grace with smiling faces. My heart clenched, and I shoved the picture in the top drawer of my dresser, out of view.

The room felt like a museum, preserving the remains of a life that no longer existed, taunting me with what I would never again have. Clothes scattered across my floor from when I had packed for Texas in a hurry. My backpack slumped in the corner, still full of last semester's notebooks.

I didn't know what to do next. How would I fit myself back into this life when my home felt like a mockery of what it once was?

I moved to clear the rest of the photos from my desk, unable to look at them for a second longer. As I shoved them in my dresser drawer, the collection of memories mixed among my socks, and I paused. I knew I shouldn't look, but my hand reached of its own accord and plucked a photo from the stack. It was small and glossy, and taken on an old camera that left the date printed in yellow at the bottom. *2005*. I must have been around five at the time. I wore a pink ruffled dress and a bow in my hair. My arms slung around pale shoulders. Grace and I stood in front of a colorful background, the kind department stores used to set up. Grace wore a pink dress, too, and a ponytail tamed her curly red hair. Neither of us looked at the camera. She smiled at me as I looked up at her.

I missed that smile. The way her eyes had sparkled when she looked at me made my heart overflow with joy. I longed for her warm embrace and the way she had held my hand when I was little. I missed seeing her eyes flutter open as I woke her up in the morning. Now I would have to wake up every day without her.

I felt my throat tighten, and I placed the photo back in the drawer, closing it shut.

How did I get to this point? When did my life take such a turn? I looked beside me, where one last picture hung on the wall of Mama, Nana, and me smiling in front of a bright floral display and remembered the moment.

It was just a few weeks ago. I had studied at the kitchen table, surrounded by notebooks and review materials for finals. I was up all night pouring over my notes, and planned to study until that Monday, but Mama had other ideas. "Come on. Close your books, we're going on a day trip," she said.

I looked at her, my mouth agape. "A day trip?"

"Yes, a day trip. It'll only take a few hours. You've been cooped up studying too long."

"But I have three more finals tomorrow." My voice came out high and stringy.

"So?"

"How am I going to transfer into a good university if I fail my finals?"

She rolled her eyes. "You are not going to fail your finals. You've been buried in textbooks for days. What you need now is fresh air."

"What I need is to study." I picked my book up and turned the page.

Mama tapped her foot while I ignored her. "You know if you keep staring at your textbook like that, you'll get a permanent frown line."

A laugh escaped me, and I set the book down. Maybe I did need a break. "Where are we going?"

She broke out in a triumphant grin. "I'm not telling you." Hurrying down the hallway, she snatched her keys and coat on the way. "I'll grab Nana, you get dressed."

I stretched as I rose from my seat and sighed.

She used to talk me into all sorts of spontaneous adventures, back when life was filled with possibilities and fun.

We spent the forty-five-minute drive singing along to the radio, Nana's melodious crooning voice clashing against Mama's tone-deaf bellowing of tunes. I laughed too hard at the spectacle to sing with them. We arrived at a brick building with a glass dome top, and Mama parked in the snow-covered lot. I looked out the window, still unable to figure out where she had taken us.

"Leave your coat in the car," Mama said.

"What, why?" The heavy wind and brisk chill warned of an approaching snowstorm. In this treacherous Chicago winter, we wouldn't last long without a coat. Nana shed her layers without question, and I narrowed my eyes at her. "Mama told you where we're going, didn't she?"

Nana looked over her shoulder. "Sorry, chickadee. My lips are sealed."

"Are you coming?" Mama asked, placing her hand on the door handle.

As I looked between the two of them, my trepidation melted into excitement. I ditched my winter coat and dashed out the door, Mama and Nana following close behind. Mama and I stood on either side of Nana, linking arms as we shuffled toward the entrance. Wind pierced through my thin, long sleeves, and I ducked my face away from the cold.

Mama jogged a few steps ahead to open the door, and a wave of balmy air greeted us. I sighed in relief as the hot, sticky warmth brought feeling to my numb fingers. I looked around and spotted a sign that read *Botanical Gardens Tropical Exhibit.*

My eyes widened. "No way. I've always wanted to come here."

Mama smiled. "I know."

I linked arms with Mama and Nana and said, "Come on, then." We headed toward the exhibit, passing a coat check on the way. "You know, we could have worn our coats inside." Though, in the exhibit's ninety-degree heat, I was glad to be rid of them.

Mama shook her head. "That coat check costs fifteen dollars a person. It's preposterous."

Nana scoffed. "Heaven forbid you splurge for our comfort."

"Who needs comfort? The experience was free," Mama said.

"Oh, hurry up." I interrupted their sparring match. They relented and we made our way into the exhibit.

A stone pathway twisted and turned through plots of exotic plants of every color and size. Vibrant-colored flowers interspersed bushes of a lavender purple and crowded the base of tall, leafy trees. I smiled with glee as I took pictures with my phone, but Mama's face had fallen flat.

"What's the matter, Mama?" I asked.

Snapping out of a daze, Mama linked arms with me once more. "Grace would love this. I wish she would come back from Texas so we could take her here." I agreed, she would have loved the floral blooms, dazzling colors, and filling her sketchbook with drawings while we perused the gardens. I liked to draw as well, but I learned everything from Grace. She was the real artist in the family.

"I wish she would visit, too," I said. "Let's take a picture for her and send it."

All three of us had gathered behind my phone screen and we sent her the picture that now hung on my wall. I remembered the text she had sent back. *I miss you guys so much. You'll have to take me there soon!*

That was the last text she sent us. We received the call from the hospital a few days after our visit to the gardens. I was at school, sitting with my group of friends, studying for my last final exam before winter break. Mama had wished me luck that morning and told me to text her after my biology exam, which I had just finished. Reaching for my phone, I remembered I had turned it off for the exams. The screen flashed as I turned it on, and I frowned at the flurry of notifications that popped up. My spine went rigid as I saw seven missed calls and twice as many texts from Mama. My thoughts went to Nana, and I jumped up from my seat, dialing Mama's number as I paced on unsteady legs.

Mama picked up.

"Hello?" I said, my voice panicked. I heard crying on the other end and my pulse raced. "What's wrong?"

"It's Grace," Mama said, her voice shaking and barely audible. She didn't have to explain further. I knew in that moment as my heart dropped, that nothing would be the same. "I got a call from a hospital in Texas. They say she's in bad shape. I don't know what happened, and we have to get there as soon as possible."

I couldn't comprehend Mama's words. "But I have one more final to take." My voice sounded hollow and slow, the crowded cafeteria blurred, and my thoughts became as indiscernible as droplets in a pond.

Mama sniffled. "Finish your final and come straight home. It'll take me that long to pack for the drive, and we'll leave right away."

We hung up and I found my way back to the table, where my friends quizzed each other for the upcoming Spanish exam. I sat, frozen in the chair. Unable to speak, unable to think. No one noticed anything amiss, or if they did, they didn't care to say anything. Except for my friend, Evan, who sat next to me, eyeing my dark laptop screen and blank sheet of paper that I was supposedly studying from. He looked at me curiously as I tried to keep my breaths even.

My group left for the Spanish final while Evan and I trailed behind.

"Are you okay?" he asked quietly.

I nodded and looked down, unable to form words. I entered the classroom and sat at my desk, hardly registering the test booklet placed in front of me. I tried to focus on the test, but my mind raced. I turned it in thirty minutes early, with half the questions answered, and walked out the door. I trembled on the bus ride home, through the drive to Texas, until Mama, Nana and I reached Grace's hospital room, and we saw her, lying there...

Feeling unsteady and shaken from my memories of Grace in the hospital, I leaned against my dresser, closing my eyes and focusing on the air passing in and out of my lungs. I shut out the world and waited until the pressure dissolved. With one last glance at the picture of us smiling at the botanical gardens, I took it down from where it hung and shoved it face-down in my closet, leaving two screws protruding from the bare wall.

As my thoughts cleared, the silence engulfing the house no longer sounded like quiet, but like a deafening scream. I wanted something to drown it out. But I didn't have any more plans or obligations to keep me busy. All the late nights of planning, endless calling, and noise just stopped and... left nothing. My head still pounded with yesterday's headache—a reminder that the surreal day of Grace's funeral actually happened. There was also the mess that enveloped the living room and kitchen. The house was always a mess when something bad happened.

While packing for Texas in a hurry, we had left with closet doors still open and everything out of place. Over a week later, we still hadn't found the energy to restore the house to normal. Mama had cleaned for last night's dinner, but most things were shoved in a drawer.

As I surveyed the mess, I felt control slipping from my grasp. Not that I had a firm handle on it to begin with, but what little I had left kept me grounded to the earth. Without it, I would certainly float away.

Papers lay stacked on my desk, and I moved to clear them. Beneath my unanswered college acceptance letters were scrap notes. Picking them up, I strained to read the scribbled handwriting. *Mass at St. Joseph's 3pm, order casket from…* The papers fluttered to the ground as they fell from my hands. Mama had made endless lists to prepare for the funeral. I must have mixed her papers up with mine. I scooped up the lists and put them in the recycling bin, but I could still see the words *funeral home* and *pallbearer* scrawled across the corners that stuck out.

Unease washed over me as the events of yesterday came flooding back. White gloves grasping the edge of a casket. The funeral home, dark and filled with strangers, closing in around me…Don't think about it.

I turned away, needing to occupy my mind with anything else. Surveying my messy room, I decided I should spend the morning cleaning up any traces of the past few weeks. Starting with the recycling, I took the small bin from its place beneath my desk and dumped the contents into the larger bin in the kitchen. Then I decided I better take the larger bins out to the curb. In her more attentive moments, Nana despised mess, and the last thing she needed was to see garbage piling up.

I took the garbage and recycling from the kitchen and paused by the entryway to shove my bare feet into snow boots and throw on a coat. As I opened the front door, freezing air shocked the warmth from my bones, and I wished I had zipped up my coat and put on gloves before rushing out of the house. After trekking through a foot of snow, I placed the bags at the curb and hurried back to the house.

With soap, water, and a drying rag, I scrubbed out all traces of the past few weeks. Though, I couldn't get rid of all the memories. The ones of Grace and me as children appeared in every crevice. Like the notches in the wall where Gramps tracked our heights, or the chip in Nana's teacup from when we had knocked it playing ball. But there was nothing I could do about that. Memories filled the house.

Soon the kitchen counters and floors sparkled, and I collapsed on the couch, feeling the weight of exhaustion that grew stronger every day. I might have stayed on that couch for the entire afternoon if my stomach hadn't started growling. I had forgotten to eat breakfast in my haste to clean the house.

Dragging my aching limbs from the couch, I walked into the small kitchen, the cool tile sending a chill up my bare feet. I cooked oatmeal and toast for the three of us, adding the remaining fresh fruit to the bowl.

The worn floors creaked under Mama's approaching footsteps.

"Morning," Mama said, rubbing her eyes as if she just woke up. Though, I knew better than to believe she slept through the morning. She would never sleep until eleven thirty. Her eyes were bloodshot and puffy, and her nose was just as red. "What's all this?" She surveyed the table I had set.

"Breakfast," I said.

She frowned as if I had given her terrible news. "I could've made something. You should've come to get me."

I shrugged. "I can make breakfast, Mama, it's not a big deal."

"You don't have to do things for me."

"I wanted to," I said.

Harry padded into the kitchen and clawed halfway up my pant leg. He cried and sniffed my spoon.

"But I'll tell you what, you can feed Harry," I said.

Mama brightened and moved to fill the food bowl. "Is Nana up yet?"

"No, she slept like a rock."

"That's a surprise, she's been having trouble sleeping at night."

I paused, spoon still in hand, and frowned. "Maybe we should tell Dr. Warren. He did mention insomnia could be a side effect of the new medication, but it might also be a progression of her condition."

Mama rolled her eyes. "What, so he can prescribe another medication to treat the side effects of her existing medication? Between the prescription costs and doctor visits, we're already up to our knees in medical bills, and her insurance doesn't cover the half of it. I just don't know how much longer we can go on like this."

"What choice do we have?"

Mama pursed her lips. "We'll tell Dr. Warren at Nana's appointment on Thursday."

I took my seat at the table across from Mama, and silence fell over both of us. We sat in the same spots we always had for the past seven years, but something felt different. Shifting in my seat, I tried to find the familiar comfort of easing into my chair and digging into breakfast. Giving up, I stirred my oatmeal and berries, which bled into a medley of reds and purples.

I stared at Mama blowing on her spoon, but she wouldn't meet my gaze. I had a mountain of questions I wanted to ask her, but the words caught in my throat, fighting for space where the oatmeal threatened to come back up. I wanted to talk like we used to every morning, about our plans for the day or the TV show we watched the night before. We had talked about everything. Now a great divide went up between us, and she seemed miles away. I doubted she could hear me even if I screamed.

We ate in silence and sipped tea over our empty bowls and bread crusts. Every morning she stirred her tea three times clockwise and drank it piping hot. But now she let it grow cold and left the teaspoon untouched. I needed her, but she retreated inward. Vacant and forlorn—her hollow shell stared out the small window just above the sink.

I had to say something, anything, to bring her back to me.

"That was some dinner," I said.

She blinked, but her eyes still rested on the window, looking at a point far off in the distance. "At least it's over," she said, her voice quiet.

I exhaled a frustrated sigh and stood up to wash the dishes. A range of emotions gripped me. Tears pricked my eyes, but my hands balled into fists. Was I mad at Mama? Was I sad because of her? No. Well, maybe. I didn't know. Why did she choose now to give up? I needed her more than ever, and she was a million miles away. But I wouldn't give up on her. Something would get through to her eventually.

I turned on the sink and scrubbed at my plate. "Can you believe the things Aunt Maeve said? You would never guess what she asked me after you left the table."

She hummed a response that sounded like a question.

"She asked me how you're *really* doing, like she wanted me to tell her you're not okay."

Mama nodded her head, but her attention remained elsewhere.

"But you are okay, aren't you?" I couldn't dance around the question anymore. Mama didn't get distracted, she didn't sit idle and stare out a window, she picked herself up, dusted off, and went back to work. I didn't know this version of her, or how to tell if she was okay.

Mama set down her teacup and folded her hands on the table, relaxing back into the wicker chair. A tight smile pulled at her lips. "Of course I'm okay."

I smiled in return, not convinced, but it was enough for now. I continued, "Typical, Aunt Maeve had to ask a bunch of questions about school, too. I didn't want to tell her I've already been accepted, then she would ask for all the details. And what was all that nonsense about taking a break? That's the last thing I would want to do. Though she would like it if I did, wouldn't she? Marco would be that much further ahead." My rambling failed to elicit a response from her. "That does remind me, I have some school payments due soon. Break is over the second week of January."

Wanting to gauge Mama's reaction, I turned to face the table. Would that blue vein pop out of her forehead in frustration? Would her brow wrinkle crease in worry? Or would she stare out the window, eyes vacant and ears unhearing?

To my surprise, she looked down and cleared her throat. "Right, of course. I'll take care of it." This seemed to bring her back into the room. A wave of relief washed over me.

"We also have to figure out housing. I missed the deadline for signing up for a dorm, but I think they have off-campus options we can look into. I know the budget will be tight, but maybe I can find roommates," I said.

The school I had decided on was a few states away, and I began to regret my rushed decision. After the other decision deadlines had passed, only two schools remained available.

One was a few hours' drive away from home, the other a few days away.

In the hotel room across the street from the hospital, I had struggled to decide. Time raced toward the deadline to commit to a school, and I wrestled with my indecision. I considered declaring a finance major and the farther school had a superior program. That was reason enough to commit to going there, right? Though, the thought occurred to me that Mama and Nana might need me in the turbulent time ahead, so the closer school could be a better option.

As my cursor moved to select the closer school, an image flashed in my mind. We had just visited Grace in the hospital for the first time. She wasn't awake. She would never be again. White sheets in a dark room, covering the bandages and injuries beneath, lay completely still. The first thing I noticed is that someone must have braided her hair. She never wore braids. The long strands interlaced, tight and neat to contain her unruly red curls. It looked wrong, as did the uncomfortable tilt of her head. The EKG kept beeping, telling us her heart still beat. They wanted to give it to someone else. A helicopter whirred outside waiting to take her away. I couldn't shed a tear because it didn't seem real.

With that image in my mind, and the memory of Mama's cries and Nana's confused terror, I couldn't fathom attending the closer school. Mama would expect me to visit on weekends, and I feared if I spent time in the place where Grace learned to ride a bike or sat at the table where we all ate dinner, it might become real. I wasn't strong enough to face that. I had made my decision and clicked to commit to the farther school.

The best scholarships had been given away with the early commitment deadline, weeks before I was forced into a decision. Overwhelmed by the chaos around me, I hadn't considered housing costs, transportation, or out-of-state fees. All I had wanted was to get as far away from home as possible, but now reality set in and made a fool of me.

Mama sighed. "I didn't think of housing, but you will need it. I can't believe you're going to be so far away." She lowered her head, and a knot formed in my stomach. "Do you have any idea how much housing will be? I didn't calculate that into the cost. You'll need a car, too. That means money for gas, car insurance, maintenance, repairs…" Her brow creased in worry. "I don't know if we can afford this. After the unexpected cost of the funeral, we're drowning here."

"We'll figure it out, we always do," I said, my voice a pitch too high.

"How?" The question burst out, as if she tried to condense the mountain of questions into a single syllable.

Shocked, I took a step back. "I don't know."

Mama rose from the table, taking the empty dishes to the sink. Frustration buzzed through my mind. Between Nana's medical bills and my upcoming school payments, I knew we were on thin ice, but school wasn't optional.

"Did you apply for the loans and scholarships like I asked you to?" Mama asked.

"Of course, but the loans won't cover everything and most of the scholarships were given away already."

Her lips set in a thin line.

We had another option, one I hadn't wanted to consider. "Maybe if we just reached out to—"

"No way," Mama said. She already knew my thoughts. "I wish Victor would step up and help support us, but he made it clear long ago that would never happen. Besides, if he wouldn't help pay for, let alone show up to, his own daughter's funeral, what makes you think he'd suddenly be willing to help you through school?"

I flinched. I knew everything Mama said to be true, but hearing it out loud broke through the appeal of my delusion. When Grace died, I wondered if he would realize his mistakes. How he abandoned his family, rejecting me and Grace. I wished guilt would consume him, drive him to despair, beg for our forgiveness. I was usually realistic enough to not entertain the idea that he could change. But hope glimmered in the darkness of my desperation. Grace was gone, the bills piled high, and the future became uncertain. As our situation worsened, I realized no ordinary solution could put the pieces of my life back together. So I began to hope for the impossible. I waited for him to visit, call, or write after Mama told him the news. But he never did. Because coming home would be like admitting he was wrong, and he would choose himself over us, every time.

"Let's take him back to court. We can't let him get away with this. He owes us this much," I said.

"Yeah, I've tried that before, remember? The divorce dragged on for years because he'd rather pay attorney fees than child support. All to get back at me. And for what? Supporting him for years? You know, I never finished school, so he could get his MBA. He made his money while I struggled for a minimum wage, all to keep him happy. Then for him to run off and—" She took a breath. "The point is, he can afford to litigate for years. I don't even have enough money for the lawyer's retainer fee."

"It's not right," I mumbled.

Mama faced me and placed a hand on my shoulder. "You don't have to worry about school, I will find a way. I won't let Victor take this from you, too, I promise."

Surprised at her serious tone, I nodded. I wanted to cling to the hope I felt at her vow, but I was doubtful. Mama made well-intentioned promises that she couldn't keep. Like when she said moving to Nana's was only temporary. I kept my stuff packed for over a year because every time I tried to unpack, she said, "We'll be out of here in no time, I promise." I didn't mind staying here, but she never stopped calling it Nana's house. It was never home to her. Mama did her best, but she did it alone, and living paycheck to paycheck didn't leave much room for the unexpected.

I needed time to think over my school plans and prepare for the possibility of not returning in the spring. I shuddered at the thought. I didn't want my future to slip away as Mama's had. She took off one semester, then two, and eventually school slipped away. Then Victor left, forcing her to spend her life struggling with multiple jobs just to stay afloat. I knew she didn't want the same for me—that's why she promised to figure out a way to pay for school. We didn't always agree on the direction she pushed me toward, but at least this time we did.

I headed out of the kitchen when Mama called. "Em? I forgot to mention, Detective Sanders will be coming by at six to discuss Grace's case. So, you'll have to be in your room when he gets here."

Stopping in the doorframe, I turned to face her, arms crossed. "Why do I have to be in my room?"

"Because," Mama declared, still facing the window. "It's not right for you to hear all those terrible things. I won't allow it."

"But I lived it! Why does it matter if I hear what Detective Sanders has to say?"

"This discussion is over. I have a lot of work to get to today, and I don't have time for this."

"Of course you don't. Not talking to me seems to be your new thing." I trembled, unmoving from the doorframe despite Mama's dismissal. When would Mama understand that I needed those answers to sleep at night?

When she turned her back to finish the dishes, I huffed and headed to my room. I paced, boxed in by my small, ten-foot by ten-foot space, and reminded myself that Mama's words held no weight. I planned to listen to Detective Sanders, even if I had to do so in secret.

• • •

Six o'clock rolled around as I finished cleaning up the leftover pasta we had eaten for dinner. I half-listened to the deep voice coming from the evening news program broadcasting tomorrow's weather. More snow and ice—no surprise there. Mama and Nana sipped coffee in front of the TV, buried under blankets on the forest green sofa. I scrubbed a dish while looking between the clock and the door. I expected Detective Sanders to arrive at any moment. That didn't appear to concern Mama, who looked like she would soon get up, stretch, and wish us good night as she did every evening after the news.

The buzzer rang, prompting me to dry my hands and hurry to my room. Nana followed me down the hall and retreated to her own room. I shut my door, loud enough for Mama to hear, then reopened it a crack. I peered past the long, thin hallway, to where Mama and Detective Sanders greeted one another near the foyer, exchanging pleasantries.

Detective Sanders wore a sympathetic smile that offset the sharp, broad lines of his face. He towered over Mama and took up too much space in the doorway. Mama motioned him into the living room and offered to get him a cup of coffee. In her absence, he took off his police officer's cap, revealing thinning blond hair that stood up at the ends. He ran a hand through his hair and shifted his feet, looking around the room with a trained eye.

I wondered what evidence he gathered. Perhaps he noticed the layer of dust on Gramps' rocking chair, or the scattered family photos which showed faces much brighter and younger than they were now. But his eyes didn't linger on any one spot for long. His posture slumped with a tired disinterest that caused my stomach to knot. I wished his eyes would catch on the mantle picture of Nana, Mama, Grace, and me, so he would understand everything at stake. Did he not realize that he investigated four deaths instead of one? Did he not care? It wasn't just Grace who had died, everyone in that photograph had died with her. I barely recognized the people in that picture: Nana's eyes bright and sharp, Mama's face round and joyful. I didn't even recognize myself. In the photo, I clung to Grace, only coming up to her elbow, and goofy smiles spread across our faces. I was happy then, fooled by the fairy tales that taught me everything would work out in the end. That person experienced joy and laughter. That person was hopeful, or maybe naïve.

Detective Sanders checked his watch and shifted his briefcase to his other hand. Whatever faith I had in him or the case quickly dissolved. He was clearly in a hurry to leave, so sticking around to ask questions and investigate seemed unlikely. In fact, he had asked only a handful of questions since the investigation started. I grew more doubtful with each passing moment.

Mama returned to the living room with his coffee, her eyes wide and alert. "Would you like to take a seat?" she asked, looking toward the sofa.

He nodded and made his way across the room. He straightened a pillow before sitting down, placing his briefcase on the coffee table. Delaying the inevitable conversation, he took a long sip from the mug and fidgeted in his seat. A vein bulged from his neck as he cleared his throat with a slight cough, a reddish hue emerging from where his skin met his collar. Then he set the mug down and leaned forward to look at Mama, who sat across from him in the armchair, just out of my view.

"I wish I had better news for you, Ms. Rizzo." He averted his eyes. "There wasn't enough evidence to continue the investigation."

My heart raced, not wanting to believe the words.

I couldn't see Mama's livid expression, but I imagined it by Sanders's nervous shifting.

"We did as promised, ma'am. All the evidence, including Grace's autopsy and the initial report, was put in her file when we began the investigation. With nothing concrete, we had to close the case. There wasn't any evidence to call for further inquiry and we had no other leads. Unfortunately, there's nothing else we can do," he said, lifting his hands in defeat.

I took a step back. I couldn't believe this. After Grace died, I clung to the investigation, counting on it to make everything right. I knew having answers wouldn't bring Grace back, but I needed some form of retribution. I needed to make sense of what had happened and what kept happening over and over again in my mind. I tried to carry on with normal activities, but every time I picked up a book or sat down to watch TV, I saw the hospital. Grace lying unnaturally still with her head skewed to one side, tubes protruding from her mouth, nose, and arms, machines beeping along with her steady heartbeat, though she was already gone.

I squeezed my eyes shut. Don't think about it, don't remember. My righteous indignation fueled me through everything following the hospital. I told myself, as long as we find some answers, everything would be okay. The delicate balance of right and wrong would be restored, and everything would go back to normal. As Detective Sanders spoke, I felt that scale tipping, irreparably. I didn't want to hear any more of his words, but I was glued to the spot.

"Since the investigation of the circumstances surrounding Grace's death was inconclusive, we closed the case and completed her file. I have the death certificate here with me now if you would like it," he said.

"Yes, that would be fine," Mama replied, her voice hollow.

He reached for his briefcase and opened the latches. I watched as he pulled out a file and handed it to Mama. She went silent, and the detective looked to the floor, blinking. I fought against a sinking feeling and wished she would protest, demanding a more thorough investigation.

Instead, Mama cleared her throat and stood with a rigid posture, coming back into my view. She reached to shake the detective's hand, who rose to meet her. "Thank you for all your help, Detective."

The detective didn't meet her eyes. "I wish there was more I could do."

Mama nodded and took the mug from him. He gathered his things and left as fast as he had arrived.

I shut my bedroom door at the same time the detective closed the front door. Hurrying away from the approaching footsteps in the hallway, I rushed for my bed. One look at me and Mama would know I had heard the conversation. I buried myself under the covers and squeezed my eyes shut, hoping Mama would think I was sleeping. My breath stilled as the door creaked open, light spilling in from the hallway.

After a moment, Mama sighed and closed my door, her footsteps retreating back down the hallway.

I shivered under the covers, wrapping them tighter as I turned to stare up at the ceiling. Glow-in-the-dark stars illuminated a small constellation. I counted them, distracting my thoughts from the crushing sadness that threatened to take over. A few tears fell, then quickened into a steady stream. I cried until my tears ran out and only an aching in my heart remained. My eyelids grew heavy, and I drifted into sleep, lulled by the memory of Grace's flaming red hair and smiling face.

FOUR

A few days later, a freezing rain showered the midafternoon, casting a steady rhythm of ice against my window. I remained in my room as I tidied the shopping bags strewn across my floor. I decided to take advantage of the New Year's Day sales and gather supplies for school. Harry sat among the bags, sniffing at the new purchases. I had bought folders, notebooks, and other essentials earlier this morning, attempting to check off the list of supplies for the upcoming semester.

My stomach fluttered at the thought of starting classes in less than two weeks. I focused all my energy on getting ready. I practically had my bags packed. I chewed my lip, feeling a sting of guilt for leaving Mama to take care of Nana. Sure, Mama could manage her before and after work, but who would help Nana make meals? Who would play her favorite movies on the TV? Who would make sure she didn't get lonely, scared, or confused?

Mama said she would come up with a solution for Nana before I went to a university. But classes would start soon, and Mama had done little else except waive off my concern, claiming that she needed to tie up loose ends with the hospital and sort out bills before we discussed school.

Until now, Nana's dementia had not been an obstacle to leaving for school. Last semester, we experienced only a few incidents where one of us returned home in the middle of the day to answer Nana's panicked calls. Then her condition had taken a turn during winter break, and now worry sat heavy in my heart. But I needed to return to school. I couldn't sit around watching my future slip away, leaving me nothing but a hole in my heart. It ached every time I slowed down enough to remember and every time I stepped foot in this house. Now more than ever, I craved my class schedule, distracting me in neat, fifty-minute packages. I would know where to be, what to do, and what to expect. Surrounded by uncertainty, I counted on the routine and structure of school to pull my life back together. Yes, that was what I needed.

I headed for the living room desk, looking for the next item on my supplies list, and found Mama sitting there with a phone to her ear. She sniffled, hunched over the same file of papers given by Detective Sanders a few days ago. She clutched a blue paper, gazing at words I couldn't see.

My stomach turned. It must be the death certificate that Detective Sanders mentioned.

Mama spoke into the phone. "I was afraid you were going to say that, and I don't agree with your decision. It's not acceptable that we will never find out the circumstances of what happened. I want to know if you pursued every possibility before closing Grace's case." She paused while the person on the phone, who I assumed to be Detective Sanders, responded. "There must be more you can do." Her shoulders shook as she began to cry. "Yes, I—I understand. Goodbye, Detective."

The floor creaked beneath my feet as Mama hung up the phone. Her eyes shot to my burning face, casting me a knowing glance. She knew I had heard the phone call.

I cleared my throat and emerged from the hallway. As I approached, she folded the blue paper into the file and closed it shut, intent on avoiding a conversation about the investigation.

It had been days since Detective Sanders's visit, and Mama still hadn't said a word about the file he had given her. She maintained a cold exterior and pretended like nothing had happened. Mama said she would always protect me, and I believed her, but that also meant she tried to keep things from me. I don't think she ever planned on discussing the truth.

Although I did not want to read the documents, she should have told me how the investigation had turned out. I had a right to know without overhearing her phone calls. Even so, I didn't want to read the death certificate myself or see the blue paper where the words sprawled.

No matter what the words said, the permanent black ink meant one thing: the end. There would be no justice, no going back. Mama's phone call made it clear that the investigation would never continue. We would never find out the circumstances of Grace's death. I saw no point in agonizing over the blue paper when it only reminded me of the unfairness and tragedy that enveloped my life.

"Mama?" I said, approaching the desk. "Why aren't you at work? I thought you were supposed to go back today?"

Mama ducked her head, wiping at the tears that ran down her red, blotchy face. She pretended as if I didn't notice, and I followed her lead. She shrugged. "I wasn't feeling well this morning, so I called in. I will try to go back tomorrow."

"Was that okay with your boss?"

"Yeah, of course."

"Well, I just figured since you went through all that trouble just to get the last couple weeks off—"

She stiffened. "It's fine, I've got it handled."

I nodded, deciding to leave the topic there. "I finished getting most of my supplies for school this morning."

Mama stood from the desk, her back facing me as she shuffled her papers together. "Are you sure you want to go back so soon? Maybe you should take some time off. It might even be good for you." Her red-rimmed eyes failed to meet mine.

"You sound like Aunt Maeve. Of course I want to go back." I eyed her, wondering why she made the suggestion.

"All right then, I have to run to the grocery store and do some errands, but I should be home before dinner." Her voice was quiet, her back still turned to me.

I narrowed my eyes. "I thought you weren't feeling well."

"I'm not. But things still have to get done around here, don't they?" Mama turned around, an ache staggering her movements. She grabbed the file as she headed to her room. Leaving me with a growing pit of worry in my stomach.

I took a deep breath and returned to my supplies list. If nothing else, at least I could control my checklists and plans.

• • •

After an hour of organizing supplies, my notebooks and folders were color-coded by class and subject, and my pencil case brimmed, but the unease left from my conversation with Mama remained. With all the recent changes, perhaps she didn't think I could handle school. She certainly thought I couldn't handle Detective Sanders' news. She treated me like glass, but I saw right through her. The way she flinched at my hugs, as if she feared shattering if I got too close. She never wanted to appear weak or less than capable of taking care of everyone. Thus, she decided I must be the breakable one, and projected onto me what she feared of herself.

I sprang from my desk chair and walked into Nana's room.

She sat in her green armchair, watching the small, boxy TV that sat on her dresser. As I plopped down on the edge of her bed, she pointed the remote to turn off the screen and greeted me with a smile. "What are you up to, my little chickadee?" Her voice was soft and lacked the sharpness of panic that had persisted the previous few days. It had been too long since she had a good day. Maybe her calmness meant the confusion had cleared. Despite my worries, my mood brightened at seeing Nana's cloudless, sparkling eyes.

"I've been packing for school. There's so much to figure out, with housing and fees, I'm afraid it won't get done on time."

She nodded. "I'm sure your mother has it handled."

"Well, that's partly why I'm worried. She acted odd this morning. I can't tell if it's because of the call—" I stopped myself before telling Nana that I had overheard Mama's phone call with Detective Sanders this morning. Learning that he wouldn't consider reopening the investigation had upset Mama and could have something to do with her unusual mood, but I couldn't explain that to Nana. Although Nana appeared to be having a good morning, I had learned the hard way that some memories would not return with the sunrise. Though, I felt certain Nana still remembered the importance Mama placed on my education. "She suggested that I take time off from school. That's strange right?" Mama seemed upset a lot recently, but she had never questioned if I wanted to return to school until now.

Nana raised her eyebrows. "That's certainly a first for Gina."

"I know. She's worked all these years to help support me through school so I can secure a future, and now she wants me to take a break? It doesn't make sense. Maybe she thinks I won't be able to handle the course load after…now." I looked away, hoping Nana wouldn't notice my omission.

She furrowed her brow. "I doubt that. Classwork has never been a problem for you. Maybe she was checking to make sure school is what you really want. She's always been insistent that you focus on your studies because she wants what's best for you. I'm proud of her for that." Nana didn't offer praise for Mama often, and never to her face. Yet, where I was concerned, they managed to find common ground.

"I know she does. Which is why I thought it was strange that she asked."

"Maybe what's best isn't what you would expect. Time off could help you decide what career you want."

"I decided on a finance major."

Her wide-eyed surprise dissolved into laughter. "You? In finance?"

I looked down. "It's…practical."

"But you don't like finance."

I stayed silent, unwilling to argue about this. Especially because she was right. But I needed a career that would give me security. Nana didn't understand that. She hadn't worked a job in her whole life, and she avoided practicality whenever possible.

"What about your sketches? Maybe you should consider art classes?"

"They're just doodles, Nana. I can't make a career out of that."

"Yes, well, you don't need to have everything figured out now."

"That's true, but I am looking forward to school."

A smile pulled at her lips. "That eager to get away from me, are you?" Guilt about leaving Nana resurfaced.

"No way. I would take you with me if I could."

"If you're really looking forward to going, then why are you worried about your conversation with your mother?"

"Everything is different now. I need this one thing to turn out as planned," I said, surprised by the urgency in my voice.

"What's different?"

I looked up at Nana's confused face. Sometimes it was easy to pretend she hadn't changed, but her question reminded me we couldn't talk like we used to. New memories hadn't stuck, old memories faded away, and she remained, living each day the same as the last.

I gave a half-hearted shrug.

"Don't you go silent on me," Nana said.

I sighed and thought of a plausible answer. "I guess I'm worried I won't make friends at my new college." Which was partially true. I didn't feel like the same person who could go to the mall and chat mindlessly with people. I didn't know how I would fit back into the world.

Nana frowned, and said, "You guard your heart closely because people who were supposed to be there for you weren't." I looked away from her observing eyes. "But you should give people a chance. The past isn't now."

I nodded, but the tightness in my chest told me Nana was wrong. The past kept happening over and over, replaying in my head, reminding me of what could never be. I had to face it every morning when I woke up and Grace wasn't there, and again when I smelled a coconut scent, reminiscent of her favorite lotion, or when I stared at her empty chair at the dinner table. I didn't want to face it anymore, that's why I had to leave.

I didn't bother to continue the conversation with Nana, and I resigned myself to watch a movie with her. We moved to the living room and sat on the sofa. I snuggled closer, clinging to all I had left.

• • •

A turning knob and thump against the front door announced Mama's return a few hours later. I hopped up from my spot next to Nana on the sofa and held open the door, expecting to take arms full of heavy bags from her.

"Where are the groceries?" I asked, frowning at Mama's empty hands. Silence stretched on as Mama took off her coat and boots, looking at anything except me. She had been gone far too long to come home empty-handed.

I tensed, feeling the small grip of control I had gained during the day slip.

She headed down the hall, slumping her shoulders, and went into her room. It was best not to pry when Mama was in such a mood, but she seemed more distraught than usual.

After glancing at Nana, who seemed content enough to be left alone, I followed Mama, then shut her bedroom door behind me. I sat next to her on the edge of the bed, picking invisible lint off the duvet. "What's going on?"

Mama inhaled a ragged breath and swallowed, stifling tears that threatened to escape. She fiddled with her hands, picking at uneven nails worn by housework and a tireless schedule. "I didn't go to the grocery store," she said, sounding small.

"I figured." I turned to face her, my eyebrows drawing together.

"I was at the bank. We're in trouble, Emma. It's not good."

My stomach lurched. We lived paycheck to paycheck for as long as I could remember, always on the brink of financial trouble. Since Nana's savings had run out, the pressure to stretch Mama's paycheck increased, and each month I worried it wouldn't be enough. I felt the strain each time Mama put back groceries at the register or told me to layer on more clothes to save on the heating bill. But Mama never showed her worry. She always insisted that everything would be fine. Before, I had bristled at her unfounded optimism, but hearing her admit to the trouble was much worse. I tried not to think about the hospital and funeral bills that Mama had spent weeks arguing about on the phone. Our financial worries had seemed small in comparison, but now those worries poured over into reality, and it seemed everything had gone wrong at once. Mama's words about the mounting cost of school resurfaced, and I pushed them to the back of my mind, warding off panic.

I stared at her, silently urging her to continue.

Mama hunched over, burying her face in her hands with only her reddened nose showing. "I got fired," she whispered.

"What?" I exclaimed. "How did this happen?"

"My boss only gave me five days off and I couldn't go back that soon." Her tears came faster as her words spilled out. "That wasn't even enough time to drive to Texas and deal with everything at the hospital." She wiped at her face. "Then there was the funeral to arrange. After that, I had to sort out the bills and answer calls from family. And that was it." She shrugged, looking at me with an expression of hopelessness that flipped my worry into anger.

"Dr. Torres has known you for almost eight years. Couldn't he give you a few more days off? And what happened to your sick days?" My words rushed out, harsh and panicked.

"All those times I had to come home early to take Nana to the doctor added up," Mama said, her voice clipped with resentment, "and Dr. Torres doesn't really care about us. Nobody does. I saw this coming for a while, actually. I went into the office early one morning and caught him interviewing a bunch of people who looked just out of college."

"Why would he do that? You're the only reason that office is still in business. Nobody would work harder at that job than you."

"It all goes back to money. He could get away with paying a younger person with no experience half of what he pays me."

I tightened my arms around myself and squeezed, hoping the pressure would keep me from flying to pieces. "What do we do now?"

"I've looked for jobs since that day I caught him interviewing people, just in case, but I've had no luck. I can try to get unemployment, and your grandma's social security will help, but it's not enough, especially with all the medical bills."

"What were you doing at the bank? Can they help?"

Mama shifted to look at me, an apology twisting her face. "I was looking into loans we could use for school."

My breath caught, my eyes widening. Not school, I couldn't lose school, too.

"And?" I squeaked.

Mama shook her head. "Not with my credit."

The air left my lungs. That meant no school next semester, possibly not for a while. The future I envisioned faded, replaced by a bleak darkness of uncertainty. All the carefully charted plans, all the vividly imagined dreams—gone in an instant. There would be no escaping this house or my reality. I would have to stay here with reminders all around me and face the truth that Grace would never come home.

My attention fixed on Mama's tired face, lined with too many wrinkles for her age and pools of purple beneath reddened eyes. A few tears escaped my wide eyes as I saw another future in front of me, one of hardship and despair, and its inevitability seemed harder and harder to escape.

"Now what?" I said, melting into a fit of sobs.

Mama took both of my shoulders and shook them. "You stop that now. We need to be strong. There's a lot to do and not a lot of time to figure it out."

"What is there to figure out? We're going to lose everything. We'll be homeless."

"We are not going to be homeless. Do you hear me?"

I nodded, wincing at Mama's fingers digging into my shoulders.

Mama released her grip and sighed. "We might have to go on public assistance. It's getting to the point where your grandma might soon need more care than we can give her. We could find her a facility paid for by the state."

"We are not putting Nana in some care facility. She needs to be with us!"

"Listen, I'm trying to take care of all of us. I made a promise to you that I would make sure you got through school, and I will. Now you already have to take the spring semester off. I will not let you miss the fall semester, too. I just need a little time, and we'll be back on our feet." She restored her composure and the glimpse of her despair faded away.

"And your solution is to send Nana away?" My eyes remained wide with shock. I couldn't blink. It was like watching a train wreck happen in front of me.

"We don't have a lot of options, Emma. When I'm looking for a new job, I'll have to take any offers I can get. I might be back to working long hours at the grocery store, or a restaurant. Do you know how hard it's been trying to juggle work and taking care of Nana? I won't have the time to take care of her like I used to. It wouldn't be fair to her." I hadn't realized how hard it had been for Mama. The exhaustion showed in her face, and I knew she couldn't continue working herself to rags taking care of everyone.

We couldn't manage Nana's condition if Mama went back to working long hours.

"What are we going to do?" I asked.

She patted my back. "It'll all be okay once we sell the house."

I gasped. "Sell the house?"

She frowned, as if it were obvious. "Yes, sell the house. Without a job, I can't afford to pay the bills, and we don't have enough savings to tide us over until I get a new one, especially with the funeral costs."

"Nana has lived in this house for fifty years. It's your childhood home, and I practically grew up here." My voice wavered, and I shook my head. "There has to be another way."

"If there was another way, don't you think I would've done it by now?" Frustration leaked through her voice.

I stood up and paced the floor, unable to sit next to her any longer. "No, actually, I don't. You never enjoyed living here. We've lived here for seven years, and you still call it Nana's house. I'm sure you still have boxes you haven't unpacked. You can't wait to get out of here. For whatever reason, you need to prove that you can take care of everything by yourself, even if it's at the expense of the people who need you."

Mama flinched at my harsh words, and my anger dissolved. I realized I wasn't only upset about Nana. I needed Mama, too. But she had become absorbed in the world she kept to herself. She wouldn't let me in; it had been weeks since had a real conversation, and she hadn't said a word about losing her job. Blindsided, I felt the rug being pulled from under my feet yet again.

She looked down. "You don't understand what it's like for me here." I turned and sat next to her again as she spoke in broken whispers, "When I look around, I see my childhood.

It wasn't fun being Al's younger sister. He tormented me, and Nana never stopped him. She wanted me to be more independent and said she would fail as a mother if I couldn't learn to stick up for myself. Some disappointment I must be." She huffed. "Your grandpa was always at work, but I looked forward to him coming home. All the loneliness and uncertainty I felt is still here, reminding me of the fact that I failed. It's supposed to be my responsibility to take care of you. I should be able to buy a house of our own, and I'm sorry I can't give that to you." Her lip quivered and I grabbed her hand. I didn't know that she felt that way about living here, but I knew what she meant; this house had a way of storing memories.

Desperation clawed at my throat, tightening it. Despite Mama's reasons, I couldn't let her sell the house, knowing it would be gone forever.

"I'll get a job." The words flew from my mouth faster than I could comprehend them. "It's not like I'll be at school, anyway. I'll pitch in until you find someplace else to work. This way, you can take your time looking for a job with more reasonable hours that'll allow you to take care of Nana. Then she could stay with us." I didn't know if the plan would work, but any plan was better than accepting our fate.

A flash of surprise showed before Mama lifted her chin. "That's nice of you to offer, but I can't let you do that. It's my responsibility to pay the bills, and you need to focus on getting back to school." To me, twenty years old seemed old enough to pay bills, but Mama never stopped treating me like a child. "It wouldn't do much good, anyway. The most you'd get is a minimum wage job, and that's not enough to keep this house, even if you did work full time," she said.

"What about our savings? I know you said we wouldn't have enough to tide us over until you find a job, but if I worked in the meantime, maybe we could make it last long enough to pay the bills and keep the house." Hope bloomed in my chest. The more I entertained the idea, the better it sounded. School wasn't an option this semester. In the back of my mind, I had seen this coming, but I hadn't wanted to believe it. If I couldn't find structure by going to school, maybe I could find it in a job, and at the same time, prevent the rest of my life from falling apart.

"Even if our savings could cover the difference, how are you supposed to find a job if I can't even get one?" Mama asked. "You don't have any real experience or a college degree for your résumé."

I paused for a moment, thinking over her words. She was right; I didn't have a degree and that limited my options. I had some experience working part-time at my college's library for a semester until the workload became too much and I quit to salvage my GPA. The only other experience I had was the volunteering I did back in high school—my one extracurricular activity. I had spent all my weekends at the retirement home a few blocks away. In return, I had earned a glowing letter of recommendation from my manager. A tentative smile spread across my face as my mind raced with possibilities.

"I know where I could work. Remember the retirement home I used to volunteer at?"

Mama narrowed her eyes. "Yes, I remember. You want to work there? Are they even hiring?"

"My manager told me when I left that if I ever wanted to come back, she would find me a position."

"Yes, as a volunteer," Mama said, shaking her head.

"I think if I just explained that I really need a job, Mrs. Hubert might be able to find me one. I worked really hard there for years; I think that earned me some goodwill."

"If the world operated on goodwill, we wouldn't be in this situation." Her voice softened. "It was kind of you to offer, but your plan is not going to work, and we have to move forward with selling the house."

My voice rose a pitch as I pleaded. "But there's no reason we shouldn't try."

"No, you need to use this time off to focus on your future, not fixing my mistakes.

"Your mistakes? How is any of this your fault? If we are blaming anyone, it should be Victor."

"Victor could never handle responsibility. He left, but it's still my job to take care of you. I was supposed to protect you, and I failed." Her voice cracked as more tears escaped. "First I failed Grace and now this."

I took her hand. "You didn't fail Grace."

She stared ahead, her eyes glazed and damp. "I worked a lot while you two were growing up. Maybe if I was home more, Grace wouldn't have run off searching for Victor. She could have gone to college, stayed close to home, and maybe…" She shook her head. "It doesn't matter anymore."

"That's not me, Mama. I can just get a job in my semester off and go right back to school."

Her quivering lips set in a hard line. "I don't agree. I won't burden you with this responsibility, too."

"But—"

She held up her hand. "I won't hear another word." Mama's face became unreadable, and she rose from her seat. "Now, I need to get in touch with my accountant and figure this mess out. I'll be busy for the rest of the evening." She ushered me out the door and shut it behind me.

Deflated, I marched into my room and slammed the door.

After losing Grace, I had wanted to run from the memories that filled this house. But as the threat of losing it forever loomed, I realized memories of Grace were not the only ones that remained here.

Nana's entire life decorated the house. The wallpaper, beige and patterned with white, budding roses, ingrained memories with pictures and paintings that covered the wall. Nana was a part of the house just as much as the solid wood beams lining the living room ceiling. Nana and Gramps had moved here fifty years ago. She watched the neighborhood turn as the suburban area industrialized and merged with the city outskirts. She remained as the trees grew into towers that lined the streets and darkened the sky. The world had changed around 402 Maple Street, but she stayed still.

That's what I needed—to be still.

If we took Nana from the house, she would surely be lost, set adrift without the steady anchor of this place. And I would drift with her, severed from the last connection to my old life, before everything went wrong. This was all I had left, and I couldn't lose it.

A mixture of anxiety and determination swirled through my veins as I paced my room. With the future uncertain, I needed Nana by my side. She had good days sometimes, and right now, that was one of the few things I could look forward to. I couldn't bear wasting the time we had left with her by leaving her in a facility.

Mama didn't want to take the chance to save the house, but I knew I had to try. It would be easy to take a semester off and let life happen around me. But, unlike Victor, I wouldn't take the easy way out when my family needed help.

I hurried to my desk, pulled open the drawer, and searched through its contents. I sifted through pens, colored pencils, and crumpled sticky notes until I spotted a white business card. *Mrs. Hubert, Manager at Riverside Retirement Center.* Without a moment's hesitation, I picked up my cell phone and dialed the number.

FIVE

The following Tuesday, I walked down the sidewalk toward Riverside Retirement Center. It was warm for early January, but I still wore my heaviest coat and wool scarf. I quickened my pace, not wanting to be late for my meeting with Mrs. Hubert.

During our call, Mrs. Hubert had agreed to meet with me and discuss whether they had any positions open. Though, I hadn't mentioned I needed a paid position. I thought Mrs. Hubert might be more agreeable if I made an appeal in person. I had been too nervous about being rejected outright. Mrs. Hubert's surprised tone had greeted me, the high pitch straining her deep, raspy voice. Quickly, her astonishment had turned to joyful conversation, and we had spent a good deal of time catching up on the phone. I hoped the meeting would go as smoothly as our polite chat.

Mama was not nearly as optimistic. She still didn't want me to go through with finding a job and reminded me at every chance that paying bills was not my responsibility. Sometimes I believed her, and that doubt shone through the holes in my plan. Even so, I had to try. In order to prevent Mama from talking me out of it, I didn't tell her about my meeting.

Determined, I trudged along the busy street. I shouldn't listen to Mama. I couldn't afford to doubt myself, with this being my last hope. All I had to do was arrive on time and somehow talk my way into a job.

Jogging in front of a line of waiting cars, I crossed the street and turned the corner. A large monolith with *Riverside Retirement Center* written across in white letters came into view from behind a row of pine trees. A long stretch of gravel road led me away from the busy street into a manicured plot of towering trees, sprawling hills, and man-made lakes. The entrance to the Center lay ahead of me at a distance far enough to block the view of the stifling city landscape that surrounded the place on all sides.

I remembered how this place had looked while I volunteered here in high school. The smell of cut grass wafting amid the manicured lawn, an ostentatious display of potted flowers, and flowing fountains had been abundant in the spring. Now, the starkness of winter made the Center look more intimidating than inviting. It resembled a row of brick mansions, echoing a colonial style and wealth that had long since left the surrounding area.

The cold air prickled at my face, and I brushed my fingers through my wind-blown hair. The large automatic door slid open. I sighed at the wave of heat that greeted me and stepped into the main entrance, which felt both spacious and homey—just as I remembered it. The smell of hand sanitizer and the bright tint of fluorescent ceiling lights contrasted dark furniture and beige carpeting. I passed the restaurant and bar, both empty during the early afternoon, and turned toward an expansive hallway meant to accommodate the bulkiest of wheelchairs. As I recalled, Mrs. Hubert's office was in the east wing of the independent living section, halfway between the music hall and the church.

The mechanical whirring of a printer echoed out of Mrs. Hubert's cracked-open door. I knocked and waited in the doorway, failing to even out my breaths.

"Come in," Mrs. Hubert said.

"Hello, Mrs. Hubert." I smiled, matching her dimpled expression.

A halo of grayish-white hair surrounded her expressive oval face, thin-framed glasses perched on the tip of her pointy nose. "Emma, have a seat." She waived me forward from behind her desk. Her brown eyes sparkled with warmth, melting the tension in my shoulders. "I have to tell you I was so glad when you called." Her raspy voice boomed. "You were one of our best volunteers."

I flashed a smile and shifted in my seat, embarrassed at the compliment. "Yes, I missed it here," I said, forcing confidence into my voice.

"So, you'd like to come back then?"

"If any positions are available." My heart picked up again. I needed to tell Mrs. Hubert the truth of why I came, but the words wouldn't come, and my courage dissolved.

"I'm sure we can find you something. We just added another weekly bingo night that we could use some help with, or maybe—"

I chewed my bottom lip. "Actually, I was looking for a paid position."

Mrs. Hubert's face fell, her thin eyebrows furrowed in an unfamiliar way. "Oh, I don't think we have any jobs available right now. I could put you on a waitlist and call you when we have something. In the meantime, we still have plenty of volunteering available."

My face burned. I didn't want to disappoint Mrs. Hubert further by continuing this pointless discussion. Perhaps I should just take a volunteering position and leave. Having volunteering on my résumé for college applications would be better than nothing. The words of surrender sat poised at the tip of my tongue, ready to assuage the situation. Mama's words echoed in my mind. My plan would fail anyway. Why bother arguing? I grew frustrated at my own weakness and sat up straighter. Mama's words held some truth—nobody else planned to swoop in and save us.

"I really need a paid position right now. I will take anything," I said, placing urgency behind my voice. My eyes burned, and I felt my composure crumbling. Not here, just hold it together. Shame enveloped me in a vice-like grip while untamed sadness overwhelmed my fragile nerves. The confusion on Mrs. Hubert's face beckoned me to explain, but I couldn't admit my recent struggles to her. I wasn't ready for that. Asking for help didn't come naturally, but I couldn't leave Mrs. Hubert's office without a job, not when I was about to lose the last remnants of my old life. I hoped Mrs. Hubert wouldn't force me to explain further.

Mrs. Hubert blinked, looking startled by my response. Stunned into silence, she paused for an infinite moment. Then her eyes brightened, and her boisterous voice lowered. "Okay, here's what I can do. We might have a use for another caregiver position. We usually expect some type of prior experience, but I know you are a quick learner and a hard worker, so I'm willing to take the chance. Because our budget didn't plan for another hire, I can't pay above minimum wage."

I grasped the side of the chair, preventing myself from jumping out of the seat. I nodded. "Yes. That would be great, I'll take it."

"Well then! Welcome aboard, Emma." Mrs. Hubert beamed, her usual vivaciousness returning.

We went over a few more details and I left with a large packet of information and a smile on my face.

I walked home, still buzzing with adrenaline. Snow fell around me, but my skin felt warm and flushed with excitement. Mrs. Hubert had given me the opportunity I needed, and if Mama agreed to my plan, I would have a chance to prevent my life from changing irreparably. I still had to convince her that accepting the job was the right thing to do. Surely, she would see reason and realize parting with both Nana and the house was the worst thing to do. I shook the snow off my boots outside and hurried into the house.

"Mama," I called from the entryway. "I'm back. I just met with Mrs. Hubert. Guess what?" Unable to contain the news, I shed my outer layers, tossed them in the closet, and rushed to Mama's desk in the living room. "She gave me a job. Like a real, paid one."

Mama turned from her computer and her eyebrows shot up, peaking over the rim of her reading glasses. "I didn't actually think you would go through with this."

I waited for her to continue, but she said nothing else. Instead, a crease formed in her forehead, and she blinked in disbelief.

My face fell. "I told you I would."

"How much does it pay?" she asked.

"Minimum wage, but—"

"And what are the hours?"

"I have to be there at eight and I'm done around five, Monday through Friday."

Mama nodded. She sat back in her chair and took off her glasses, setting them on the desk. "I still don't think this is a good idea. I don't think you should be working when you could focus on getting back to school. Why don't you leave the bills to me and spend your time building your résumé or reconnecting with your friends from school?"

I hadn't spoken to any of my friends since the hospital called us about Grace. I had canceled plans with them to drive down to the hospital in Texas. So, I was obligated to tell them why I had left, but I hadn't heard from them since. At first, I thought they were just giving me space, but the longer they stayed away, the more I realized I wouldn't fit in with them anymore. Most of them couldn't understand that kind of loss, and I couldn't be who I was before. Next week, they would head into their final semester of community college. Meanwhile, I had pressed pause on my life. It was better to just let them move on.

I looked down. "I don't think I'll be hanging out with them anytime soon. Besides, having this job on my résumé will help when I reapply for the fall semester."

"Why can't you just let me handle this?" Mama wouldn't admit she needed my help, but I stood my ground.

"I'm not giving up on the house and Nana. I can't deal with everything changing all at once. Just give me some time. We'll figure this out."

She looked crushed. "Well, if this is what you want to do, I guess I can't stop you."

"It is. As long as you promise not to send Nana away and sell the house."

"I'll do what I can, but it still might not be enough."

My fingers clenched around the information packet. "If I give you my entire paycheck, shouldn't that be enough until you find another job?"

"These things take time, and we might not have enough savings to cover whatever expenses are left." She crossed her arms. "Also, I don't think we should use all our savings to keep the house. It's not a wise decision, and I need to look out for our futures."

Our futures. I wondered if she worried about Nana's future and what would happen if she sent her to a facility. I knew Nana wouldn't want to be away from her house and everything she still found familiar. Mama knew how important it was to me that Nana stayed with us. Yet, she refused to consider any other possibility, all because she didn't want to ask for help.

"Whose future? Because if you were looking out for my future, then you would make sure Nana stays with us."

"We've all had to sacrifice a lot, Emma. After what happened, you can't just expect things to go back to normal," Mama said.

"Well, I'm not giving up."

"I'll do what I can, but I can't promise it will turn out how you want it to."

I nodded and headed to my room, swallowing tears. I stood between the rumpled sheets of my unmade bed and obsolete textbooks strewn across the floor. The silence radiated with uninviting emptiness that amplified the volume of my worried thoughts. My mind looped on the impending possibility of Mama sending Nana away if my plan failed. Nana was all I had left, and then I would be alone.

The familiar stir of clawing sadness and panicked loneliness set in, forcing me out of the room. I opened Nana's door across the hall, risking the wrath of confusion for the chance of familiar warmth. It wasn't a gamble I took often, fearing for the fragility of my heart, but I feared losing Nana more.

I stopped in the doorway, watching her with guarded expectations.

Nana stood at her bookshelf, looking over the titles that covered most of the wall. Her mouth gaped slightly in thought, and she balanced herself with one hand on the shelf while reaching for a worn, red book. Nana read each of her books at least once, her favorites four or five times. I noticed how she held the book in her hands and flipped through the pages, frowning in concentration at the first few lines.

I looked closer at the title, *The Catcher in the Rye*, and smiled, knowing it was one of Nana's favorites.

Nana looked up, noticed my presence, and closed the book. "Emma, dear, what's wrong?" she said.

"What? Oh nothing," I said, ducking my head to wipe at my nose and tear-stained cheeks.

She tilted her head. "I can tell something is bothering you."

I nodded, my lip quivering.

Nana moved to the beige floral armchair and lowered herself. She scooted to one side and held her arms out. I ran to the chair and snuggled up next to her. The two of us were just small enough to fit in the oversized chair if I sat sideways. My arm and shoulder draped over Nana, who hugged me in return.

Nana's fingers combed through my hair and my jumbled nerves untangled. I rested my head on her shoulder, hiding my tears. I squeezed my eyes shut. Listening to the steady beating of her heart, I breathed in deeper, the smell of lavender and something woodsy tickling my nose. I hugged her tighter, wanting to capture the moment in my memory, storing up enough warmth to last through her bad days.

"What's the matter, dear?"

"I'm scared, Nana. I don't know what's going to happen."

"Is this about Grace?" I blinked in surprise and looked up at her. I thought she couldn't remember. The fog blurring her memories was getting worse, but I needed her more than ever. I dared to hope that she could be her old self for a while longer. Nana patted my shoulder. "I know she hasn't been home in a while, but she will come home, eventually."

My hopes deflated. It was too painful to tell Nana that Grace was gone for good this time. I wouldn't try to explain it when she couldn't remember.

Nana continued, oblivious to my disappointment. "Now, I told Gina to stop pressuring that girl to go to college or she would never want to come home. We just have to let her live her life, even if we don't like it."

I should have ended the conversation there, but something prodded me further. Mama never talked about Grace, so Nana was the only one I could talk to. All the conversations Mama and I never had and the questions I couldn't ask boiled over.

"What if she doesn't come home? What if she's gone for good this time?" I asked.

"Well, then, that's her choice, and we have to accept her decision."

For all her aloofness, Nana had a remarkable ability to accept life as it happened. She didn't feel the need to fight against the tide. Instead, she let life happen around her, as if she were a character in one of her books, following the words written for her. I never had that kind of passivity. I wanted to write the words, control how the story turned out. Was that so wrong? Nana thought so. When I was younger, she scolded me for reading the last chapter of a book first. She told me the enjoyment was in the journey. I never saw the point in reading a book that would disappoint me in the end.

"What if it turns out badly?"

"The Lord knows we've done what we can. At some point, we have to let go. We can't control what happens, and we just have to accept that."

I accepted the fact that Grace had left home when I was eleven and she was eighteen. She and Mama had different ideas of what her life should look like. Grace spent years looking for Victor, but he didn't want to be found. She wanted to spend her future chasing the past, and the fairy-tale image she had of Victor. Mama wanted her to move on. Grace was never more than a tourist in every place she ended up, never had a consistent address, only offered scattered phone calls across the years. But I never let go. I always had hope that she would give up and come home. I hoped that when we grew older, we would be close again, and talk about all the things we didn't get to say in our time apart. But that never happened, and now it never could.

"She didn't even say goodbye."

"You know her leaving had nothing to do with you. You two were always inseparable. I remember when you were just a brand-new baby and Grace was almost eight, she would carry you around everywhere, dressing you up like a doll come to life. I think you even preferred Grace over your own mother."

"What am I going to do without her?" I said, my voice barely a whisper.

Nana gave me a light squeeze. "You always have me, and don't you forget it."

On December twelfth, I became an only child.

That was the moment my life became ruled by necessity. What they don't tell you is that grief is overwhelming in the way it strips everything bare. Silence becomes noise, noise becomes silence, routines become survival. First you forget breakfast, then you forget to sleep, soon you find yourself doing these things only when you collapse from exhaustion or shrink a clothing size. For a while, that was my every day. Stuck in the middle of an endless push and pull. I yearned for my old life, lulled by the memory of Grace's flaming red hair and smiling face, while the same memories prompted me to run as far from home as I could. But no matter how far you try to run, the truth catches up. Denial doesn't last forever. The sooner you turn and face the truth, the sooner you can accept it. I knew the clock ticked on my avoidance. With every reminder, like Mama shedding tears over that blue paper, family pictures hanging in their faded frames, and flashing ambulances racing down the street, reality chipped away at my wall of thin ice. Simmering just beneath the surface, a swirl of emotions threatened to erupt. I pushed them away, fearing they would sweep me under the current and I would drown in them. But I already floated beneath the water—and called it air.

Because she didn't say goodbye, and neither could I.

PART TWO

SIX

———

My training period at the Center ended after three weeks. Then, I slid into a blur of routines and monotonous schedules. The days crawled by at the pace of sluggish wheelchairs and leisurely walks, though it felt like six months passed in a blink.

So far, Mrs. Hubert seemed pleased with my work. She said I was made for the job. In some ways, I was. I received a list of residents to look after every week. Some I saw once, some I saw every few days. From eight in the morning to five in the evening, I delivered meals, helped administer medication, steered wheelchairs, and accompanied residents to activities. Then I went home and did the same for Nana.

Nana's memory deteriorated, and the doctor's visits grew more frequent. Mama did her best to keep up, but between taking care of Nana during the day and trying to find a job, the stress was becoming unmanageable. With each passing day, Mama seemed more exhausted. She limped from the ache in her joints and the toll of sleepless nights. More than the workload, I think she tired under the weight of that blue paper she still carried around.

The late nights and early mornings also took a toll on me, but I liked my job. Most of my coworkers were pleasant, though I didn't talk to them much. Except for Natalia, a waitress who worked in the Center's restaurant. We ate lunch together as an unspoken agreement to avoid solitude in the crowded breakroom. Natalia said she was tired of the noisy conversations at her previous table and preferred to eat with one person. Since no other coworkers were willing to disrupt their long-standing lunch plans, I was glad to be that person. Aside from lunch breaks, I my spent days by myself or with the residents. I grew fond of the residents that I saw every week, but I tried not to get attached to my regulars.

During my training period, I had made that mistake. Mrs. Johnson from apartment 304C. A small woman with large, dark eyes that sparkled whenever she spoke of gardening or evenings at her old lake house. Mrs. Hubert assigned me to wheel her to a knitting circle three times a week, but she refused a wheelchair despite her weak bones. So, I accompanied her as we meandered from one end of the Center to the other, joining her in lively conversation and admiring the independent spirit that reminded me of Nana. After a few weeks, I was reassigned. Since that happened all the time, I didn't think much of it until another assignment took me to the hospice wing, and I saw her frail body in one of the beds, connected to tubes and IVs. One of the nurses said her attitude was more stubborn than her brittle bones. They had given out. She would not return to independent living.

After seeing Mrs. Johnson, I felt a sting like a scab torn open, and suppressed thoughts flowed freely. Flashbacks of seeing Grace in the hospital returned that night after work, worse than before. I thought I had moved on, dusted myself off, and left my troubles in the past, but I realized I was wrong. Like a shadow, the memories followed me wherever I went. Haunting like a quiet hum in the background—I could hear it in the silence, see it in my reflection, feel it hovering behind me. After that, I didn't talk to the residents as much; I couldn't risk it.

Then June approached with another round of college application deadlines. I had a choice to make. I could apply, take student loans, and leave Mama to take care of Nana alone, or I could defer another semester. I had thought the finances would have been sorted by then, but Mama remained jobless, and we had no other solutions. I suggested that we find Nana a caretaker, but we couldn't afford it. I hadn't planned to spend more than one semester away from school, but giving up my job meant selling the house and sending Nana to a care facility. Mama said it was only a matter of time before it happened, and I should focus on my future instead of this pointless plan, but I couldn't quit, even if that meant postponing school again.

Mama wasn't happy when I decided to take another semester off from school, but a small part of her must have wanted to keep Nana and our home, otherwise, she would have forced us to move out already, and I would be in a cramped dorm studying finance.

Sometimes I wondered what would've happened if I had gone back to school. I wasn't sure I fit into that life anymore. Worrying about grades and classes, making friends for a semester, and never seeing them again. That used to be my world. Now it all seemed futile. I would never admit it to Mama, but I was glad I wasn't at school.

I opened the kitchen window, inhaling the heavy floral scent of early June. I moved to the refrigerator and looked over the mostly empty shelves. Then I tried the pantry, opened the doors, and peered at the remaining few jars of Nana's jam. The jars, almost two years old, were soon to spoil. But I couldn't bring myself to open them. Once they ran out, that spot would stay empty—Nana didn't make jam anymore. I liked seeing it on the shelf, knowing every time I opened the pantry, I would still have five jars left.

Butter on toast would have to do. I could come up with something better than that, but I was almost late for work again. The past few weeks, my mornings had consisted of sleeping through alarms and late starts. At first, I had attributed late nights to helping Mama with the unsuccessful job search and researching loans. But after accepting another semester off school, and finding no solution in sight, I had nothing to blame for my sleepless nights other than the nightmares and flashbacks that I tried to avoid by watching my alarm clock count the minutes until six in the morning.

Something happened when I closed my eyes. All I could see was tubes and cords tangled into flaming red hair and the beeping of a machine murmuring under Mama's cries. Everyone said time would fix all, but six months had passed, the memories did not fade, and I didn't feel any different since I had stood above her grave, wondering what had gone so wrong. Some nights, I lay there waiting for the sunrise to cast the shadows away, hoping for the moment I could jump out of bed and busy my mind with work, chores, schedules—anything to keep the memories at bay. I tried to push the memories back during the day, and with my schedule, I wouldn't have the chance to ponder the past, anyway.

With toast in one hand and my bag in the other, I rushed from the kitchen, looking for Mama. "Mama, I'm heading to work, okay?" I stopped in her doorway.

Mama looked up from where she sat on the bed, wrapped in a warm blanket. She held a familiar blue paper that I saw her reading often. Each time I caught her, Mama wiped away any tears and hid the blue paper in Detective Sander's file, which I suspected she tucked somewhere in her closet. I never brought it up. I wanted to forget the file existed.

"Not so loud, you'll wake your grandma," Mama said.

"Nana finally fell asleep?"

"Just a couple of hours ago, I think. We'll have to tell Dr. Warren the new medication isn't helping her sleep."

"None of the medication seems to be working," I said, not realizing I spoke my worries out loud.

Mama sagged in her chair. Darkness cast over her face, emphasizing the hollow of her high cheekbones, and the lines and creases that began to appear six months ago. Every day Mama ate less and slept more, complaining about mysterious pains that tormented her joints, head, and stomach.

"And how are you feeling?" I asked, frowning.

"A bit better. I think I'll try eating some breakfast today."

"Good. But you might not have many options. I have to run to the grocery store after work. Do you need me to pick up anything?"

"Just the usual is fine."

I nodded. "I have to leave before I'm late for work, but I'll be home around six thirty to make dinner. Do you have any interviews today?"

"No," Mama said, her voice hollow. Over the past few months, her high-strung disposition and endless to-do lists unraveled into apathy and fatigue.

I decided not to push her and instead headed out the front door just in time to catch the bus, jogging and out of breath.

• • •

Later in the day at work, I pushed a bulky wheelchair down the hall, straining with some effort at the incline. Mary Anne Turner was a small woman, but the chair itself must have been at least half her weight.

"Come on then, Emma, you can go faster than that. Put some muscle into it," Mary Anne said in her high, tremored voice. Her auburn-dyed curls bounced as she laughed at my expense.

I accompanied Mary Anne to the music hall every Friday for the weekly performances. She was a lovely woman, vibrant, traveled, and exceedingly quick-witted. I reminded myself of that whenever she felt the need to give me an unsolicited performance review. During lunch, Natalia liked to look at my assignment sheet at the start of each week. She had grimaced after seeing Mary Anne's name under my list of regulars. As a waitress, Natalia witnessed first-hand Mary Anne's constant complaining and returning of her uneaten food to the kitchen. Yet, I didn't mind Mary Anne's company. Besides her occasional remarks or requests for help, we hardly spoke.

I assisted many other residents as a caregiver, most assignments changing from week to week. But my Fridays in the music hall were consistent, and I began to look forward to the live music and Mary Anne's indifference. In comfortable silence, we made the trip from her small, dorm-like apartment, through endless hallways walled with glass windows, and up the ramp to the music hall. I wheeled her into the large hall, which could easily seat two hundred people. We were the first to arrive. Mary Anne insisted on being twenty minutes early to secure her spot in the front row. The static shuffling of my uniform and the squeak of my white tennis shoes echoed in the empty hall. I pushed the wheelchair to the outside of the front row and took a seat beside Mary Anne.

"Emma, could you help me with my glasses?" Mary Anne asked. Her hands shook too badly to do most tasks herself, like operating an electric wheelchair or putting on her glasses.

"Of course," I replied, grabbing the glasses from the wheelchair's pouch. Carefully, I placed the wired frame on Mary Anne's delicately pointed nose.

Mary Anne blinked a few times and nodded in thanks. She crossed her hands on her lap, signaling the start of our comfortable silence. I tried to prevent my mind from wandering unoccupied for long, so I pulled a book from my bag, one I took from Nana's shelf, and read.

The shuffling of a cane and approaching steps pulled my concentration. A tall, sturdy man with wisps of white hair and sparkling blue eyes slowly headed our way. I recognized him from his bright yellow hooded sweatshirt, which he wore each time I saw him in the music hall. He seemed to share Mary Anne's penchant for punctuality and always arrived just five minutes after us. He nodded in greeting and gave me a warm smile and a wave. Like Mary Anne and me, he took his seat in the front row, leaving a few empty chairs between us. He reclined and let out a contented hum. He often tried to converse with me before others came and filled the seats between us, but I soon learned to bury my nose in a book before his arrival. He seemed nice enough, but his polite questions about my school plans and interests put me on edge.

He cleared his throat once, then twice.

I would not look up from my book. Nope, definitely not falling into that trap again.

He didn't give me an opportunity to refuse the bait. "You sure do like to read, don't you?" His gruff voice boomed with enthusiasm.

I sighed and looked up, forcing a tight smile. "Yes, I do, I must get it from my grandma." I laughed politely and returned to the book, hoping to end the conversation there.

"You're lucky. All I ever got from my grandma was a sore ear for sneaking extra helpings of dessert, bless her heart."

I let out a surprised laugh despite myself.

The Yellow Hoodie Man turned forward, his eyes sparkling with humor. With a toothless smile, he raised his chin, pleased with himself. Then he looked at me again, and I clutched the book tighter. "As a retired English teacher, I've read quite a few books in my day. My wife complained I always had my nose in a book. She reminded me to go and live a real life, but I think books are as real as it gets, except, unlike real life, they actually have tidy conclusions and happy endings. But I'm sure you know all about that, don't you?"

My eyebrows shot up. What did he mean by that? Did I have *bereaved* written across my forehead, or did he just assume that I knew a lot about books? I didn't get the chance to ask before others filed in, murmuring in anticipation for the night's entertainment.

A hunched woman with a gray bob sat next to me, forming a barrier between us. I breathed a sigh of relief and subsequently choked on the woman's overwhelming geranium-scented perfume. A string quartet entered the stage and played scales to warm up while the rest of the rows filled.

The lights dimmed, and I relaxed into my seat, content to occupy my mind with nothing else but instrumental melodies. I pushed the Yellow Hoodie Man's words aside, determined not to ponder their meaning. Darkness enveloped the room as the stage cast a warm glow of spotlights over the performers and the first few rows of the audience. After a silent pause, the wooden instruments started, volatile and quick. The music rose and fell with a gripping intensity, the effort beading sweat on the musicians' foreheads. Eventually, the relentless sawing of bows on strings slowed, and the music seceded into a mellow confluence of final, resonant notes. The next set had the same exciting pace as the first, but with a distinctly Latin beat. I couldn't help but tap my foot.

Heads craned as a middle-aged woman appeared at the foot of the raised stage, swaying and swinging her arms along with the beat. Her carefree smile beamed, and she earned additional applause from the audience. I smiled, recognizing her as Daisy Martin. She often gave impromptu dance performances whenever she liked a particular song. Daisy should have been too young to live here, but because of her intellectual disability, the Center allowed her to move in with her mother.

The string quartet noticed their new performer and played with renewed vivacity. Typically, she danced alone, but now another person appeared beside her, bowed slightly with his hand outstretched. I blinked in surprise. It was the Yellow Hoodie Man. Daisy's smile intensified, and they joined hands, stepping side-to-side in a clumsy box step. The pair pivoted, and I smiled at the look of determination on the Yellow Hoodie Man's serious face. The audience's expression varied from adoration to amusement, except for a few disgruntled onlookers.

He gave Daisy a few gentle spins and some grand arm swinging as the music slowed to an end. He bowed and gestured applause for Daisy before taking his seat, his focused face never cracking.

I joined in the applause while Mary Anne huffed in annoyance. I turned to see her casting a scrutinizing look toward the man, mumbling something about him being a nuisance. She obviously knew him in some capacity.

"Mary Anne, who is that?" I whispered.

"That's Ken." Her tone sharpened. "He's an odd one."

After the musicians took their final bow, I shifted forward, looking to my right to get another glance at Ken, but his seat was empty. I found him shaking hands and exchanging smiles with the musicians before heading toward the door. Most of the residents arrived and left in groups, but he was alone, weaving between the packs of chattering people who cast speculative glances at him as he disappeared into the crowd.

"Shall we go?" Mary Anne said with a hint of impatience, pulling my attention from my curious gaze.

"Yes, of course. I'll take you back." I wheeled Mary Anne toward the exit and frowned, realizing I looked for bright yellow in the lingering crowd.

SEVEN

Monday marked the start of a new schedule and a list of people to care for. The weekly caregiver meeting started at seven-thirty, a half an hour before work, and the halls remained empty except for a few lingering janitors cleaning up for the day ahead.

The ache in my feet protested the prospect of pushing wheelchairs and traversing the endless halls with carts of food and medication. The blisters on my heels hadn't recovered from the ballet flats I foolishly chose to wear last week instead of gym shoes. I wouldn't make that mistake again, even if I had to wear my worn sneakers that had turned from white to tan and expelled air with each step. But I couldn't justify buying a new pair; every penny went to keeping the house.

I smoothed down the wrinkles of my light pink top and matching pants before walking into the hallway where Mrs. Hubert's office was located. I hoped she wouldn't give me any difficult assignments that would require me to rush from one end of the Center to the other. My mornings and evenings helping Nana wore me thin, but I tried to pick up the slack for Mama. Before I had left this morning, it took a good half an hour to convince Nana to swallow her medications and even longer to make sure she ate breakfast, leaving me no choice but to run out the door with partially combed hair, a creased uniform, and a buzz of anxiety that marked the start of most days. I left early and Mama slept late, so I didn't see her aside from dinner, but when I did, she looked frail and distant, as if her mind were somewhere else.

I entered the office, where a group of ten other caregivers waited for Mrs. Hubert to arrive with the assignments. They clustered into three groups seemingly arranged by age. One group, a varying mix of brunette thirty-somethings, lounged in chairs. They were young enough to gossip about which TV shows they had started and finished that weekend but were old enough to call me "sweetie." The group of middle-aged caregivers kept to themselves. A burly man with an unkempt beard and boisterous personality chatted loudly with a stout woman who ended all her sentences with a self-qualifying laugh. A short woman with frizzy black hair and warm, beige skin nodded repeatedly at their exchange.

I stood next to the silent few, an elderly woman named Dorris, who had worked there as long as anyone could remember, and a girl who looked around my age. The girl had dyed-black hair and chomped on strictly prohibited gum. She hardly ever looked up from her phone, leaving me to exchange polite smiles of greeting with Dorris, a woman of few words. I shifted on my feet, still feeling uncomfortable among the group despite working here for over six months. Self-consciousness washed over me. It was the same feeling that appeared at school, at the store, any place with a gathering of people. I didn't belong to the same world as those who could discuss their lives with ease.

I rehearsed my responses and practiced my smile each morning. How are you? Fine, I would answer. What did you do this weekend? Oh, I just caught up on some errands, I would lie. I couldn't mention taking care of Nana, worrying about Mama, or grieving Grace. I hadn't done anything else this weekend, but I couldn't tell anyone that. I could just talk about the weather. People loved to talk about the weather. In conversation, the weather was safe, no matter if it was rainy, sunny, unseasonably cool, or temperate. Sometimes we could see the storms rolling in, sometimes the lightning struck without thunder, occasionally we would catch a break in the clouds, the sky transforming into a clear blue for a while. Who knew what tomorrow would bring; we couldn't control it, but we all shared it. A lot like loss. But no one talked about grief like we talked about the weather. It made them sad.

Mrs. Hubert breezed through the door, files in hand, cutting off the tinkling laughter of one of the brunettes. "Good morning," she announced in a singsong voice, quieting the room. "I hope you all had a lovely weekend." She cleared her throat, masking the breathlessness of her voice. She plopped down behind her desk and straightened her green-cabled cardigan before setting out the files.

The room answered with a mix of friendly hellos and good mornings. I stood straighter and stepped to the side, my view of Mrs. Hubert concealed by the burly man's large frame.

Mrs. Hubert looked up with attentive brown eyes and placed her clasped hands on her desk. "So, I have all your assignments for this week. You all know the drill. Make sure to fill out the charts and put them on my desk at the end of the day. Let me know if you have any questions." She gave a toothy smile and looked pointedly around the room. Then she motioned for us to grab the folders, dismissing us from the room.

The room buzzed with talk of the new assignments, gossip, and groans of disappointment as if this week would be any different from the last. I retrieved my folder and scanned the list of assignments. Many names I expected: Mary Anne at her usual time on Friday, meals for Harold in assisted living, bingo with Martha.

I turned over the paper, looking for new assignments. These were called the temps, the assignments that were only given if a resident unexpectedly felt sick and needed a caregiver for a short time. I usually had a list of five or six temps, so I frowned when I saw an almost-blank page. Only a single name was printed at the top: *Ken Gallagher.* Could it be the same Ken I saw in the music hall? He was the only Ken I knew of, but I hoped it wasn't him. Placing his name on that list meant that he was ill, and in most cases, temps eventually needed full-time caregivers.

Though I had shied from his questions, he seemed kind. Maybe if I had been brave enough to answer, we could have been friends. And he was the only one to get up on that stage to dance with Daisy. It couldn't be him, the same Ken who had danced and waltzed in front of the audience on Friday. That Ken was too lively, too sturdy to have landed on this list just two days later. I also wondered at the lack of other names. Maybe Mrs. Hubert made a mistake?

"Mrs. Hubert, I have a question about my assignment. I think I might be missing part of my list," I said, approaching the desk tentatively.

"No, that's right. It should all be there." The other caregivers filed out, heading toward their first assignments. Distracted by her computer screen, Mrs. Hubert turned away.

Maybe I only received one assignment because someone had complained. Perhaps Mrs. Hubert felt I couldn't handle a full workload and put me on probation? Mama wouldn't be able to pay all the bills if my hours were cut. I was always polite and tried to be exceedingly patient even with the most difficult of residents. Nobody had ever complained about me before, except Mary Ann, of course, but all her words were laced with some degree of derision, and she preferred to complain directly to me.

Mrs. Hubert looked up, noticing that I lingered. "Is there something else, dear?"

"Oh, um…" I hesitated, knowing Mrs. Hubert expected a question and not anxious rambling. "I just wanted to double-check that I'm only assigned to one temp this week. It just seems unusual. Is something wrong? Did I do something wrong?" I couldn't keep the worry from my voice.

Mrs. Hubert waved a dismissive hand. "It's nothing like that. You're a star. Once you check in with Mr. Gallagher's nurse and get his schedule, you'll see that you're booked to take care of him all week."

"I've never been assigned to a temp for more than an afternoon before."

"I don't arrange the schedule like this often, but Mr. Gallagher asked specifically for you." Mrs. Hubert looked curiously over her glasses.

I swallowed hard as I realized Mr. Gallagher must be the Yellow Hoodie Man. Hopefully nothing serious had happened. I frowned, wondering why he had asked for me. "I didn't know that was allowed."

Mrs. Hubert shrugged. "Yes, well, he insisted. You are becoming quite popular, Emma."

I gave a polite laugh, though she couldn't be more wrong.

Mrs. Hubert waved me off with a cheerful goodbye and I headed out the door with a torrent of questions on my mind.

• • •

I had a fifteen-minute break before the morning rounds started. I sat across from Natalia, pretending to look at the pictures she showed me of her one-year-old son.

"Look at Mateo walking! He's finally taking steps on his own. I was so worried when he hadn't hit that milestone before turning one last week, but I guess he's just a late bloomer."

"I told you he would be fine," I said as she slid to the next video. Her eyes never left the screen, and sometimes I thought she forgot I was there.

During my first week on the job, I had lost my way to the pharmacy and found myself in the first-floor restaurant where Natalia waitressed. Later she told me the panic on my face made her maternal instincts kick into overdrive, and she took me under her wing. She told me who to watch out for, which coworkers to avoid, and how to find my way around the Center. We exchanged numbers and started meeting for lunch. She talked a lot, and I mostly listened.

Over the past six months, I learned an absurd amount of information about babies. Natalia wasn't much older than me, and she never mentioned Mateo's father, but at least her family helped watch him while she worked. Aside from her dreams of nursing school and disdain for most of our coworkers, I didn't know much else about her. In fact, our lunchtime conversations revealed much more about Mateo than her. We all had our reasons why we worked here. Mateo was hers. I was glad she never asked for mine. It was an easy dynamic, and I was relieved to have someone to sit with since I hadn't connected with anyone else here.

I checked the time on my phone for the third time in ten minutes. I needed to leave for my assignment soon; Ken's apartment was located at the far end of the independent wing.

"Natalia, do you know a resident named Ken Gallagher?"

It was impossible to know everyone in the Center, but Natalia gossiped enough with the other waitresses to know the good tippers and the picky eaters.

She took my assignment sheet and looked it over while munching on cheese puffs. "I think I do know him." She tapped on the paper while swallowing her snack. "Ken comes to the restaurant all the time. He always requests a table for one, which I thought was odd since most of the residents eat in bigger groups. Also, he's really chatty, and almost too good to be true, like nobody is that cheery all the time, you know? But now that you mention it, I haven't seen him in a couple of weeks." She handed over the paper, and I wiped off the orange dust left from her fingers.

"He's the only temp I have for the entire week. I'm not sure what to expect."

She shrugged. "I'm sure it'll be fine."

"I might not be able to make it for lunch the next week. His apartment is near the side entrance to independent living. By the time I go to the resident dining hall and bring him his food, I won't have time to make it here."

We ate in the break room in the assisted living wing, which was a ten-minute journey from the independent wing. Branching off from the main common areas, the Center divided into three wings: assisted, independent, and hospice. Caregivers were most needed in the assisted wing, but some of the temps, like Ken, lived in the independent wing. Hospice was the farthest away. I had been there only a few times.

"That's okay. I won't be able to make it either. I was transferred to the kitchen in the hospice wing," she said as she scrolled on her phone.

"You were? When?"

She scrunched her nose. "Just a couple of days ago. I thought I told you?"

"You didn't."

"Well, I'm super excited about it. I heard they had some openings, so I applied a while back. I won't be waitressing anymore, thank goodness. The transfer comes with a raise, and my friend Jada works over there, too."

"That's great," I said, my voice flat.

She patted my arm. "Don't worry, I'm sure we'll still see each other even though we can't spend our breaks together anymore."

I doubted that was true. I gave her a strained smile and averted my attention to packing up my things.

A maze of window-lined corridors, keycard access doorways, and wheelchair traffic lay between our usual lunch area in the assisted wing and Natalia's new job. We made plans to meet up before work next week. Though, I had a feeling it wouldn't happen. I scanned the break room. The tables crowded with people laughing and whispering, their attention focusing within their small groups. Not a single gaze wandered around the room as mine did, searching for an unfamiliar but welcoming face. I left with a sinking feeling that I would return to eating lunch alone.

• • •

I found my way to Ken's room after wandering the confusing third-floor corridors. I lingered for a moment, clutching my assignment folder tightly. I had spent six months making small talk and delivering meals with a momentum that propelled me through the day. This assignment was different from my previous ones, and the familiar procedure I was accustomed to wouldn't apply. Usually, I didn't linger in the rooms. And I was glad for the long list of activities that allowed me to avoid lengthy conversations with the residents. Now I had hours of open space left for Ken to fill with whatever activities he wanted. I hoped it didn't include the chatting that Natalia had complained about.

I looked again at the single name written on the sheet and checked the room number next to it. The wooden plaque on the wall confirmed the match, and I scowled at the closed door. Why had he requested me, anyway? The Center had plenty of other volunteers just as capable of helping all week, couldn't he have occupied one of their schedules? Although we hardly spoke, I knew of Ken's talkative and outgoing nature—two things I was not. I supposed I should be flattered to have been requested. After all, it wasn't Ken's fault I found it difficult to connect with people since Grace died.

Reluctant, and feeling like I had no other choice, I knocked on the door. Pulling at my wrinkled uniform, I resented the clingy cotton that stuck to my warm skin. The hallway smelled of chalk, or maybe baby powder, something dusty and antiseptic that irritated my nose as I waited, pondering the tasks ahead of me.

Life had taught me to beware of the unexpected, which whispered warnings of misfortune. I thought I could hear a whisper then, in the footsteps nearing the other side of the door. But perhaps it was only an echo of warnings long past, of footsteps leaving rather than approaching.

The door swung open. I blinked in surprise at the male nurse in front of me. I had prepared myself to encounter Ken's stoic oval face with tufts of bushy gray eyebrows above laughing blue eyes. The eyes that greeted me were a darker blue and shone in a way that made the unfamiliar nurse seem approachable, even though we hadn't met. A smile pulled at his thin lips, softening his long and angular features.

I smiled back. "Hi. I'm Emma. I'm here to take care of Mr. Gallagher. Sorry if I'm a bit early, but I was told someone here would instruct me on what to do."

"That someone would be me. I'm Thomas, Mr. Gallagher's nurse. Come on in," he said in a honeyed voice. He opened the door wider, and I stepped inside.

I gasped softly, taken aback by the overwhelming display of what looked like the condensed belongings of an entire house. Even so, the room could hold three people comfortably, and walking around still seemed to be an option, but not an inch of the place remained untouched. Intricately carved furnishings and the musky smell of aged leather filled the apartment. Most of the residents moved into prefurnished apartments with just their practical belongings. I looked around and couldn't spot a single piece of standard-issue furniture. Even the regulation-white walls were indiscernible behind large paintings and an antique-looking armoire.

"Thomas, what did I tell you about calling me Mr. Gallagher," Ken said in his gruff voice. I jumped, frightened by his unexpected proximity.

Ken sat unmoving in an armchair just a few feet from the entrance. The chair faced away from the door, and only wisps of white hair showed over the top. "Mr. Gallagher was my old man. You call me Ken."

"Sorry," Thomas said, elongating the word with amused sarcasm.

"Is that Emma?" Ken asked.

"Yes, it is," I said. I hurried over to the chair, almost tripping over an oxygen tank on my way. I faced Ken and held back a gasp. His full oval face seemed sunken, dark circles pooled under his eyes, tubes protruded from his prominent nose and fed into the tank next to his chair. He looked so small tucked under the blanket, it seemed impossible that he had danced around the music hall just a few days ago. "Hi, Mr. Gallagh—I mean Ken." My voice was high and stringy.

Ken responded with a booming laugh that descended into a coughing fit. His chest heaved as he struggled for air while Thomas adjusted something on the tank.

I looked between Ken and the tank, wondering just how serious his condition was.

"Please, take a seat. Make yourself at home," Ken said, his spirits undamped.

I stepped around the coffee table and sat on the end of the worn leather sofa. I looked around the room again, unsure where to put my attention, while Thomas made more adjustments.

A picture on the side table caught my eye, the metal frame reflecting morning light streaming in from the window. It displayed a family of three wearing matching tropical button-up shirts on a beach. The tall figure in the center had to be Ken, the depth of his blue eyes unmistakable. He was younger there, with blond hair and pale skin free of age spots and lines. He stood with his arm around a beautiful woman with long black hair and large eyes. She must have been his wife. His other arm rested on the shoulder of a girl who had to be their daughter. She had a striking combination of her dad's blue eyes and her mother's dark hair. Dimples dotted her goofy smile and she posed with a large cotton candy. She seemed to be in her late teens. I wondered what she looked like now, but the apartment held no other pictures. It seemed unusual that despite having an apartment filled with sentimental odds and ends, Ken displayed a single photograph. I felt compelled to ask about it, but as far as I knew, he lived at the Center alone. I wouldn't risk upsetting him to indulge my curiosity.

"Okay, Ken you're all set. I'll be back after lunch to check on things," Thomas said.

"That's really not necessary. It's just a little angina, nothing to make a fuss about," Ken said.

"Well, I insist on visiting anyway. I would miss that sense of humor of yours."

Ken scoffed, feigning disbelief, but his face relaxed into contentment as Thomas turned away.

"Emma, I have your assignment sheet here somewhere. I'll get it for you," Thomas said, digging through his bag near the door.

Unease crept up again at the thought of Thomas leaving. I fell into a comfortable silence while they conversed, but I couldn't be a spectator for much longer.

Thomas handed me a clipboard of scheduled tasks. "You should be familiar with everything there. It's pretty standard stuff. You'll bring up breakfast in fifteen or so minutes, followed by medication. After that you can go check on your other residents and come back for lunch and dinner," he said.

I jotted his instructions on the clipboard as he spoke. "Sounds easy enough," I said. I looked up to his perplexed gaze, as if he had never seen someone take notes before.

"Don't worry, he's not as difficult as he looks." Thomas spoke loud enough for Ken to hear. "But if he gives you any trouble, my direct line is at the top of the sheet."

I nodded and flashed a smile. "Thanks for your help. I appreciate it."

"Sure. You'll be here all week, right?"

I glanced at Ken, who seemed preoccupied adjusting his blankets around the oxygen tubes. "That's what I hear."

"Well good. It's such a pain to explain everything to a new person every day. And you strike me as the responsible, overachiever type, so that'll make my job much easier."

I tilted my head, going over his assessment of me, and smiled, deciding by his innocent expression that he meant it as a compliment.

Thomas grabbed his bag from the table and headed for the door. "Goodbye, Ken, don't miss me too much while I'm gone," he said in a singsong voice.

"Oh, I won't," Ken replied. The door shut, rattling the hanging paintings with a shudder. "He's a good kid," Ken said to nobody in particular.

I squeezed my hands together and shifted in my seat. There was no reason to be nervous, but I squirmed like it was my first day on the job. It wasn't even Ken that put me on edge. In fact, I found him to be quite subdued. The loquaciousness I anticipated was nowhere to be found. It could have been the fact that he was sick, or the calming coziness of the apartment. Either way, my thoughts wandered to the mystery of it all. Why me? What could be so interesting about me that he decided to request my help for a whole week? He would be much more suited to someone like Natalia, who spoke in an unending stream of thoughts and opinions. It wasn't my job requirement to talk. Meals and medication were my responsibility.

Ken cleared his throat, and I stood, snapping into action. "Breakfast will be served downstairs in ten minutes. I should go and pick it up. What would you like today?" I restored my voice to a confident tone that I had practiced to sound both official and capable.

"Just the special is fine: eggs and pancakes."

"Any dietary restrictions I should be aware of?"

"Doc says no red meat. I've gone my whole life with steaks every Friday and bacon with every breakfast. I don't see what good it'll do now." His sentence ended in a wheeze, and I looked toward the door, wanting to chase down Thomas and ask him to take my place. My usual skill at putting on a bright and brave face for sick residents faltered at the sight of Ken's rapid deterioration. I needed to escape the overwhelming room and gather my thoughts.

"All right, the special minus the bacon, then. Coming right up," I said, hurrying toward the door.

He nodded a thanks. I caught the shuddering inhale and tired expression he wore as I left. I shook off a feeling of concern as I headed downstairs to the first-floor kitchen.

EIGHT

I knocked on Ken's door twice before letting myself in, pulling a cart that held his breakfast and a cup full of colorful pills.

The tick of the clock on the wall permeated the silence. Ken straightened in his chair and stretched out his neck. His tired eyes and ruffled hair made him look like he had awoken from a deep sleep, though I had left him for only twenty minutes.

"Sorry that took so long. There was a pancake shortage," I said.

His eyes lit up as I approached with the breakfast tray. "That's quite all right."

I positioned his food on the foldable table in front of him, arranging his water and pills on the side. He dug into the stack of pancakes. I took that as a good sign. Since his appetite appeared to be intact, he must be on the mend.

"Have a seat," Ken said, his mouth full.

I sank into the sofa. The leather was still indented from when I had sat here before.

In my typical schedule, it was around this time that I typically excused myself to serve another room, but I had no other residents on my schedule until this afternoon.

"So Emma, tell me something about yourself," he said between bites.

I inwardly cringed at the question, but I was not all that surprised that he asked.

"There's not much to tell, really. I would rather hear about you." I wondered how far deflection would get me.

"Can't eat and talk." He pointed to his full mouth and shrugged. "The only time you'll persuade me to stop talking is when there's a plate of food in front of me. At least that's what my wife used to say." He glanced solemnly at the photograph before returning his attention to his plate.

My heart lurched at the longing in his eyes. It was a particular form of grief that I knew well. I wondered if my eyes also gave away the secrets I desperately tried to hide. The words he spoke in the music hall returned to mind, "Books are as real as it gets, except, unlike real life, they actually have tidy conclusions and happy endings," and I began to understand what he meant. I felt compelled to say anything to distract the forlorn man from his thoughts.

In my haste to fill the pained silence, I could only find the words for the bare truth, which always sat on the tip of my tongue, wild and on a short leash. Before I opened my mouth, my mind usually pared, primped, and groomed the words, but that took time. The words tumbled out of my mouth faster than I could hold them back. "It was never my plan to work here. I volunteered back in high school, but truthfully, I only did it to have extracurriculars on my college applications. Now college is on hold, and I ended up back here. Not that there's anything wrong with working here. I am grateful for the job, but it's just not where I thought I would be at this point."

Ken's pained expression dissolved as I spoke, convincing me to divulge more than I had planned. He frowned and tilted his head. "Education is very important to a bright, young mind. Why did you place your college plans on hold?"

None of what I had shared was part of my predetermined set of answers. That left loose ends and footholds for more questions. I shifted in my seat. I had no way to contain the conversation after what I had said. Maybe I should excuse myself? I wondered how much I would tell this newly acquainted person. I considered not responding and staying silent for the rest of the meal. Though, he would likely think I was very odd, or at least rude, and I didn't want to hurt his feelings by rejecting his kindness. I wondered what would be worse: being the rude girl who didn't answer questions or being the mess of a girl with a past worthy of ridicule and unending gossip.

Ken's frown deepened at my hesitation to answer. He set down his fork and reclined into the chair. "Touchy subject, eh? You don't have to tell me, but I've had a lot of experience giving advice to kids around your age." I raised an eyebrow, casting him a questioning glance. "I was a high school teacher," he explained with a wry smile.

Something about his patient gaze and understanding nature reminded me of Nana's intuitive perception. Like Nana, he was not the kind of person you could hide things from. Besides, he probably heard it all before. My problems wouldn't be much of a surprise. Still, I hadn't shared details of my life with anyone, and my mouth felt dry as I spoke. "Money, mostly. My mom lost her job and needed help taking care of my grandma, so I decided to help out by getting a job."

Ken nodded and resumed eating. In between bites, he said, "What line of work is your mom in?"

"She was a receptionist at a dentist's office for many years, but she has worked a couple different clerical jobs when I was growing up."

"And your dad, what does he do?"

"He's…not in the picture." I looked at my hands folded on my lap and waited for his response.

He sighed and shook his head thoughtfully. "You know my college experience wasn't all that conventional either. I went to college for teaching back in the early seventies. Finished up in seventy-two. Then I was drafted, one of the last to be called, and I served two years in the national guard. Luckily my troop was never deployed, and it worked out okay." He paused to swallow his pills.

"That is lucky." I couldn't imagine getting drafted and going to war straight out of college. I felt the gravity of my situation shrink.

He drank the rest of his water, struggling around the oxygen tubes, and continued, "I found a teaching job at a Chicago public school when I came back. The area turned rougher over the years and forced the principal into early retirement." He chuckled, shaking his head. "Poor old Mr. Leary. He was in way over his head. Contractors built row after row of towering apartment buildings in the neighborhood. If you could even call them apartments. I could fit one in a shoe box. The things those places saw. I'm telling you, it's a wonder they stayed upright. When the kids bothered showing up to school, they were bloodied, bruised, and only came to cause trouble. It was a shame, seeing all those kids wasting their potential, because they didn't know how to live any differently. So, I did the only thing I could." He wiped his mouth with a napkin and crumpled it onto the tray, stacking his plates with a show of concentration.

"What did you do?" I asked eagerly, hoping to divert him back to the story.

He looked up, a humorous twinkle in his eyes. "Are you sure you want to hear? You seemed anxious to run out of here earlier." He teased like a parent baiting a toddler.

"Oh, no I wasn't—I mean I do want to hear. Really," I said, stumbling over my words.

He cut me off with a laugh. "All right, all right. If you say so." He smiled, and I settled back into my seat. "I couldn't just sit there and watch the school fall apart. One day, Mr. Leary told me he would retire soon. Who knew what his replacement would be like? So, I went back to school. Twenty years since I last set foot on a college campus, I went back for my master's degree. And let me tell you, school was different from the first time around. There was internet, for one, and they gave a lot more homework than I remembered. I was old enough to be the students' father!" He threw his hands up and I laughed in response. "But I managed through it, graduated, and applied for the position of principal at the high school. Luckily, I still got to teach English class; the school was understaffed. Mr. Leary was over the moon the day I walked into his office and agreed to take his position. He lost most of his hair in the two years I was getting my degree. He handed over the keys and went on a vacation somewhere. I think he retired to Florida, and he still calls from time to time."

"If Mr. Leary was so eager to leave, why did you go through all that trouble to take his spot? It seems like he was stressed for a reason." I understood he wanted to help the school, but going back for a master's degree to work at the same school seemed like a big risk.

"I had a duty to those kids. I knew they weren't getting a proper education. I refused to worry about what I might lose in the process. I knew I was meant to help that school, and I had faith that everything would work out."

I leaned forward. "And did it work out?"

"I would say so. I ran that school for nearly twenty-five years before retiring here over a year ago. It wasn't always easy. I encountered some tough students, but I never gave up hope that I could make a difference for them." He looked at me pointedly while I wondered at his meaning. "Although, I did have some judo training which came in handy quite a few times. I was a state champ back in high school. I think Mr. Leary gave up his job because he was afraid when some of the more hardened kids became angry. Luckily, I knew a thing or two about diffusing anger, and they learned pretty quickly not to mess with a judo champ." He pointed his thumb to his chest.

I imagined that Ken was quite an intimidating force in his earlier years.

A knock at the door pulled my attention from the conversation. A key rattled in the lock and Thomas stepped in.

"All right, Ken, are you ready for your checkup and washup?" Thomas asked. He saw me and stopped short. "Oh, Emma, you're still here. I thought that you would've left by now."

"Ken is my only temp this week, so I stuck around. But I'll go and leave you two. I'll just do some paperwork and I'll be back with lunch. Is that okay, Ken?"

He dipped his head in agreement, avoiding my eyes.

I waited for him to offer a goodbye, but he remained silent, the joy in his face fading as his lips pulled in a grimace. After a moment, I slipped out of the room, wondering about Ken's reaction. Revisiting the warm memories of his earlier years, only to be yanked back to the present where he needed tubes to breathe and a nurse to bathe him must have been painful. All his questions and stories…maybe that was his way of holding on to the good memories.

I still felt shaky after talking about my money troubles and Nana. I feared what else might come up in our conversations, but it seemed like he needed my company. How could I refuse? The least I could do was help him remember, even just for a little while.

• • •

After stopping by the pharmacy for another cup of Ken's medication, I headed down to the kitchen, and stood in the caregivers' line for his salad.

"Hey, Emma!" I looked up from my list of Ken's food orders. Natalia waived at me from behind the counter.

"Hey, what are you doing here? I thought you were transferred to the kitchen in the hospice wing." I smiled.

"I was, but it turns out they're having me train here in the independent wing's kitchen because it's not as busy." Most of the residents in independent living dined at one of the restaurants in the Center, rather than from the kitchen. The kitchen food, while not terrible, couldn't compare to the gourmet options. Usually, the only residents who ate kitchen food were the ones who needed a caregiver to bring it to them.

"How's training going?"

"It's a lot easier than my last job. I should have applied ages ago."

Someone cleared their throat behind me, and I remembered my reason for coming here.

"I have an order for you." I handed her my slip of paper. She frowned in concentration as she gathered the materials behind the counter. Hoping to remind her of our earlier conversation, I continued, "That's Ken's order. I just came from his room."

"Who? The talkative guy?" she said as she piled salad into a container.

"Yeah, the one I asked you about this morning. It turns out he's actually more of a listener than a talker. But I still wonder why he requested me to be his caregiver all week."

Natalia shrugged. "You should ask him that." She turned away to grab plastic dinnerware. I wouldn't ask Ken, to avoid the risk of offending him, and Natalia seemed unwilling to offer any more insights, so his reasoning would likely remain a mystery. She handed me Ken's lunch. "Is there anything else you need?"

"No, that's all." I thought about leaving but paused. "Do you want to eat lunch together while you're still here?"

Her cheery expression wavered. "I already promised my new coworkers I would eat with them at a place down the street. Mateo's been a handful the past few days and I've been living off mac and cheese, so it'll be nice to go out somewhere.

"Oh, okay."

"But I'll see you around, I'm sure," she said, her smile stretching too wide.

I wished her good luck with the new job and left the kitchen.

• • •

When I arrived at Ken's apartment with lunch, he sat in the same chair, reading the newspaper. Although he looked like he hadn't moved, I knew he had worked with Thomas.

Ken didn't pay any attention as I walked into the room and called out a greeting. I approached with the tray and placed it on the table while he muttered a thanks. He turned the page slowly while the food sat in front of him.

I took my seat on the sofa and waited for him to finish reading. Absorbed in the task, his gaze never lifted from the page. What did he read that demanded his undivided attention? Maybe reading the paper before lunch was simply part of his routine—something he absolutely must finish before moving on with his day. Either way, I felt oddly disappointed while he stayed silent. I wondered if he was still upset about Thomas' interruption. The brown paper bag crumpled in my hand as I shifted in my seat. I had brought my homemade lunch from the break room in case Ken wanted me to stay. Though the caregivers were not required to eat with their residents, I knew Ken didn't have anyone to eat with either. I hoped he wouldn't mind if I joined him for lunch. Otherwise, without Natalia, I would have to brave the break room alone. A fearful prospect, indeed.

He looked over the newspaper toward the bag in my hand. "What's that?"

"Oh, that's my lunch. Just in case you needed me to stay through my break."

"You don't have to do that. I won't ask you to sit here and eat with an old man, go eat with your friends." His tone was light, but it didn't match his solemn expression.

I hesitated, remaining seated. I looked down at the bag I clutched between my hands, cheeks burning. "Are you sure? I really don't mind." My voice came out higher than normal.

"Go on," he said, waving me out.

I nodded and left quickly. What had I said to earn a dismissal? I rode the elevator to the first floor and walked down the sun-filled hallway. Laughter echoed out from the break room, and I couldn't bring myself to enter. I breezed right past the door, heading for the side entrance.

Hot, sticky air enveloped me as I pushed open the door. The heatwave didn't invite long outdoor lunches, but I welcomed beading sweat and runny peanut butter over sitting alone in the loud break room. I walked through the grass, taking a shortcut toward the gardens. Rows of tall lilac bushes lined the large plot of land. A sweet smell wafted from the small purple buds, mixing with cut grass and heavy florals. Daffodils, peonies, and rose bushes bloomed proudly from ornate planters and organized sections of land.

I hurried through the rest of the garden toward one of the sparkling lakes. The two lakes of the same size and shape stretched a football field-sized length on either side of a paved path. They mirrored each other in the placement of benches, manicured ferns, and fake swans that hovered in the very center, bobbing along with the gentle ripples. A single weeping willow towered next to the left lake. It was the only mark distinguishing the lakes. The trunk, thicker than an arm span, spoke to its age. Patches of fuzzy green moss gathered at the base and spotted up toward the branches. Long, knotted fingers pointed upward, splaying into mops of green that clumped at the top and fell, surrounding the sides with a veil of roped leaves. Its shadow blanketed a bench, offering a cool reprieve. Despite being shielded from the sun, the surface of the bench still burned through the thin cotton of my uniform.

The morning hadn't gone as I predicted, and Ken wasn't what I expected. Mary Anne had called Ken odd, and Natalia had described him as too chatty and cheery. He wasn't chatty; in fact, I found him to be a great listener. Maybe it was just the burden of his condition, but he wasn't all that cheery either. Humorous and good-spirited, maybe, but not too good to be true. I knew his laughter and smiles were real; he didn't pretend. Ken wasn't odd, he was genuine. I didn't even regret answering his questions. Not yet, anyway.

I didn't tell many people what had gone on in my life. Of the few times I revealed the truth to my friends from school, they responded with pitiful stares, blanketed optimism, or just silence. People didn't act the same around me after they found out my sister died. But Ken did. He acted like what I said was the most normal thing in the world. Of course, I didn't tell him about Grace, or why Nana needed taking care of, but still, it was more than anyone else at work knew about me. I didn't have friends here, and I suspected it had something to do with my tendency to hide. How could I do anything else when sharing my difficult experiences terrified me?

I focused on concealing the past because I couldn't accept what had happened. The tragedy felt shameful, like my pain and grief were weaknesses. Mama always told me we had to be strong, no matter how tough things became. But I didn't feel strong.

The bite of my peanut butter and jelly sandwich turned to sand in my mouth and I struggled to swallow. I discarded my half-eaten lunch back into the bag and clasped my shaking hands together. Unexpected emotions swirled, and I grasped the edge of the bench. Typically, solitude provided me with relief from the pressure of maintaining a brave face. But now I felt fragile, like I would blow away with the slightest breeze, and no one would notice.

Maybe Ken would notice. He saw me even when I hid, and somehow peeked through my many barriers. Such as when he spoke to me in the music hall and seemed to know things about me that I had yet to share. I was a balloon, but he held on to my string.

He had looked disappointed despite insisting I leave. Maybe something in his story or the reality of his condition had shifted his mood. He probably just didn't feel well. Either way, I didn't like leaving him in that condition, and I hoped to smooth things over at dinner. Truthfully, I would rather eat lunch in his eclectic apartment, but something about Ken demanded honesty. I feared admitting many things, like I had no other friends to eat with, and that was why we both ate alone. Maybe being honest was worth the risk to have a friend.

I remembered the last time I had a true friend. When I was ten, I had made a secret pact with my sister. We promised to be best friends forever. We would never leave each other. We swore it. Nothing worked out how it was supposed to, but it seemed like Ken understood that.

• • •

At around four o'clock, I took Martha home from bingo and prepared for my last task. Exhaustion weighed on me as I walked to Ken's door. I hoped bringing him dinner would go smoother than lunch. Stepping around my food cart, I knocked on the door twice before entering the room, pulling the cart with me.

When I turned around, I found Ken missing from his chair. To my surprise, he sat at the small table next to the kitchenette, leaning over a mug as steam rose from it.

He inclined his head in greeting, his expression seemingly content. I supposed that was a good sign.

"Hi Ken, I brought dinner. Roasted salmon and asparagus, as you requested this morning." I placed the plates on the table as Ken moved his mug aside. The burnt, sharp smell of coffee lingered in the air. I narrowed my eyes at him. "Is that contraband?" I asked, raising an eyebrow.

Ken's eyes widened, his mouth gaping in feigned shock. "I can't believe you would accuse me of such a thing. I thought we were friends." He bowed his head solemnly.

I recognized the olive branch and smiled. "We are," I said firmly.

He sat back, his eyes smiling in return.

"But I'm still taking that away from you," I said.

Ken grabbed the cup with both hands and pulled it up near his chest. "Doc says I can have one cup a day."

I eyed the small counter, where the coffee pot sat mostly empty. "And what number cup is that?"

"Two," he grumbled, relinquishing the cup back on to the table. "But I earned it! I had to haul this thing all the way from the living room." He kicked the oxygen tank lightly, which resounded with a metallic ping. I placed a hand on my hip and outstretched the other. He set the mug in my hand, and I dumped its contents down the sink.

With my back turned, he was brave enough to call me a spoilsport. I smiled to myself, feeling more at ease about our friendship. It felt natural and easy, like two children who met on a playground and decided they would be close friends after just a few minutes. Although it was not quite the same, Ken offered an openness that reminded me of a child's unapologetic authenticity. I hoped one day I could offer that same openness in return.

NINE

———

"Emma, go in that armoire over there and open it," Ken said, pointing to the large armoire across the room.

I set Ken's lunch tray on the side table and looked between the armoire and the clock. Ken was aware it was time for my lunch break, so I wondered if that meant I would be eating with him.

He looked at me expectantly. I frowned at his vagueness but followed the instruction. I tugged at the door of the armoire, the swollen joints creaking as it popped open, revealing shelves full of books and papers with no particular organization. I turned to Ken with a questioning look.

"Second shelf on the left," he said.

I stood on my tiptoes and grabbed a rectangular wooden box from the spot. "Checkers?"

"Yeah, I never was much of a chess person. Checkers are simple, straightforward. All the pieces do the same thing." I walked over and handed the box to him. He frowned. "Don't just stand there. Grab your lunch, have a seat, and set up the game. What, are you afraid of a little competition?" He smirked.

I grabbed my lunch from the counter, then I cleared off the coffee table, placing the box on top. "You know, I was the champion of my junior high school chess team. It was quite a distinction at the time."

"All the more reason to play checkers. At least this way I'll have a fighting chance against you."

I laughed. I couldn't remember the last time I played a board game. Well, there was bingo with Martha every week, but that was work so it didn't count. Although I was technically still at work with Ken, it felt more like fun. The constant stress of taking care of Nana and scrambling to pay bills didn't leave time for frivolities like board games. Even if I did have time, who would I play with? Nana couldn't remember the rules, and Mama was far too overwhelmed to bother.

"So you were a champ then, eh? That's mighty impressive," Ken said, bringing my thoughts back to the room. He looked directly at me; his head tilted. He seemed focused on me rather than the words he spoke. It was our second day working together, and a pattern had emerged. Sometimes I would become distracted and quiet, wrapped in my own thoughts. Most people didn't notice, since I was quiet anyway, but Ken did. He always said something to bring me back to the moment, wearing an expression that could be curiosity or wariness. I was glad he never asked me what I was thinking; I didn't want to explain my worries.

Keeping my focus on unfolding the rectangular box, I set out the board and arranged the pieces, which had small scuffs from age and repeated use. "That's right. We had small tournaments and I came out on top two years in a row. Believe it or not, it didn't make me very popular."

"Well, that's because all the cool kids played checkers." Ken gave a goofy grin.

I shook my head. "Right, of course they did." I finished arranging the pieces and took the first turn, sliding a carved cedar piece diagonally across the board. "My mom and I played chess for fun growing up. After some time, she refused to play with me anymore. Apparently, losing every game in under ten minutes isn't all that fun. That's when she signed me up for the chess club and insisted I make friends. But I was so focused on winning the matches that I missed out on the making friends part." I smiled ruefully, recalling my blue ribbons and disgruntled opponents.

Ken inhaled with effort as he leaned over to look at the board. While he appeared to have regained some strength, his hands still shook with exertion, and his breath labored with effort. He didn't need an oxygen tank anymore, which meant his new medication had worked, but I knew he didn't always feel as well as he let on. His hand hovered over one of his pieces for a moment. Then he narrowed his eyes and landed his pointer finger on the next piece over, moving it forward. "Well, it is an unspoken rule: sometimes people have a duty to let their friends win."

I rolled my eyes. "You're just as competitive as me, except I would never stoop to such blatant tricks."

"I can't get anything past you, can I?"

"Nope," I replied with a bemused expression.

"Well, if you saw my siblings play board games, you would understand. I was one of five siblings; Arleen was the eldest. Then there was Colin, Timothy, me, and then Ruth. The biggest bunch of cheaters you'd ever met. It's just me and Ruth left now. Do you have any siblings?"

"Yeah, I have a sister—" I froze, panic washing over me. Ken's eyes focused on me, but I averted my gaze as my heart beat faster and my palms sweat when I realized what I had said.

That was the worst part—forgetting. Even just for a moment. It happened all the time. I would see something at a store and think: that has Grace written all over it. I would daydream about buying it for her as a birthday gift. Only, nobody noticed when I slipped into denial because I had never spoken the thoughts out loud before. Gone was my filter and out spilled everything I had tried to hide. I wanted to call the words back, but they wouldn't come. There would be no explaining my momentary lapse.

"Had a sister," I finished, my voice quiet. "She passed away about six months ago."

"I'm very sorry to hear that. You must miss her a lot."

I nodded, unable to form words.

"I had a feeling something was going on with you."

"How?" I asked, alarmed. With Ken, I put less effort into appearances than with others. Still, I thought my sunny façade and our easy conversations were enough to make me seem normal.

"When you laugh, there's no joy behind it. Almost like you're too overwhelmed to enjoy the moment. It's just something I noticed about you."

I frowned. His words were soft rather than critical, and I knew instantly they were true. Sometimes I wondered if I had lost the ability to feel joy completely. Sure, I could laugh. I might feel amused or even happy. But there was a dull flatness where joy used to be.

"It'll come back to you with time," he said, as if reading my thoughts, "but only if you really let yourself feel the loss. You can try to ignore it, but grief has a funny way of coming out no matter what you do."

"How do you know?"

He shrugged. "I've lived a long life, Emma. Loss is just a part of it."

I had spent the last six months pretending I was fine, not realizing how badly I wanted someone to realize that I wasn't.

Of course, Mama suspected that I struggled to move forward, but neither of us knew what to say to the other. We became isolated by our own grief. To comfort the other would be to confront our own sadness. I knew Mama avoided those feelings as much as I did. It was what we did to survive. But Ken understood what I felt. If he could overcome loss, why couldn't I?

Conflicted, I longed to be free of the constant ache in my heart, but I also wanted to run out of Ken's apartment, knowing that happiness would come at a cost. That cost was acceptance. I would never make sense of Grace's death, and somehow, I needed to accept that. What kind of sister, what kind of person, would simply move on, knowing how unjust life turned out to be?

I shook my head. "I don't see it. I don't see how I could possibly feel joy or happiness or normal, ever again." My words came out bitter and harsh, but my shoulders wilted with a sadness that betrayed my sharp tongue. I felt tempted by the prospect of hope but defeated by my own doubt; I could never do what he described.

Ken seemed unfazed by my outburst and spoke without pause, "I said nothing about going back to normal. Joy and happiness are attainable, going back in time is not. Your old normal is gone, but you can create a new normal. This loss changed the meaning, perhaps even the direction of your life. You have to rediscover it. It will take time to redefine your life's purpose, and it's important to find support to help you get there." He spoke with such certainty I almost believed him.

"I would hardly know where to start."

"Many people feel that way. Moving forward often sounds too overwhelming. It starts with making a healthy choice to move forward in this moment and then again in the next moment. Pretty soon each of those moments adds up to create positive changes. Don't worry about having it all figured out. When you don't know what direction to go in, any step forward is the right one. Each step paves a new path toward healing. It's okay to take a break or a pause just as long as you get back on the path." Maybe it was time for me to take a step forward. At the thought alone, it almost felt like I already took one.

Remembering our game, I picked up one of my pieces and moved it forward, taking one of Ken's pieces captive. I smiled at his exasperated sigh.

Nothing would ever be the same, no matter how hard I tried. Ken was right about that. And maybe he was right about some other things as well. It seemed impossible to be happy again after everything I had lost, but Ken believed I could do it. I knew I must do something; my life stood still. My school plans were uncertain, and after all I had been through, there was still no reprieve from life's constant hurdles. I wasn't at college, I wasn't figuring out a career, and Mama still didn't have a job. I ran as fast as I could just to stay in place. Maybe I stalled because I chased a life that no longer existed.

I had grown tired. Tired of lying awake at night, unable to block out a torrent of anxious thoughts. Tossing and turning as memories played, grinding my teeth against regret that twisted in my gut. It was exhausting. A new normal didn't seem so bad compared to what I had, and for the first time in a while, I hoped for something different.

But part of me latched on to the past, too afraid of the unknown to abandon the familiarity of loneliness and pain. It was that fearful part that propelled me through the funeral, past the investigation, and into Mrs. Hubert's office. That part told me to save my tears and get to work. Crying wouldn't accomplish anything but a headache. Things needed to get done, and that part figured out how. It told me, "Don't stop and think about what you've lost for too long, it'll be painful. Just keep busy and always keep moving." I kept moving but I never took a step forward. I couldn't move forward because that meant facing things too bleak and agonizing to bear. The fear allowed me to survive, but I realized surviving wasn't living. A mountain of memories, questions, and regrets stood between me and peaceful acceptance. In the back of my mind I heard, "Don't risk it, the grief will be too much." But Ken's eyes held a challenge, and I wasn't a quitter.

TEN

After work the following day, Mama and I prepared dinner. She stirred a pot on the stove, combining a thick mixture of pasta, homemade sauce, and meatballs. Familiarity crept up on me as Mama hummed. I eyed her from the side as she handed me plates and silverware to set the table. The gesture reminded me of how life had been before Grace died and Nana's mind deteriorated. It had been a while since we ate a meal together. Between Mama's interviews, Nana's appointments, and my job, most evenings ended with us eating takeout alone in our rooms.

In the past, we rarely went out for dinner. Mama always said, "It's an awful waste of money to pay a restaurant to cook our food wrong when we could just stay home and do it ourselves." So, we stayed home and enjoyed each meal, finding peace in the simplicity of each other's company. Our family dinners were not like that anymore. Now they brewed from Mama's guilt, like an attempt at a normal that no longer existed. But she never stopped trying, so I wouldn't either.

We used to set the table with Nana's inherited lace tablecloths, each intricate stitch crocheted by her mother's hand. Determined, I walked into Nana's room where we stored them.

"Hi Nana, what are you up to?"

She sat in her armchair, her hands clasped together, staring at some point on the wall. "Just reading." She didn't have a book in her hand.

"Which book?

She looked at the stack on her side table and frowned, answering with a confused hum.

I crossed the room toward her linen closet, refocusing my attention on the tablecloths. "I was thinking of setting the table like we used to since we're eating together for once," I said as I pulled open the closet door.

"Oh."

"Do you know where the lace tablecloths went?"

"I'm not sure," she mumbled.

I sifted through towels and bedsheets until finding the linen box labeled *tablecloths*. "Here they are." I placed the box on her bed and lifted the lid. "What's all this?" Our missing mugs, pens, and handfuls of sugar packets filled the box that once contained our treasured tablecloths.

She jumped up from her armchair. "Don't touch that!"

I took a step back as she took the box from me. "Do you want me to help you organize this?"

"No, that's for safekeeping."

"Our mugs will be safe in the cabinet, where they belong." She put the box back into the closet and I didn't try to reason with her. "Do you remember where you put the tablecloths that were in that box?"

"What tablecloths?"

I deflated. "It's okay. We'll look for them another time. Let's go eat. What do you say, chickadee?"

She brushed past me without a word, and my heart clenched as I tried to fend off tears. Like the tablecloths and her books, our special phrase meant nothing to her. She was supposed to answer, "Together is my favorite place to be." She used to ask, and I would answer. But now my only hope remained that she would echo the phrase back to me one day.

I left her room without any table dressings. It was a silly idea, trying to make the table look how it used to for dinner. It wouldn't have mattered, anyway. Just because things looked the same didn't mean they would be. Like Nana, appearing unchanged on the outside, but changing underneath, slipping more and more with every moment until eventually…I didn't want to think about what would happen eventually.

In the kitchen, Mama set the food on the table. She remained in good spirits, oblivious to my troubling conversation with Nana. So, I forced a smile, reluctant to ruin her rare mood, and sat across from her and Nana.

Nana stared at her plate, shoulders hunched, grumbling as she struggled to cut a large meatball into smaller pieces. Mama took the plate and sliced effortlessly through Nana's food. In days past, Nana might have protested, insisting she didn't need help, but today, she sat back, retreating into a world of her own.

"How was work today, Emma?" Mama asked.

"It was interesting. Mrs. Hubert gave me a new placement on Monday. I only have to take care of one temporary resident for the entire week. His name is Ken, and he's quite the character."

"Uh oh," Mama said, eyebrows raised.

My smile became genuine as I recalled the past few afternoons working with Ken. "In a good way, I mean. At first, I was worried that he would be a lot to deal with, but he turned out to be really kind. He tells the best stories."

"What kind of stories?"

"Mostly about the school he worked at. It was a public high school in the inner city. It seems like it was a tough job," I replied, digging into my plate.

Mama nodded while pushing Nana's plate closer in front of her. The gesture brought Nana's attention back to the table and she took a bite.

"I'm sure it was a difficult job, trying to run a large school without enough funding," Mama said. She twirled pasta on her fork as if she were going to take a bite.

I knew that Mama didn't actually eat the food. Instead, she kept busy dissecting her meal into tiny pieces, taking a small bite every once in a while so I wouldn't worry. But I did worry. Each time Mama faltered, wincing in pain, she pressed her hand to her stomach. Her body seemed to revolt against food. But no one could figure out why. The doctors said it could be from stress—a common psychosomatic reaction after a major loss. They told her to take it easy, but our life didn't allow for that. The pressure to find a job loomed, and I started to feel guilty about begging her to keep the house.

"Well, at least you have a good placement this week. How come you only have one temporary resident? That seems like a light workload." Mama said.

"Don't worry, it's the same amount of work and salary, but I just have Ken taking up most of my time slots. Mrs. Hubert said that he requested me while he recovers."

Mama twirled her fork before setting it down again. "I see. What is he recovering from?"

"He had something going on with his heart. Thomas, his nurse, said he'll make a full recovery. In fact, he looked much better today." This morning I had noticed brightness in his eyes and color returning to his face. "He even walked around a bit this morning and Thomas lowered his oxygen."

"Well, that's wonderful. I'm glad you're happy at your job," Mama said.

"I had a good day," I said tentatively.

After fluctuating between numb and sad for so long, it felt unfamiliar to say those words honestly. I tried to put on a brave face because I knew it upset Mama when I struggled. But I often failed to hide what I was feeling.

"You must've made quite an impression to be requested all week."

I shrugged. "We understand one another. He likes to read a lot, too."

Mama smiled. Then to my surprise, she lifted the fork to her mouth and took a large bite. All this time I thought Mama didn't feel well because she couldn't deal with losing Grace, but perhaps it had more to do with me than I realized.

Nana sat back in her chair with an almost dreamlike expression and spoke. "That's my girl. A love of books is a fine quality to have. You get that from me, you know." I didn't know Nana was listening to our conversation. She continued, "Although, I do have to give some credit to your great-grandpa. He worked long hours doing construction. He would come home full of dirt and dust, his hands chapped and bleeding. He would always say something…" She looked up, frowning. "What was it now?" Moments passed and her mouth moved wordlessly, likely searching for the right memory. Her frown deepened.

I cast Mama a worried look and prepared to assuage whichever of Nana's moods would emerge from her confusion. "Remember he used to say—"

"Hush." Nana put up a hand and scowled at me. I used to know exactly what to say to her, and now offering help was like navigating a minefield of her fluctuating moods.

We waited in silence, careful not to disturb Nana's concentration. Then, recognition sparked in her eyes, and she finished her story. "'Pick a book,' he would say. By the time he finished washing up, I would be waiting with my book in front of the fireplace. He asked me to read three chapters every night. He only spoke broken English, but he made sure that my sisters and I had proper schooling." Nana beamed as she finished.

I knew her joy came from the love she had for her dad, but also from her ability to retell the story. Nana's memories were puzzle pieces, taken one by one. Just enough of the picture remained for her to know what had gone missing, but not enough to pretend like nothing was wrong. The first time Nana told that story, I bloomed with hope. I thought the medication might be effective after all, but in the past few weeks, she told that story every day. Sometimes Nana latched on to an idea or memory. She held on to them as long as she could, until she couldn't remember anymore. When it reached that point, and it always did, her cheeks would turn red with frustration and embarrassment as she failed to recall the details, no matter how long we waited in silence. She would inhale deeply and go silent. Sometimes she stood up and walked away. I expected her to tell the story again tonight or tomorrow as if she was telling it for the first time, but I didn't mind. I hoped she could hang on to that memory for a long time.

"Mom, you didn't eat much. Do you want me to heat that up again for you?" Mama asked her.

Nana just shook her head, smacking her lips. "There's something wrong with it, you didn't make it right," she said, her voice shrill.

Mama blinked, taken aback. "Well, it's your recipe. It's not my fault if you don't like it all of a sudden."

I tensed at Mama's defensive words. I hated getting in the middle of their arguments.

"Don't use that tone with me. You live in my house, and I deserve some respect." Nana pushed away from the table and tossed her napkin on her plate. She shuffled out of the room with a scowl.

Mama huffed and put her head in her hands. "She's impossible sometimes, you know. I just can't deal with it. This is why I didn't want to live here. She will never let me forget that we're guests under her roof. And I'm always doing something wrong. How is that? After all I do for her, and everything is still my fault!"

As she did tonight, Mama often took the majority of Nana's frustration. She hadn't been an angry person before, but it was getting harder to remember the Nana we knew.

"I know," I said. "But remember what Dr. Webster told us? He warned us that she might start struggling with food textures. He said it's just part of the adjustment process. Maybe that's what happened here."

Mama shook her head. "I don't know anymore. We used to argue like this all the time before I moved out. That's why I left not long after Uncle Al. Without him, all her attention focused on why I couldn't be more like him, independent and living on his own. Maybe she really does feel that way, like I can't do anything right."

I frowned. "I'm sure that's not true. Maybe that's just how she shows that she cares."

"Yeah, maybe." Mama's attention trailed off, and she rose, taking the plates with her. I saw why they argued when Mama was younger. They were too similar. Neither could accept help, and both ended conversations by storming off. And yet, Mama insisted they couldn't be more different. I hadn't seen that angry side of Nana until recently, but I figured her dementia caused irritability. I only hoped that Mama had enough resolve to keep taking care of Nana.

"You just have to be patient with her," I said.

"I'm trying." She rubbed her hands over her face. "But you're not home to deal with her. This is my every day. I don't know how much more I can take."

I stared at her in disbelief. "I'm not home because I'm at work trying to save this house and Nana. After what happened with Grace, I can't believe you still want to send Nana away."

She turned toward me, her brow pinched, and eyes narrowed. "What do you mean?"

I ducked my head, wishing I could call my frustrated words back. "Once Grace moved out, we barely heard from her. I don't want us to make the same mistake with Nana by sending her to a nursing home." I swallowed the lump in my throat and crossed my arms.

She had a pained expression as she sat next to me. "Of course I regret how I left things with Grace. I wish I'd been more patient with her insistence on finding your father. But we couldn't have known what would happen." Mama's refusal to help Grace find Victor caused a divide that splintered a thousand ways, and Grace hardly called in the years before she died. The distance left us with so many questions and too much room for regret. "I wanted what was best for her, just like I do with Nana."

"I don't think sending her away is what's best for her."

"Soon we might have no other choice. I was rejected from another job this morning and the bills keep piling up." Her forehead creased with worry. "And since it's been six months, my unemployment benefits are about to run out. I'm applying for an extension but there's a chance I won't get approved. Your income and Nana's social security help to buffer costs, but without that unemployment, we'll have to sell the house."

"How much time do we have left?"

She shook her head. "Without unemployment benefits, we'll have to sell right away, but if I can get the extension, maybe six more months at the most."

After the evening we just had, I wondered if we could keep it together that long.

ELEVEN

A couple of days later, I sat on Ken's couch, quieter than usual. I leaned my elbow on the worn arm rest with my head in my hand. Strands of hair fell out of my disheveled ponytail and tickled my cheek. The dark bags under my eyes and mismatched socks, one black and the other navy blue, resulted from yesterday's sleepless night. I had tossed and turned in my bed, thinking over a conversation I'd had with Mama that evening, until the first rays of sunlight peaked through my window. Again, her words echoed in my head.

"We have something to discuss," she had said. I put my bag down after a tiring day, stiffening when I noticed her solemn expression. I knew it was something bad. It was always something bad. I was right. Mama had been denied an extension of the unemployment benefits that morning. There would be no more checks. I tried not to panic. I figured we made it this far, what's a few hundred dollars more a month taken from savings? Mama must be close to getting a job, right? After all, I had found a job to save our home. Surely this setback wouldn't impede my plan.

Except it did. Mama didn't want to use any more of the savings, she didn't think it was wise. And no amount of crying or pleading had changed her mind.

My eyes were still swollen and puffy from all the tears I had shed yesterday, begging Mama to hang on for just a couple more months.

Pushing the memory away, I busied myself with the forms in front of me, masking my disappointment with focus as I filled out rows of checkboxes for Ken's symptoms and affect.

"How is your mood today, Ken?" I asked, forcing levity into my voice.

Ken looked up from his dinner plate and studied my face for a moment, as if he wanted to say something. Instead, he yawned and stretched, pushing away his food. "I feel like I've been cooped up here for far too long. What do you say we take a trip outside?"

It took me a moment to register his words. "Outside?"

Ken nodded his head toward the door with a conspiratorial smile. "Come on, let's break out of here."

"All right, I don't see why not." I stood to gather my things.

"Good, it looks like we could both use some sun." Ken looked me over with concern as I handed him a walker. He obviously meant to point out the stark paleness that replaced my normally rosy complexion. Ken's skin naturally had the translucence of a ghost and showed maps of blue and purple veins in his hands and arms. He was right—we could use some time outdoors.

I zipped up my bag after making sure I had Ken's emergency heart medication and my phone. When I looked up, Ken had made it to the door. His steps were stiff, but sturdier than I expected. Considering he had spent the last week on the couch recovering from what he described as "a minor heart thing," he looked well. Perhaps it was also the yellow hoodie he wore that made him seem like his usual self. After a week of wearing grayish crewnecks and blankets tucked up to his neck, it was nice to see him back in his self-assigned uniform. I didn't look in his closet, but if I did, I was certain it would be full of those yellow hoodies.

"Ready?" I asked.

He extended an arm toward the door. "After you."

I winced at the fluorescent ceiling lights in the hallway. Ken's apartment had them as well, but he refused to turn them on. He said they reminded him of a hospital, so he opted for a couple of floor lamps instead. I always liked how he dimmed the apartment to feel like thirty minutes past sundown compared to the flood of artificial light everywhere else in the facility. It was a nice place to spend my day, just another comfort I would miss next week. I surprised myself at the thought. I usually felt too anxious to feel comfortable anywhere but at home.

We took the elevator and slowly walked to the side entrance. I wondered if I should have brought Ken a wheelchair. All that walking might be too much for him. He was certainly going a lot faster without the bulkiness of an oxygen tank, but we were still passed by electric scooters as we inched down the hall. Ken would never agree to a wheelchair, anyway. He focused on the ground and pressed his lips together in a tight line. His breaths gave the occasional wheeze, but they came steadily. At the end of a long hallway, we reached the door.

I held the door open, inhaling the fresh air and warm breeze. Ever since I started eating lunch with him, I hadn't found a chance to visit the gardens.

"Let's go this way," I said, pointing in the lake's direction. "There's a bench on the other side of the garden where I ate lunch one time, but it might be too far."

He gave a quick nod. "That's just fine."

After five minutes, we plopped down on the bench. I was grateful for the breeze and the shade of the willow tree on such a warm day.

I should have enjoyed such refreshing scenery, but the distraction of last night's events weighed on my shoulders. My single consolation was that Nana would stay with us when we moved. Right now, Mama needed to focus on finding a new place to live, but she said I must prepare for the possibility of sending Nana to a care facility soon. If those arrangements became necessary, we would discuss our options with Dr. Webster. To make matters worse, today would be my last day taking care of Ken. Come Monday, I would return to a normal schedule of three different temps, and none of them would include my new friend.

We sat looking forward, avoiding one another. Often, we spent decent amounts of time in comfortable silence. This was not one of those times. I fidgeted in my seat and squeezed one hand in the other. I noticed Ken's sideways glances, but he was too polite to pry. Instead, he had given me an excuse to escape the confines of the Center. Somehow, he knew that my sadness and worries were too big to fit within four walls. I wanted to tell Ken what was going on, but how could I find the words to explain? Would he even want to know? I had to tell someone. The burden of all my worries had become too much to bear alone. Proving that I would be okay on my own only made things worse. I tried to protect Nana and help Mama, but we only ended up in a more difficult position than before. An overwhelming swell of guilt and sadness threatened to burst out. I imagined what a relief it would be to spill all the details from the previous night.

"You look exhausted today. Are you all right?" he asked gently.

"I just have a lot on my mind." I was relieved that he was the first to break the silence. I didn't know how to start a conversation like this. Luckily, he did it for me. "I was up pretty late last night just thinking and worrying. Mostly worrying."

He stared at me intently, waiting for me to explain further.

I focused on the fake swan bobbing up and down in the lake and rambled on. "My mom still hasn't found a job When we were first at risk of losing our house, I took this job. Between my income and her unemployment benefits, we managed to buffer costs and conserve our savings. But it's been six months, which means her unemployment benefits ran out." I told him what Mama had said yesterday, how she spent a few days negotiating her benefits, until it became clear that she wouldn't get an extension, leaving us to sell the house. I could only watch as everything fell apart. "I don't know where we're going to live, or what we're going to do. This is everything I was trying to avoid. Now my life is going to change again," I finished, my voice quiet.

Ken nodded, his gaze steady. A moment passed as Ken drummed his fingers on the armrest, gathering a response. His calming presence remained unfazed, and a bit of my own tension eased.

After a few moments, I thought he would say nothing at all. Then he looked at me and asked, "Have you ever flown somewhere in an airplane?"

I blinked, my head tilted slightly in confusion. "Um, well yes. I have a few times. Why?"

"Before a flight, when the flight attendants go over the instructions in case of emergency, they mention something about oxygen masks. Do you remember what they always say?"

I frowned and shook my head.

"They tell you to put your own oxygen mask on first before trying to help anyone else."

I took a moment to think over his cryptic advice. "So, you're saying I couldn't save my house because I tried to take care of everything else before myself?"

"I doubt there's anything you could've done to save your house. It's a noble thing you did, getting a job to help, but some things you can't control. If you're in a plane and it's going to crash, I doubt you could do anything to stop it. But what you can do is take care of yourself and prepare. By putting on your oxygen mask and bracing for impact, you set yourself up for the best possible landing. That's what you have to do right now. Breathe and brace yourself. I'm sure it won't be easy over the next few months. The move will be hard on everyone, and you will all have to grieve the loss of what was your home. That's why I mentioned the oxygen masks. Just make sure to take care of yourself, get a proper night's rest. You won't be much use to anyone if you're too tired to make it through a day."

"You're probably right."

"I'm not usually wrong," he replied, raising his bushy eyebrows with playful smugness.

I smiled appreciatively.

"I am sorry about your house," he said. "Although you might not be able to control what happens next, you can control how you react. You didn't fail just because things didn't work out as smoothly as you would like them to. Things rarely do. Now it's time to take a pause, step back, and change direction."

Ken was right, of course. If I had a say in life's unexpected events, things would be very different. Everything changed so fast, I found it difficult to adapt. It felt scary heading into the unknown, but clinging to a foiled plan would only make a terrible situation worse. A tiny shimmer of hope swelled in me, replacing the pit of helplessness I had felt all day. Moving wasn't ideal, but Mama and I would manage. We always did.

"You always know exactly what to say," I said in awe.

He looked down and shrugged in an unexpected show of bashfulness. It differed from his usual bravado, and I wondered if he was much more used to giving out compliments rather than receiving them.

He cleared his throat before responding. "I was an English teacher after all. Words are kind of my specialty."

"I will miss our afternoons discussions." I failed to hide the sadness in my voice. Talking about books was something dear I shared with Nana. It was nice to have that again; I could relive a simpler time. I would miss those conversations come Monday.

Since he no longer required a caregiver, the doctors must have cleared Ken to be on his own again; it would be selfish to be upset about that. But after the past week, it would be difficult returning to the way things were, pretending it didn't bother me to scurry past the break room just to eat alone. Even the normal parts of my routine without Ken seemed monotonous and lonely. I tried to stay positive. It was good news, after all.

He nudged my shoulder and said, "I'll make you a deal. How about we keep meeting here for lunch? Then we can continue our discussions. This spot is as good as any, and it certainly beats the stuffy dining hall."

A smile bloomed across my face. "I would really like that."

I couldn't believe I shrank away from this assignment at first, fearing Ken's sociability and judgment. I realized just how sorry I would have been if we had remained strangers because of my trepidation. Without the assignment, our conversations would have remained in the music hall. I almost missed out on a true friend because I feared scrutiny. I admired how Ken had a levelheaded acceptance of someone who made peace with their life and acknowledged their experiences as part of growing. Plagued by a torrent of guilt, regret, and sadness about Grace, I wanted his courage. Perhaps if I stuck with him, I could figure out how to live my life again.

"You know, I never thanked you for requesting me to be your caregiver all week."

"Mrs. Hubert told you about that, did she? I just had this feeling we would get along well." I waited, but he didn't explain further. Though, he was right. We were an unlikely pair, but somehow we related to each other.

"We should probably head back in soon," I said, showing Ken the time on my phone. "But we'll meet right here for lunch."

Ken nodded and stood up slowly, reaching for his walker.

"We will have to meet a bit later than you're used to, during my lunch break instead of yours, and I assume I'll have a new list of temps to bring meals to. But I'll be here right when I'm done."

"In that case, I might come early and bring a fishing pole to keep busy while I wait," he said.

"Sounds like a plan."

He departed with a quick nod and a wave. I smiled in return. It was strange, parting at the door, watching him shuffle down the hallway, back to the confines of his small apartment without me. I didn't want to move from the spot, fearing that the spell of our promise would break if I left. But it was the end of the week, time to drop off paperwork in Mrs. Hubert's office before heading home.

Home. I couldn't really call it that anymore. I thought it would feel much worse, going about my day with nowhere certain to return to. Except that wasn't exactly true, I realized. I had a bench and a willow tree that I would return to every day for lunch. Nothing could replace the comfort of Nana's house. But I had found a piece of it sitting by the lake with Ken. The next few months would not be easy. Yet, for the first time in a while, I felt like I had gained, instead of lost, something. That something might just make this all bearable. As I left to go inside, I looked back at the sparkling lake, a promise of a new beginning.

TWELVE

I blinked through half-open eyes as rays of early morning sunshine peaked through my window. Exhaustion gripped me, threatening to pull me back to sleep. Usually, I tore off the covers anyway, ignoring the fatigue that made my limbs feel like jelly. But it was Saturday, and I reached over to turn off my alarm before it had a chance to ring. I could sleep in for one day.

I knew when I woke, Mama's near-frantic packing and precarious mood swings would shatter the fragile peacefulness. For just a few more hours, I wanted to hang on to yesterday's feeling that everything would be okay.

After what had turned out to be a nice last day working with Ken, I returned home and ate dinner in my room before turning in early. In an effort to not disturb the unfamiliar peace of a lovely day, I had avoided Mama and Nana. I would deal with it all soon enough, but not just yet. I sealed my eyes shut and burrowed deeper under the covers.

My eyes flew open as the sound of breaking glass and a muffled shout echoed down the hall. I hopped out of bed, leaving the covers in a trail behind me as I hurried toward the commotion. There was a reason I never slept in.

Mama crouched on the living room floor, picking up pieces of glass and putting them in a garbage bag. A stack of toppled boxes surrounded my feet, spilling out of the hall closet.

"What happened?" I asked, my voice still hoarse from sleep.

"I was looking for some more boxes to go through and pack when this one fell from the top shelf," she answered, not bothering to look up. Pointing to the pile of glass and cardboard she said, "It was just an old vase, I didn't realize it was up there."

I retrieved a broom from the kitchen and started sweeping up the shards. I shifted around boxes to sweep under them, seeing the sparkling reflection of tiny crystals scattering the floor. It didn't help that indiscernible piles of forgotten belongings covered the living room, obstructing my movements.

"Don't move that!" Mama said. "I have a system. Don't worry, I'll take care of this mess."

I set down the box precisely where I found it and retreated farther into the living room.

On Thursday night, after Mama had made her decision to sell the house, she entered a frantic state of packing. However, she still slept for a good portion of the day, weakened by a sudden and unexplained fatigue. One moment she would attack the closets with ferocity, pulling out belongings and throwing them into donation piles or packing boxes. The next, she would collapse on the couch, complaining of stomach pains and exhaustion, only to fall asleep seconds later. I wasn't sure how long she had been awake, but red rimmed her eyes. Judging by the growing pile of belongings emerging from the corners of untouched closets, she had been working for quite some time.

Perusing the piles, I picked up and inspected the worn wool of an old beret that lay atop a pile on the couch. Mounds of forgotten things surrounded me and made me feel small among the chaotic disorder of our house. I couldn't remember the place ever looking this messy and unorganized. In the past, every surface would gleam, not a thing remaining out of place for long. Not because we had an abundance of time for meticulous cleaning, but because Nana had insisted on keeping the house spotless.

Before she was unwell, Nana had spent every weekend of her life ensuring her house had been swept, washed, and smelled like lemon soap. When the dementia had set in, she lost track of schedules and her days melted together. Layers of dust accumulated on her bookshelf and forgotten objects lined the counters. Nana even neglected to clean herself. Together, Nana and her house became discarded and unkempt.

Then, when Nana had tried to leave the house with matted knots in her gray hair and days-old clothes, we had realized something was wrong. At first, Mama and I hadn't tried to clean the house for her. Nana liked things a certain way, and she would have rebuked us if something ended up out of place. But after a few months, Nana remained unbothered by the accumulating mess. The tangled muddling of her thoughts spilled over into the house's disarray. A cup left lying here, a scrap of paper there. Each item that Nana left out of place struck me with a warning.

After a fateful doctor's visit and diagnosis, Mama and I picked up Nana's cleaning schedule and did what she could not. Nana would have wanted it that way if she still had the sentience to cast disdainful looks at window streaks or purse her lips at perspiring cups on her hardwood table. In a way, the clutter became a symptom of her disease. I had known the mess signified something was very wrong in the same way it now foreboded unwelcome change.

I looked down, realizing I gripped the beret in my white-knuckled hand. Tossing it back onto the couch, I looked around, resting my hands on my hips. There was a lot to be done, and Mama surely couldn't do it alone.

"What do you need me to do?" I asked Mama, who crouched beside the broken vase.

"In just a few minutes I'll need your help in the basement. We have a lot of boxes down there to go through." Her voice waivered. "No excuses this time."

I shifted on my feet and glanced around the room, not meeting Mama's eyes as she stood. "There seems to be plenty to do around here in the living room, can't we just keep doing that?" Nobody had been in the basement in six months. It was easy to ignore the mahogany door standing a few paces away from the kitchen. Sometimes it still caught the corner of my eye as I passed by, but if I walked quickly enough, I could pretend it wasn't even there. No mahogany door, no crooked steps, no rows of boxes holding piles of Grace's things.

When Grace left home with just a small duffel bag, Mama had shut her bedroom door where her things remained untouched. Then when we moved into Nana's house a of couple years later, Mama had boxed up the contents of Grace's room and put them in the basement. We didn't part with a single clothing item, journal, or teddy bear. After Grace died, we never discussed the boxes or dared to venture downstairs.

"I can finish the living room while you're at work next week. I really need your help in the basement," Mama replied.

I crossed my arms. "We haven't even sold the house yet. I don't understand why you're in such a big hurry to pack."

"It'll sell sooner than you think. I've asked the realtor to list it at a very reasonable price. Right now, I'm just try-ing to prevent foreclosure. We'll take whatever we can get for the house." She grabbed a pair of scissors and a roll of garbage bags from the couch and stopped in front of the basement door. "Coming?" she asked, her hand hovering on the doorknob. Her question sounded demanding, but her eyes watered, and she softened my reluctance. Going through Grace's belongings was the last thing I wanted to do, but I wouldn't leave Mama to face that by herself.

I nodded and walked over to the door. Once I reached Mama's side, the doorknob turned with a click. The door creaked, revealing a steep set of stairs shrouded in darkness. I descended the first few steps while gliding my hand against the wall in search of the light switch. The textured wallpaper grated lightly against my skin, and I felt smooth patches where it had peeled. The sunlight streaming into the kitchen carried just enough to reflect off the plastic switch. With a flick, the staircase and basement flooded with dim, yellow light, and we made our way into the crowded room.

One side of the room held a tall brass floor lamp and worn green sofa that sagged in the cushions. They had belonged to my great-grandmother. Nana kept them stored among the weathered boxes of heirlooms and childhood memories. A tower of newer boxes covered the other side of the room. Mama and I stood inspecting the sharpie letters that labeled Grace's things. I eyed a box labeled *favorite toys*. Memories of countless days playing with plastic horses and dolls flooded my mind. No, we really should not start there. Perhaps we shouldn't go through that box at all. We searched for the weakest point in the impenetrable fortress.

Mama shifted boxes and pointed to a large one labeled *clothes*. I took a breath and nodded. Clothes didn't seem so bad. It's just clothing, nothing more. I helped Mama drag the box into the center of the room to empty its contents. While still huffing with effort, I tore off the tape and unfolded the flaps in one motion. I already felt fatigued by the anxious knot in my stomach, and delaying further would only make it worse. I picked up the item on top: a light pink jacket. I ran my hand over the soft fleece fabric. A memory of curly red hair bouncing against the collar flashed in my mind.

Something snapped and sealed memories rushed back.

The smell of fallen leaves, a brisk chill, my excited heart pumping as I raced Grace to the playground. My feet slammed against the sidewalk, my arms swinging. Only one more block until we would reach the swing set, and Grace was still ahead. The cold air bit at my lungs through rapid breaths, but I wouldn't slow down. Chasing the pink and red figure through trees and bushes, I only trailed by an arm's length now. I could almost reach out and take her hand, but I could never catch Grace.

Instinctively, I clutched the jacket to my chest, burying my face in the well-worn fabric. My legs suddenly felt weak. I lowered to the floor and leaned my back against the large box. Mama crouched beside me and wrapped outstretched arms around my shaking shoulders. I couldn't stop the tears that fell.

"I know, Emma. I know," Mama whispered.

We stayed sitting like that while I cried. Tears dotted Mama's cheeks.

Eventually, my tears ran out and I stood, taking shuddering breaths. A dull imprint of sadness replaced the overwhelming pangs of grief. I realized the pain of holding in my tears and sadness far outweighed the pain of actually expressing it. I felt lighter without the tears I had held in for so long. Slowly, we resumed our task to empty and sort out the box.

We bagged most of Grace's things to donate and placed a few items in a box for safekeeping, including her Girl Scout sash, a pair of purple winter gloves, and a denim backpack. The rest piled on the couch in a growing stack of things I rescued from Mama's donation bag.

"I'll use this, I swear. It looks like a perfect fit," I pleaded. I held on to one sleeve of a T-shirt while the rest of it crumpled into a ball in Mama's hands. Mama raised a doubtful eyebrow and conceded by releasing her grip on the shirt. The words *Sarasota, Florida* encased a seascape on the front side. Mama had bought it for Grace while we were on spring break. It turned out to be our last vacation together.

Mama tore through the boxes with relentless determination. Often, she stopped to linger over something, her brow furrowing as she decided if she should keep it or not. However, most things ended up in the donation pile. Though her face was unreadable, I knew she was hurting, too.

I felt guilty about the rescued pile. I wouldn't wear the T-shirt. More likely it would remain somewhere tucked under my bed, but I couldn't get rid of it, either. It seemed wrong to imagine someone else wearing any of Grace's clothes. I didn't know how Mama parted with so much.

Mama held up a pair of black flats that Grace had worn almost every day. Mama admired them for a moment before placing them in the donate pile.

I panicked at the sight of the shoes in a black garbage bag. "Wait! Are you sure we should give those away?"

"What would we do with these? Neither of us are her size."

I shrugged and looked away. "I don't know. I just think we should keep them."

"Emma. You know that our future apartment is going to be very small. We will only have room for the most special things."

My lip began to quiver. "But those were her favorites."

Mama walked over and took my hands in hers. "These things are not Grace. Hanging on to all these things will not bring her back, and I'm sure someone else could really use them. I know this is difficult. It is for me, too. The process would be much better if we had time to do this slowly and unbox one at a time. But we don't have a choice. I shouldn't have put this off for so long. I'm sorry we have to do this all at once." She bowed her head and her voice cracked. "I just couldn't face all this knowing she'll never come home. It's time that I stopped living in denial, for both of our sake."

"It's okay, Mama." I hugged her tightly and suggested we take a break.

Mama agreed, and we gathered our keep pile, full of sentimental objects and Grace's drawings, and brought them upstairs.

For the rest of the afternoon, sorting went easier. I no longer felt like I lost a piece of Grace with every item we gave away. They were just things; they were not Grace. By the time we reached the trophy box, Mama and I began enjoying ourselves. After discovering Grace's participation award for softball, we knelt on the floor, laughing uncontrollably.

Mama's face crinkled and turned red as she gasped for air between words. "I was terrified she would get hurt. She just stood there, staring at the birds while the ball passed right over her head."

I erupted in more laughter as I pictured a young Grace wandering cluelessly around the field.

"I begged her to quit, she just wouldn't," Mama said, her voice quiet.

"I think we've done enough for today, don't you?" I asked. I felt battered and bruised. Physically, I was tired from a full day of lifting boxes and sorting, but emotionally, I was completely drained.

Mama yawned and nodded.

I dragged myself up the basement stairs, feeling like I had just returned from battle. I wasn't looking forward to finishing the task, but I held my chin a bit higher, knowing that I could face it now and be okay. We had a lot left to do in a short time, but at least we had a start.

THIRTEEN

The hands on the clock seemed to stand still while Monday afternoon dragged on. As the hour hand inched toward twelve, I grew restless. Silently, I sat in Mr. Wilks's apartment and sliced his food into pea-sized bites. Realizing I would be late for my lunch with Ken, I sawed hurriedly at the food with a dull knife.

Roger Wilks needed more help than my usual assignments. He sat in a large hospital bed. An elaborate setup of monitors and equipment beeped and hummed throughout his living room. His sofa and coffee table were pushed against the wall to make space. He remained in his independent living apartment, and I wondered why he hadn't transitioned to the assisted wing. Maybe his condition was temporary. Looking at him, however, that didn't seem to be the case. The quiet man labored to breathe. The thinness of his frame only exaggerated the slow expansion of his diaphragm. Like filling a balloon, his stomach rounded, then quickly deflated with a wheeze. Occasionally his ribs shook as his breath stuttered over a fluid-filled cough. The purple that surrounded his brown eyes didn't look temporary.

He needed to be in hospice, or in the assisted wing, at the very least. Instead, Mr. Wilks had an around-the-clock nurse.

Mrs. Hubert must have made an exception allowing him to stay in his apartment. She did everything possible to make her residents happy, including assigning me to check on his room every half hour. As a result, I had come and gone from Mr. Wilks's room at least ten times today, and each time he frowned and shouted, "Who are you?"

I repeated my name and assured him I was there to help. I used the same tone that calmed Nana when we traveled to an unfamiliar place. I knew how frightening it could be, especially to someone fighting to hang on to their memories. At that moment, I felt grateful toward Mrs. Hubert for allowing Mr. Wilks to stay in his own home even after his health failed. It would've been horrible trying to move him into the sterile and foreign rooms of the hospice wing.

Forcing him to move would have gone a lot like the past few weeks at my house. Nana had protested every box we packed while preparing to sell. With a pang of sadness, I recalled her confused expression as she saw half-packed boxes scattered around the living room floor. Her hands clenched and unclenched as she gaped at the disheveled remnants left in the basement. Mama assured her we had only been cleaning, which was true for the most part. The slight deception eased Nana's distress, but it left me with dread. At some point, we would have to tell Nana about selling the house. I didn't want to imagine how difficult that would be.

I accepted the fact that I couldn't change whether we kept or sold the house, or where we ended up next. However, I doubted Nana could come to the same conclusion. I worried about what the added disruption would do to Nana while she fought for control of herself every day. I wished she could have the same luxury as Mr. Wilks, staying in his home instead of moving.

I stepped around the bulky monitors and placed the minced food on the hospital bed's side table. Mr. Wilks grimaced and struggled to lean toward the plate. I waited while he took a few bites before collapsing back onto the bed. I urged him to try eating more, but he only shook his head and closed his eyes. My brow furrowed with worry, and I felt sorry to leave the sick man alone, but then his jaw opened slightly and relaxed. Even breaths echoed a steady beep on the monitor. He had fallen asleep after the exertion of lunchtime, so I tiptoed out with the mangled Shepherd's pie.

Startled by Mr. Wilks's condition, I thought I should mention his lack of appetite to his nurse, but I couldn't stay here and wait for someone to come in. The nurses wouldn't make another round until after lunch, and I would be with other residents by then. Looking for the name of his nurse, I searched the chart on his counter. *Thomas Fey*—the same nurse that helped Ken. Mr. Wilks's apartment was down the hall from Ken's, and the third floor only had a handful of nurses. I was glad for the coincidence; it would make my task a lot easier explaining Mr. Wilks's symptoms to a familiar face. Perhaps leaving Mr. Wilks in independent living would do more harm than good. I hoped Nana wouldn't follow a similar prognosis, forcing us to send her away for better care.

I packed my things and hurried down the hall, hoping to catch Thomas in the break room. At a quarter past noon, I worried about Ken sitting alone on the bench, thinking that I forgot all about our plan to meet. Though, I didn't think Ken would be upset if I explained. Searching the room for platinum-blond hair, I passed the tables crowded with my chattering coworkers.

On a typical break, my feet carried me straight toward the refrigerator to grab my packed lunch, and then swiftly out the door. Now as I walked up and down the aisles, I couldn't avoid overhearing my coworkers' carefree laughter as they shared hushed details of their day. I reminded myself that fitting in didn't matter for a temporary job. When I planned on leaving in less than six months, I didn't see the point in introducing myself. But since I decided to take another semester off of school, six months would eventually become a year, and I would still be the perpetual new girl because no one knew my name. Well, almost no one.

"Hey, Emma." Thomas greeted me with a wave as I approached him. He leaned over to grab a bag of chips from the vending machine's dispenser.

I forced a calm smile. "Hi, how's it going?"

"Busy, but good. You know how it is." Pretending to understand his vagueness, I nodded and smiled. He shoved change in his pocket and turned away as if he expected that to be the end of the conversation.

"I was hoping to talk with you about something."

He tipped his head to the side. "Sure."

"I was with a resident, Mr. Wilks, earlier this afternoon, and I'm concerned about him. He hardly touched his lunch. I thought I should tell someone, and I saw on his chart that you're his nurse."

His eyes widened into disks. "That's not good at all. I'll have to make a note in his chart. Thank you for letting me know."

"Of course." I shifted on my feet, wondering if I should leave the conversation there, but the situation with Mr. Wilks still left me feeling unsettled. "Do you think he's all right in that apartment, instead of hospice?"

Thomas turned to face me again, wearing a blank expression, as if he forgot what we were talking about, then shrugged.

"I'm sure it's fine. I don't think he has much time left, anyway—there's no point in moving him to hospice. There's nothing more we can do than give him oxygen." He looked over my head and nodded a greeting to someone who approached from behind me. "I should go, but don't worry about Mr. Wilks." He walked over to a table with a group of other nurses and sat down.

I grabbed my lunch bag before leaving the crowded room. The conversation didn't soothe my worries about Mr. Wilks, but at least Thomas would make a note of his decreased appetite. How could Thomas talk about Mr. Wilks' deteriorating condition with such nonchalance? Sure, he was a nurse and likely encountered that prognosis daily, but his hollow tone and flat expression showed a kind of desensitization that I could never have. Not after seeing Grace fade from existence in a hospital bed, just like the one Mr. Wilks currently lay in. But I couldn't blame people for what they didn't understand.

I hurried down the hall, toward someone who did understand. I hoped Ken waited for me. I was at least ten minutes late for our lunch plans.

· · ·

I pushed open the doors and followed the familiar paved path toward the twin lakes. After passing a group of residents meandering near the garden, I picked up my pace. Angling my body, I avoided colliding with a St. Francis statue. I ducked under a trellis overgrown with hanging ivy and finally emerged to the plain fields surrounding the lakes. Narrowing my eyes, I struggled to see the bench from behind the veil of swaying willow branches. The downward slope of the manicured hill carried me faster toward the lake, which reflected the sparkling intensity of the hot afternoon sun. A splash rippled near the shore and a red bobber appeared on the surface. A glimpse of yellow peaked through parting willow branches as the bobber flew back into the leafy cover. The stiffness in my limbs melted at the sight, and I crossed the final distance with the relaxed ease of a gentle wind.

"Ken," I said, my voice filled with surprise and elation.

His warm eyes smiled a greeting, and he put a finger to his lips. He motioned his head toward the water, where the line of his fishing pole disappeared beneath the surface.

I nodded in understanding and sat on the bench a few steps behind him. With his feet planted on the ground, he waited with the stillness of a statue. His shoulders hunched forward, and his head bowed as if it grew heavy, but no other signs of his previous illness showed.

After I finished scarfing down my sandwich, Ken reeled in his line and sat next to me on the bench.

"Nothing," he said while shaking his head. He scowled. "There used to be fish in that lake. I swear, last year I came down here every other day and bass practically jumped on my line, left and right. I doubt they stocked the ponds this year because nothing gets past my lucky hook."

I laughed at the indignant shake of his index finger.

Ken wiped his sleeve across his forehead, which reddened with early signs of sunburn. He must have been out for a long while to get a burn, despite standing under the willow's shade. He probably didn't notice I had shown up late. Even so, I explained what happened with Mr. Wilks.

"It's a good thing you were there for the poor fellow and that you said something to Thomas," he said.

"Yeah, I just hope they can make Mr. Wilks more comfortable."

Ken fiddled with his fishing pole, a grim expression showing on his face. "I've seen Wilks around, since he lives on my floor. I'll stop by and check on him from time to time, and I'll make sure Thomas made that note about his appetite."

My stiff posture slumped. Ken took my concern seriously, and I knew he would follow through on his word. "That would make me feel much better. I worried that Thomas would forget."

"Thomas is a good kid, but you never know what's going on in his head."

I stifled a laugh.

"It's true. You know, he was my nurse for almost two weeks, and the only information I know about him is that he's a Gemini and he likes frozen yogurt. And I only know that because he ate mine whenever it came with breakfast. Doctor's orders apparently."

"Have you had any checkups recently?" Ken looked good as new, but looks could be deceiving.

"Yes, just the other day. Everything looks just fine." He patted his left chest pocket.

A quiet moment passed. On a whim of fate, Mr. Wilks remained confined to his bed, slipping in and out of sleep, while Ken took advantage of his near-miraculous recovery by fishing for hours. Just as easily, their fates could have been reversed.

"So how was your weekend?" Ken asked, his voice loud and full of enthusiasm. He had a way of brightening the mood with just the tone of his words. The shock of his boisterous voice startled me from my somber thoughts and made me laugh every time. Like a bubble of joy that burst forth, my amusement came from a fascination with his spontaneous and nonsensical humor. He was unlike anyone I knew.

"It was a very busy weekend. I helped my mom pack up the house. Then we were so sore from lifting boxes on Saturday that we spent most of Sunday on the couch. Although it wasn't a total waste since we did an online search for apartments."

"That sounds like quite a bit of work you did."

I took a sip from my thermos, savoring the bitter taste of iced tea. "I had no idea that one family could acquire so many things, but it wasn't as bad as I thought it would be. Except for the basement, which was almost as difficult as I expected."

He furrowed his bushy brows, prompting me to explain further.

"We kept all my sister's belongings down there. Now my mom and I have to go through everything. She says we can only take a few boxes of Grace's stuff with us, and we have to donate the rest. I really didn't want to give her things away, but we can't afford a storage unit, and the new apartment won't have room to hang on to everything."

"You tackled a lot this weekend. Sorting through a loved one's items can be overwhelming, to say the least. All those memories, all that importance placed in objects. It's natural to want to cling to those things. I've had to go through the process many times. It never gets easier, but I've found that it's manageable with help, planning, and time." Ken's serious expression reflected his deep understanding of the process.

I rested my head on my hand and my elbow on the armrest. "Unfortunately, we have none of those. It's just me and my mom, and we need to have everything packed within two months. We're planning to move in early August." Mama explained we would move as soon as possible, but the upcoming deadline still startled me as I repeated it. It became even more real when Mama requested that I look up apartments available in August.

"Ripping off the bandage, eh? I'm sure that was very stressful. How did you cope?"

I frowned. How did I cope? I made it through Saturday somehow, but nothing really stood out that made the process easier. I doubted that I did any coping at all, considering I cried through most of it and kept trying to rescue her belongings from the giveaway pile. "Well, I'm not sure. I definitely wasn't very good at the whole sorting thing. I cried a lot, and I'm fairly certain that I'm still dehydrated."

Something resembling frustration crossed his face. "You don't give yourself enough credit. Did you go through Grace's belongings, or look at even just one item?"

"Yes," I answered, conceding to his line of reasoning.

"Then you did a good job. A great job, even. And crying is good, too. You should do a lot of crying. It's actually proven to aid a healthy grieving process. Sometimes that's how you cope. Just let it all out. You like scheduling, so pencil in a time to observe the sadness and cry if you feel like it. At least every week, I insist."

Crying, on purpose, every week? Why would anyone do such a thing? Ken said it helped the grieving process, but wouldn't that just make it worse? I couldn't cry on demand, it only snuck up at the strangest and most inconvenient times.

"Really?" I said, incredulous.

"Really." He didn't offer further explanation, but for some reason, I believed him.

"I did feel slightly better after my meltdown on Saturday, but I hope that I won't have to do that ever again. The buildup to facing that amount of sadness overwhelms me, and I can't imagine doing it voluntarily."

"It's better than doing it involuntarily," he said.

I looked up, realizing I voiced my thoughts out loud.

He shifted sideways in his seat to face me. "One day you might find yourself so full of suppressed grief that the smallest things set you off for no reason at all. It doesn't go away just because you ignore it."

His words rang true. Lately, agitation buzzed beneath the surface like a rumble of thunder before a lightning storm. It surfaced most with Mama and caused a rift to form between us. We used to be close, almost like we shared one mind and one heart. After Grace died, something changed, and we became uneasy around one another. Mama's presence elicited the emotions I tried to ignore. So, it became simple—to shut out the sadness, I shut out Mama. Back in December, before the shock of everything wore off, I had no concept of healthy grieving. I slid down the path of least resistance by trying to ignore the loss. It worked. I had great success pushing away my emotions and Mama, the only true family I had left besides Nana. With Ken's advice, I could look to move forward, but the feelings I ignored stood in my way.

"All the memories, all the thoughts—I'm afraid to face them because when I do, it consumes me. It's not that I don't want to remember, it's that I can't stop the intrusive memories. But I'm also afraid to stop remembering because I'm afraid she will really be gone. The memories are all I have left, and once those fade, so will she. I want to hang on to them, but sometimes it's just too painful."

"I know it feels that way now, but Grace was more to you than a memory. Wait with patience, because one day you'll find the sadness has drained away, and when a memory surfaces, the happiness it once brought will be returned to you."

I looked up at the sky and winced at the afternoon sun. Inhaling a deep breath, I prepared myself to speak the thoughts that ran through my head and sat on my tongue.

"When I was going through Grace's things, I found her favorite old teddy bear named Apple. My mom gave it to her in the hospital after her tonsils were removed. She never let me play with it because she loved it so much. Even as she grew older, she still set it on top of her bed every day, right up until she left." I paused. I had told Ken about Grace before, but not this part of the story. I told no one. "Grace left home shortly after she turned eighteen. I saw it coming for a while. I just never thought she would leave like that, without saying goodbye. She went looking for our dad."

I told Ken about how my dad had lost contact after the divorce. For the first few years after he left, Victor sent postcards for birthdays and Christmas. Around those times, I ran out to the mailbox in my pajamas every morning to check. I treasured the postcards he sent from New York, South Carolina, and even a few places in Europe. Mama's mood soured whenever I ran into the house, waiving around my cards.

One Christmas in particular, nine years ago, she had heard enough of his empty promises.

"It's here! It's here! Gracie, come look!" Grace and I gathered on the old gray sofa. She peered over my shoulder as we admired the shining cities displayed on the front of the card. We read the scribbled lines of writing over and over again. *Merry Christmas to my favorite girls. You're both growing up so fast. I'll visit soon, I promise. From, Dad.*

My heart soared as Grace and I fantasized about running off to one of Dad's postcard cities. We dreamed of packing a bag and escaping in the night to find him, wanting more than anything to uncover the idolized father figure we built up in our minds.

I overheard Mama on the phone with him a few days later. He hardly ever called, so I ran to grab Grace from her room. We approached the kitchen quietly, hearing the anger in Mama's whispered voice.

"I can't do this by myself anymore, Victor. I've paid for everything, done everything for our girls for years. You might have fancy attorneys, but you can't hide your money forever." She paused, blinking rapidly. An angry red hue came to her cheeks and nose. "That's a lie, and you know it." She turned and started pacing within the confines of the corded wall phone. Grace and I ducked farther into the hallway, remaining hidden. "I know very well you make a pretty penny. Tell me, how do you sleep at night knowing that we're barely making rent, or that I couldn't send Emma on her fifth-grade field trip because I could either pay for that or groceries?"

I looked at Grace, eyes wide with confusion. "But Mama said I couldn't go because she wanted to spend the day with me," I said.

"Hush," Grace said, focused on hearing the conversation.

Mama continued, "Grace has to go to college next year, and I don't have a way to pay for it. It's time for you to step up." Mama's pacing footsteps silenced. "Then stop lying to those girls! Stop pretending to be something you're not. I will not have you messing with their minds like you did with me. Don't even think of contacting them again." She slammed the phone into the wall receiver. It fell, a pendulum swinging back and forth while a dial tone played.

Grace stormed into the kitchen, shrugging me off as I grasped for her arm. "How could you do that? How could you tell Dad he can't talk to us? I always knew you were keeping him away!"

Mama turned, her mouth gaping.

"I hate you," Grace cried. "I hate you. I'm going to find Dad and live with him, and you can't stop me. I can't even stand to look at you anymore." She turned and blew past me as I stood silently in the hallway. I jumped as a door slammed somewhere in the house.

The memory of Mama standing in our old kitchen, wiping away her tears, burned in my mind.

Ken shook his head while absorbing the story. "Victor sounds like a difficult man to forgive."

I shrugged and looked at my hands folded on my lap. "I was eleven at the time. Grace was eighteen. For once Victor listened and hasn't contacted us since then. I stopped hoping for him to come around, but Grace was different after we overheard that call. She had the kindest heart, and Victor just shattered it. I never really knew him; all I had was Mama. Grace wanted nothing more than for him to come back to us. She became more distant, and then after graduating high school she left without a word, taking nothing but a small bag of clothes. Eventually, she tracked down Victor. At the time, he lived somewhere in Texas. She moved into an apartment near his place after he turned her away. Devastated, she called us crying every time he refused to see her. We thought the postcards meant something to him, but obviously they were only a gesture for appearances. Perhaps he even sent them just to upset my mom, but I'll probably never know his reasoning. My mom begged her to come home, start over, enroll in college, but she wouldn't. Refusing to give up, Grace settled not too far from where Victor lived. Years went by, and then she was gone. I want to remember the good things, but all I can think of is how complicated and messed up everything became." My shoulders wilted from the toll of reliving that time. "I have so many regrets. All I can think about is what if. What if there was something I could have said or done, she could still be here—"

He put up a palm. "That guilt you feel, it's natural. You search for answers, a way for everything to make sense. But we are not meant to know why these things happen, only that they do. That's part of the deal."

"It's just not fair."

Ken's mouth pulled to one side in a rueful smile. "My students used to come to me with that same declaration all the time. Now mind you, those kids saw horrible things. They lost siblings, parents, their homes. It was just heartbreaking. I'll tell you what I told each one of them." He sat up taller in his seat and puffed out his chest. "Fairness, while a noble concept, becomes arbitrary when invoked by the individual. To say that something is unfair would be to claim that one person understands all that has happened, and all that has yet to be. More often, fair is a word applied when an observable outcome is deemed satisfactory or not by individual standards. People are limited in their understanding and knowledge; thus, the concept of fairness must also be limited to the mundane. We could hardly expect it to apply to matters as important as life and death."

"If that is true, I expect a great number of events in my life were considered important."

He smiled at my quip and reclined back into the seat.

Time ran short and my break would end soon, but I was glued to the bench, weighed by the levity of his words and one last admission that hung over my head. "When I found that teddy bear in a box of old stuff, I remembered seeing it on her bed every day. Even after she left, her room stayed the same, and I would check every day to make sure it was still there on her bed. It's silly, but I thought she left it for me, as a sign. I knew she would never leave it behind if she never planned on coming back. I was certain it meant she would come home someday. When she didn't, I was devastated—angry, even. I feel guilty for being angry about it. I just wish it wasn't complicated so I could miss her properly without all the anger."

"Anger is a part of the process; you just need healthy ways to express it. Besides, everyone's relationships are complicated. Your relationship was imperfect, all of them are. One day, after you find a way to forgive her shortcomings and your own, you will look back on your memories and hopefully see the gifts in them. Appreciate them for what they are—pieces of her that stay with you forever."

I admitted more to Ken than anyone else. I spoke now with relief instead of fear because we shared a truth. It was one that made strangers of everyone else: fairness did not always apply.

FOURTEEN

The Center made a spectacle of holidays. Red, white, and blue filled the halls in streamers, flags, and flowers, and a few of the employees dressed in festive gear. Full-skirted dresses with stars and stripes swished down the halls as the overzealous employees donned passing residents with cheap, beaded necklaces.

Most of the caregivers left with their assignments ten minutes ago, but Mrs. Hubert requested her "A team," as she called us with a wink, to stay back in her office for an unusual assignment of decorating. Spending the morning hauling boxes and decorating under the hot sun didn't thrill most. However, some of my purest, most joyful memories were of decorating every surface, corner, and wall of Nana's house for the Fourth of July. I smiled inwardly at the prospect.

Mrs. Hubert spilled over with merriment and frantic bustling. She tapped her red and white painted fingernails on the back of her clipboard as she inspected the task list. Her pen doubled as a miniature flag and swished as she wrote in careful, curling letters.

Then she turned her nose up, her wide, unblinking eyes peering through small-framed glasses. "All right," she said, dragging out the words, shifting her attention between her clipboard and a large stack of boxes next to her desk. Finally, Mrs. Hubert gathered her focus. "Russell, you can help get the last few boxes from the storage closet?"

"Yes, ma'am," said the burly man.

The group of indistinguishable brunette thirty-somethings commiserated amongst themselves while Mrs. Hubert jotted something down on the page. Then Mrs. Hubert focused her determined gaze on their group, silencing their whispered complaints. "Jenna, you can cut and serve the cake in the atrium. There should be a nurse coming to help as well." She turned to face me. "Emma, you will join her."

My face fell. I hoped for something like flag hanging or flower arranging—something individual. Now I would spend the morning forcing small talk.

Jenna's group turned to look at me, wearing expressions with varying amounts of disdain, as if I split them up on purpose. I shrank away from their glaring looks and shifted my weight to conceal myself with Russell's large frame, who stood between me and the group. My cheeks burned, and I looked forward, pretending to pay close attention to the rest of Mrs. Hubert's assignments. She said something about the golf cart parade in the afternoon, but my efforts to avoid the glances cast from Jenna's group distracted my attention.

After Mrs. Hubert finished rattling off orders, she waved her flag pen and declared, "Off you go."

I hesitated, causing Dorris to huff in irritation. Realizing I blocked her way to the door, I hurried out of the room with the rest of the group, trying not to inconvenience the one coworker who tolerated my proximity. I ended up walking the entire length of the hallway just a few paces behind Jenna. The uncomfortable silence, I assumed, went unnoticed by Jenna, who had her head bowed toward her phone the entire time. In the sunlight, and without the company of her group, her chin-length hair looked more dirty-blond than brown, and her face turned down in a permanent scowl.

Why couldn't I work with someone friendly, like the elderly caregiver, Dorris, who was reserved but polite? Instead, Mrs. Hubert paired me with someone who showed obvious disinterest in making my acquaintance.

The atrium flooded with light from the skylights. The room held no trace of the Center's usual brisk chill. Someone had pushed the hibiscus trees and tall potted plants to the side walls. Instead, three large, foldable tables with festive tablecloths sat in the middle of the room. How large was this cake to require three tables?

"Coming through," a deep voice shouted from behind me.

A group of three custodians and a nurse shuffled toward the table, each holding a corner of an enormous rectangular box. Struggling to keep it upright, they took turns interjecting half-uttered directions. Once they placed it on the table, the custodians left, looking winded despite their stocky frames.

The nurse, a young guy with blackish-brown hair that fell over his face, nearly concealing his eyes, stayed behind.

"Hey, Derek," Jenna said. She tucked her phone in her pocket and strolled over to him.

They knew each other. At least the morning would be less uncomfortable this way. Derek nodded a greeting. He didn't talk much. We stood around in silence, looking for direction.

"Um, I guess we're supposed to start cutting and serving the cake now," I said.

Jenna and Derek gave each other a look. It became clear I was the odd one out.

I took off the lid and a sickly-sweet vanilla scent wafted from the box. The box held a flag cake at least three feet long.

Instructions were left on the supplies cart. One fork, one napkin, one palm-sized slice per resident. Intent on finishing on time, I started slicing while Derek and Jenna stood near the table.

When I realized they wouldn't come to help, I spoke up. "Why don't you guys set out the plates and napkins while I do this?" Derek shrugged and grabbed the bags of forks from the cart, but Jenna remained intractable, sending me daggers from her eyes. Now I missed when Jenna had ignored my presence. She snatched the plates from the carts, casting me one last glare, and we started working in silence.

I pushed with all my effort as the knife struggled to cut through thick layers of frosting. But the knife slid through with the same languid glide of a string through clay. Beads of condensation glistened on the cake's surface and rings of red and white drooped down the side.

Derek's white gym shoe tapped against the floor while our assembly line stuttered to a stop. He offered to take over. Relieved, I handed him the serving knife.

I took his job of setting the table with napkins and forks as Jenna set out plates.

Jenna shot me a sideways glance from across the table as if trying to confirm a suspicion. She led with anger that hummed like a live wire. The type of anger someone else might have mistaken for confidence or brash authenticity. In comparison, Derek's calm demeanor was a welcome reprieve, but I had yet to find out if he stayed quiet because he possessed gentle shyness or hardened disinterest.

I turned toward Derek. "So, what floor do you work on?"

His pointy chin remained tucked toward his chest while he sliced in even motions. "Second. Sometimes third if they're short-staffed."

Jenna planted her palms on the table as if the room had gone off-kilter while we conversed. I feared she might leap across it, right at me.

"I was on second the other day and was stuck with the worst resident," she said.

Derek raised an eyebrow, a smile transforming his bored expression. "Oh yeah? Who was it?"

"Connie Lin. Do you know her?"

"Short with black hair and mopes around all the time? Yeah, I know exactly who you're talking about. I tried getting a buddy of mine to trade floors with me, but he didn't go for it."

"Me too." Jenna threw up her hands. "People are the worst. I even offered to buy Ashley lunch if she switched with me. Although maybe she knew that anybody who gets stuck with Connie Lin never makes it to the break room."

Somehow, I was on the outside again, peering in at the strayed conversation. "What's so bad about Connie Lin?" I asked.

Derek and Jenna looked at me like they had forgotten I was there.

"She just rambles on and on about nothing and always insists I sit and listen," Derek said.

Jenna turned her back on me and faced Derek. "Yeah, she honestly gives me the creeps. She always talks about her husband who died over a year ago, like personal stories, too. I'm sorry, but I don't need her entire life story." She leaned toward Derek. "And sometimes, while she rambles on, her eyes get all glossy and she just stares off into space, like she's not totally there. I've heard her talking out loud, to no one in particular. I think she's talking to her husband, like his ghost or something. Freaky, right?"

I sniffled, trying to hold in the frustrated tears brimming my eyes. How terrible for that poor woman. She was alone, suffering from loneliness pouring from a lifetime of memories. She only wanted to share them, to have someone else hold on to them with her. I knew how it felt to be ostracized because of grief. My heart broke for Connie Lin. I hoped Jenna and Derek did not know the cruelness of their words. They left her alone to cope, in a time of great need for compassion and comfort. How did they become so cold and uncaring? Because they didn't know how to respond? Because they felt uncomfortable? I had experienced some hurtful and uncaring responses to my loss, some people avoided me, some only offered meaningless platitudes, and some criticized, but few things affected me as deeply as hearing Jenna paint Connie Lin as a witch to round up and burn at the stake. Like her grief was a form of dark magic threatening to encroach on Jenna's perfect bubble of contentment.

I stayed silent until the residents began showing up for a slice of cake. Then I served the slices while Jenna and Derek talked on the side, uninterested in helping me manage the long line of people.

My face bloomed pink and my eyes watered. The overall effect gave me a feverish look. More than one resident asked if I felt all right.

The line slowed, dwindling to stragglers and the sneaky few looking for seconds. The staff would come around soon for their slices, so I pulled up a foldable chair to regain my strength. A while later, a few nurses joined Derek and Jenna, excessively greeting them.

Though Derek had not helped me serve the residents, he found himself capable enough to serve his friends each a slice of cake. They gathered in a group at the farthest end of the table from me. Though I didn't wish to partake in their lively conversation, sitting with my hands folded in my lap was a pitiful alternative, and I wished I hadn't left my book in the break room.

I spotted blond hair on a tall, thin frame approaching the table. Thomas chatted with a group in blue uniforms and they each grabbed a plate. His eyes met mine for a moment, and his thin lips curved up in a brief smile. I gave a small wave in return, but it was too late. He turned toward the growing group, shifting his weight as he settled into their conversation about the new rule outlawing open-toed footwear. His eyes crinkled as Jenna complained about life without flip-flops and the futility of work uniforms, her voice loud and gestures wide as she addressed her audience.

Thomas said little and stood listening. Nevertheless, he surprised me by partaking in the group. Sure, I could stand there too, but I didn't want to plaster on a pretend smile. The morning had been long, and Jenna sucked all the energy out of the room. I excused the uncomfortable encounters and the burden of doing all the work, but I couldn't brush off the pit of sorrow that remained for Connie Lin. Something needed to be done, but I couldn't visit residents who were not assigned to me, even if I found out which apartment she lived in.

I only knew one person who could help her.

A while later, the group of nurses headed toward the door, and I shot from my seat, hurrying after Thomas to share my rehearsed thoughts. "Hey, could I bother you for a moment?"

"Yeah, what's up?" he said, his eyes darting between me and his friends who disappeared further down the hallway.

"There's a resident on second that I'm concerned about. Her name is Connie Lin, and I heard she might not be doing well after her husband died. I thought maybe you could check on her once in a while? I would do it, but I don't have clearance."

The amused glimmer that seemed like a permanent fixture in his eyes dimmed. "I remember who you're talking about. I feel so bad for her, but I'm not sure I would be much help. Maybe you should mention it to the social worker?"

"We have a social worker here?"

"Yeah, his name is Mr. Lewis. His office is down the hall from Mrs. Hubert's."

"Isn't there a protocol for this kind of problem?"

He shrugged. "I'm not sure, but Mr. Lewis might know."

"Okay, thanks," I said. I could see he wouldn't help any further. So, I said goodbye, and he turned, hurrying to catch up with his coworkers.

I wondered about Thomas; this person who seemed as vague as he did familiar. Everything about him was fleeting. His thin frame, restless feet, and eyes that shone with ocean blue and shifted with the tides. He never stayed in one place for long. I knew people like him. From what I remember, my dad had the same inattentiveness, always chasing something on impulse. Everyone knew of him, but no one truly knew him. His aloof attitude might have bothered me if it weren't for Ken's words. "Some people are there for a lifetime, others a moment. You can only take what people offer, and you cannot expect more than that." So, I took the advice Thomas offered and headed to the social worker's office.

• • •

I knocked on the door of the social worker's office once, and then twice. The plaque confirmed this office belonged to Leonard Lewis, licensed clinical social worker, and I waited outside the door, exchanging greetings with those who passed by. I hoped they didn't think I waited for an appointment of my own. A terrifying thought, to sit across from a stranger who poked, prodded, and dissected one's most private feelings. A slight panic washed over me as if I were going to my own appointment. I turned to leave when the door opened.

Mr. Lewis was a short, balding middle-aged man with round spectacles too large for his face. He wore a crisp white shirt with a notepad and pen tucked in the breast pocket, as if he prepared to jot down a stranger's inner-most worries at any given notice. Despite his orderly and high-strung appearance, he exuded warmth, and I was first struck by his welcoming smile.

"Hello there," he said.

"Hi Mr. Lewis, my name is Emma. I'm a caregiver, and I was hoping you could help me with a concern I have about a resident?"

"Of course, Emma, come right in. And please, call me Leonard." His voice seemed quieter than it should have been, as if he restrained a booming tenor to prevent me from startling.

I took a seat in the small office, which had a single window and many plants.

He took a seat across from me and said, "I have a few minutes if you want to tell me what's going on."

"A few of my coworkers told me about a resident named Connie Lin and described symptoms that made me think she's struggling with the loss of her husband. I don't know too much about the situation, but I thought she might need your services if that's something you deal with."

He jotted down a note and then leaned back in his chair. "Certainly, I deal with those issues all the time. In fact, that's my specialty."

"Really?"

He nodded. "At the residents' age, many people are dealing with loss, or making end-of-life preparations. Those issues can be difficult, to say the least. That's what I'm here for."

"Great, do you think you can help her?"

He sighed and leaned forward, resting his elbow on the desk. "I can't force her into counseling. But I can visit her and tell her about the different programs we offer. Some people are hesitant at first, but I've seen great success with those who choose to join."

"What kind of programs?"

"We have a grief and loss group that I run every week in the Assembly Hall where the residents gather and share with each other. Then we run group activities and I lead them through some coping exercises. If the residents still have off-site transportation, I run another group on Saturdays at the recreation center down the street."

"Is…that open to anyone?"

He paused, reevaluating me. "Yes, anyone can come to the recreation center group."

I thought of how Mama had physically deteriorated and changed into someone I could no longer talk to. Maybe the support group could help her. "I might know someone who would be interested in going to that. Would they have to sign up in advance?"

He smiled. "I'll tell you what. Let me give you my card and I'll write the information on the back. And there's no sign-up necessary; they can come whenever they would like."

He scribbled on the card and handed it over.

I took it and edged toward the door. "Thanks for this," I said, holding up the card, "and for Connie Lin."

"Of course. It was great to meet you, Emma. I hope to see you soon."

• • •

I enjoyed the afternoon away from Jenna and Derek while I helped residents from their rooms to the main entrance. They made a fuss about finding the best seats for the annual golf cart parade, but really, they would all have the same view. The entryway road carved a straight path through the oak forest that divided the busy outside street from the main entrance. Sirens and fire engines blared from a parade that happened just outside the barrier of trees. Residents who sat at the end of the road could have seen both parades, but only those in automated wheelchairs made it that far down.

The younger staff occupied the end of the road, away from residents and managers. From where I stood on the opposite side of the street, their pink and blue uniforms blended into a tight clump, and they made far too much noise for workers still on the clock.

I leaned against a tree a few paces behind the wall of foldable chairs, excited chatter, and red coolers. Like a bear scratching its back I rolled slightly from side to side, distributing the pressure of the biting bark against my sunburnt skin, the rough surface still more tolerable than my otherwise aching legs and the stinging afternoon sun.

A throat-clearing cough from behind startled me, and I turned to see Ken balancing against the uneven grass with a cane. A Vietnam veteran cap partially hid his face, but I could tell by his broad smile and puffed posture that he had been enjoying the day's festivities.

"Are you staying for the parade?" he asked.

"Of course. Fourth of July is my second favorite holiday, behind Christmas, but tied with Easter. My mom, Nana, and I used to go to the parade every year. Then we would spend the rest of the holiday trading the candy we collected and making hamburgers on the grill. We're not doing any of that this year, so I wouldn't miss this parade." Though trivial amid the chaos of packing up the house, I looked forward to the parade and a day of levity.

"Why aren't you doing anything this year?"

"My mom isn't in the celebrating mood. She loves the holiday just as much as I do, but this year is different. She just changed the topic every time I asked about plans." With Grace gone and Nana unwell, the day served as a reminder of what we had lost. Birthdays came and went, Valentine's Day, Easter, all our happiest times and traditions had been discarded this year. No holidays, no celebrations, no big events, nothing to mark the passage of time. We had pressed pause. "I wasn't even sure if I wanted to celebrate. It didn't seem right to make a big deal out of a holiday right now. Before, I was too distraught to even think of a holiday with anything other than dread. But now I'm left with a longing for how things used to be." It's like we took up a solemn oath, silently swearing to avoid all the things we had enjoyed as a family.

"Eventually the time comes to focus on your current life. It may never feel like the right time, but you deserve to enjoy your life."

"How could a new normal ever compare to how things used to be? I'm worried the happiest times are in the past."

He braced against the tree and looked ahead. "I remember when my dad passed, holidays became a real challenge for me. My siblings and I scattered all over once we moved out. All five of us split up into our own corners of the world." He chuckled and shook his head. "I guess being stuck living on top of each other in such a small place growing up, we just wanted some space. But for Thanksgiving and Christmas, we would head home every year without fail. None of us wanted to face the phone call we would get from Dad if we tried to skip. He said we would send our mother to an early grave. He was the glue of the family. No matter how far away we moved, he would always make sure we came home." He paused for a breath and looked toward me. "After he died, the family fell apart. I think it was too hard for some of my siblings to face an empty chair at the dining table. They stopped coming home completely."

He didn't talk about his family often. So, I listened intently, unwilling to interrupt the story he divulged.

"I was always close with my mom, and we tried to continue the tradition together, but it was never the same. Ruth, the youngest, started coming to Christmas after a few years passed. I remember the great big turkey my dad used to make. Everyone was thankful just to be together. It almost seemed pointless to try to recreate it, since nothing could compare."

"That's how I feel now," I said.

"You have to adapt. After a while, when it was clear the others wouldn't visit home, we simplified. Besides, my mom was getting up in years, and it wasn't right that she made an entire table full of food for people who never showed up. One year, I convinced her that we should make a reservation at a restaurant. There was only one fancy restaurant within twenty miles of the house, and they only served seafood. She had an absolute fit at first and said it wasn't right to eat lobster on Christmas. But it turned out, that was the first Christmas we enjoyed in a long while. My advice: simplify. You already have a lot going on. You don't need the added pressure of impossible expectations to recreate the past. Shrimp and dip weren't anything like the home-cooked feast we used to have, but it wasn't just the tradition that we missed, it was the connection. Once we stopped trying to make life as it was before, we were free to enjoy a different life after. Look at it as an opportunity for new traditions. What did you enjoy before, what do you enjoy now? Take inventory, set some goals, but try to start small. Pick just one thing to do at first. Those hamburgers you mentioned sound like a good start."

"I agree, I could go for one of those right about now." I smiled at the fond memory of picnics and burning charcoal wafting through the air. "Thank you for telling me that story about your family. I don't understand how, but when you explain something, it always makes perfect sense." Without Ken, I was sure my life would resemble a scattered puzzle, with no idea what it should look like.

His shoulders lifted and fell. "I'm old, I've had a long time to figure things out."

"Is that your answer to everything, that you're old?" I said, placing a hand on my hip.

Acting as if my words had struck him, he placed a hand on his chest. "I couldn't possibly know what you mean."

"Last week, you skipped a physical therapy appointment to have lunch with me, and when your physical therapist caught us walking back inside, your excuse was, 'I'm old, it happens.'"

His eyes crinkled. "I did say that, didn't I?"

"She was not very happy with you. And neither was I for that matter."

"Well, you're much better company. They make me do laps like some kind of lab rat. Besides, I'm in great shape," he said, broadening his stance and standing up straighter.

I didn't want to remind him that just last month he needed oxygen to breathe. He looked like his normal self, but that didn't mean I would let him rebel against physical therapy. I found him to be the type to tough things out. Back when I worked with him for that week, he only asked for help on a few occasions. Puzzling, how someone who constantly helped me refused it for himself. Maybe he didn't need it. With all his wisdom and strength, it was hard to believe he could need help from anyone.

"You have to go to physical therapy this week. What day is it?" I asked.

"Tuesday and Thursday at noon." My lunch break, the time we ate together, was at noon.

"Oh. For how long?"

Grimacing, his mouth pulled to the side. "The next few months, at least."

I nodded. Disappointment washed over me. I didn't think it would be for that long. I would have to get used to eating my lunch alone again for a few days during the week. "Well, at least we can still have lunch the other days, and I'll see you in the music hall on Fridays."

He nudged my shoulder. "Hey, who knows, you might like your lunch breaks better without me talking your ear off."

"No way. I would much rather listen to you talk my ear off than listen to anyone in the break room." I nodded my head toward my coworkers who grew rowdier by the moment.

"Oh, come on. They're not so bad."

"I'm not saying they're bad. I just—I feel distant from them. It's hard for me to force myself to have a conversation about a TV show I've never seen when I have so much going on. When someone asks me how my day was, the only acceptable answer is 'fine.' It's not like how I can talk with you, answering questions honestly."

"That's right, I would know you were fibbing."

I narrowed my eyes, shooting him an inquisitive look.

"You have a tell, a nose twitch. That's how I keep winning at cards."

My eyes widened, and my hand shot to my nose. "I do not."

He smiled triumphantly before growing more serious. "I know it's hard to be around people who don't understand what you're going through, but it's important to find good, supportive people. Some days you'll be more sensitive to what people say. But most people can't fully understand what they haven't experienced, it doesn't mean they say insensitive things on purpose."

Today must have been one of those sensitive days. I told Ken what happened earlier with Jenna.

He shook an accusatory finger in the air. "You know what I said about people not trying to be insensitive? Jenna is an exception. I encountered her a few times. She seems like the type who lacks empathy. I'm not sure how she stumbled into this profession."

"Me, either," I said. We observed Jenna, who celebrated with her group. "I went to talk to the Center's social worker about Connie Lin."

"How'd that go?"

"Good. He said he would talk to her about weekly support groups. He even mentioned a public group he runs at the recreation center down the street. I was thinking about telling my mom about it, but I'm not sure it's a good idea. I wouldn't want to push her. I just worry sometimes about how she's dealing with everything. She doesn't like to talk about it with me."

"I think that's a great idea. You should tell her about it."

I looked up at him. "You think so?"

"Absolutely. And you should go with her."

I scoffed. "Sharing in front of all those people? No way."

"It's only scary at first. You would be surprised at the things you can learn."

"I don't know."

"Hey, If I have to go to therapy, so do you."

"You have to go to *physical* therapy, that's different."

He frowned. "No, it isn't. Emotional health is just as important as physical health."

I opened my mouth to argue but couldn't object to anything. "I'll think about it."

Faint red lights caught my eye farther down the road, and a few moments later, a siren started. It wailed with a high-pitched ring that resembled a fire engine, but was quieter and static-filled, like it came from a speakerphone straining at maximum volume. People cheered as the golf cart parade began.

Ken and I found some seats along the road for a better view, and we settled in as the first cart passed. It bore a speaker in the front for the symbolic siren and a disco ball on top, which shot weak beams of red that faded in comparison to the hot sun. Mrs. Hubert drove the cart with one hand and waved with the other. Three residents packed around Mrs. Hubert in the tiny cart, throwing candy on both sides of the street.

The other carts were decorated for style and ranged in their adornments from painted flag posters to buckets of red and white tulips. Candy littered the street and grandchildren, great-grandchildren, and the occasional employee picked over the asphalt like birds in the early morning. A tropical-themed cart slipped in the mix, but no one complained about the popsicles they handed out instead. I gathered a small stash of candy, which Ken sifted through for all the caramel and chocolate treats.

I chewed on licorice as the bittersweet taste dissolved in my mouth. Ken wore an expression reminiscent of complete contentment, his calming presence unchanged amidst the vivacious and loud surroundings. Joyful laughter and celebratory cheers sent tendrils of hope piercing through my heart. Just because Mama and I stopped living life didn't mean it would wait. It slipped past while we longed for things to go back to normal. Maybe we wouldn't have the big celebrations that we used to, and maybe I would always have the nagging feeling of something missing, but the parade offered me a moment of the simple joys that I longed for. Right now, those small moments were few and far between, but as they continued to add up, finding a new normal didn't seem so out of reach.

As the parade came to a close, the golf carts cleared the street and made way for the finale. Engines revved as antique cars drove in a line at a crawling pace. I recognized a few from the Center's parking lot and figured they belonged to the residents.

"Oh Ken, look at that one," I said, pointing to a baby blue Pontiac Grand Ville convertible that looked like it belonged in an old Hollywood movie.

When he didn't respond, I looked over.

His expression clouded over, and he gripped the armrests of his chair until his knuckles turned white.

"What's wrong?

He stiffened. "I'm going to head back."

"Right now? I think it's almost over if you want to wait a few more minutes."

He inhaled a sharp breath and rose from his seat.

"Do you want me to walk back with you?"

"That's all right. You stay and have fun."

"Oh—okay," I said, but he had already turned to leave.

FIFTEEN

The early August air held an unseasonably brisk chill, which prickled my face and the exposed skin of my arms. I would have put on a jacket, but all my clothes were packed in boxes. Mama and I had set our alarms for four-thirty in the morning and worked on piling our belongings into the moving van since then.

Mama closed the back door to the van and wiped her palms on her old jeans. "Ready to go?"

"Sure. How many more trips to the apartment do you think we have?" I asked. This would be our third so far.

"This is your last trip. I need you at the apartment unpacking and sorting the boxes while I drive back and forth."

I looked between Mama and the house. "I—I could take the trips back and forth with you."

Mama shook her head. "I need you there unpacking and making room to unload new boxes. If you come with me, we'll never finish in time. I have to get the truck back by six o'clock."

Panic gripped me. This would be my last time seeing the house. Once I drove away in that truck, I could never come back. I knew it was inevitable, and we had spent last night at the new apartment, where Nana and my cat, Harry, waited, but I thought I had at least a few more hours to accept my new reality. "I think I forgot something inside. I'll be back." I turned on my heels and raced up the sidewalk toward the bright, red door. Closing it behind me, I took in my surroundings, one last time.

Everywhere I looked there was Grace, Nana, Mama, and Gramps—how my family used to be. I ran my fingers down the doorway where Gramps had marked mine and Grace's heights growing up. When I looked around, I saw Grace, young and vivacious. The thought of someone else living here felt like a dishonor to Grace's memory. I didn't want to lose those moments. When I closed my eyes and blocked out the bare walls around me, all that remained were visions of the hospital. Although it hurt to remember, I wanted the good memories back. I needed to keep them fresh and preserved. Soon they would fade, and all I would have left is the image of her casket lowering into the ground, playing over and over in my mind. How could I leave, knowing all that remained of Grace would be lost?

I startled as the door creaked open. Mama entered, her misty eyes mirroring my own. She outstretched her arms, and I had the urge to run into my old room and slam the door. But it wasn't my room anymore. Frustration brimmed as I stood among the remnants of my house. I wished Mama had stuck to my plan for just a few more months. Now I had lost the last piece of my old life.

I remembered talking with Ken when I first started packing for the move, realizing that I shut out Mama and the memories that I had been afraid to face. "Wait with patience," he had told me, "because one day you'll find the sadness has drained away, and when a memory surfaces, the happiness it once brought will be returned to you." At first, I didn't want to remember, but the thought of losing the memories that lay within this place made me realize just how much I needed them, and how much I needed Mama. I ran to her outstretched arms.

"I don't want to go, Mama."

She patted my back. "Me either."

"I'm afraid I'll forget…"

She pulled away. "Forget what?"

"I'm afraid I'll forget my memories of Grace."

She looked around before focusing her gaze on me. "We had a lot of happy moments with her in this house. But those memories aren't stored in things or in these walls. You can find them right here." She pointed to my heart and brought me in for another hug. "One day, your memories might fade. You might struggle to remember what her laugh sounded like, but you'll always remember how it made you feel, and that she loved you more than anything."

After lingering in the house for a while longer, Mama and I meandered to the doorway, stretching our last moments here. With a rueful smile, Mama left first, beckoning me to follow. I took a breath, stepped outside, and shut the door.

• • •

We arrived at the apartment twenty minutes later. I yawned and rubbed my eyes. Exhaustion set in, though the time neared seven o'clock in the morning. An electric shade of coral pink cast over the dark sky in streaks. The first slip of morning shone between the tall pine trees, illuminating everything it touched in burnt gold. The sunrise made me wary of the long day ahead as I leaned on the van's open back. We had many more trips left, and already the boxes crowded our doll-sized apartment. At least my bedroom had a view of the gazebo. It would be a good place to read, nestled between trees and hidden from the busy street. Although, only leaves stirred at this quiet hour. The gazebo might not be as serene once my two hundred neighbors awakened.

"Em, can you help me carry up the floor lamp?" Mama said as she opened the back of the truck. Pulling it from the truck, she grunted with effort, and I knew she struggled to make the trips up and down the stairs. I worried she might not be able to help move boxes at all after spending the last few days suffering from exhaustion and joint pain.

Coordinating our steps, we ascended the stairs with Nana's antique lamp. Movers came the day before with the heavy furniture, but we took the irreplaceable items.

I set the lamp in the far corner of the indistinct living room space. The entire apartment could have fit in the basement of our old house. The old sofas crowded the living space and encroached on the assumed dining area. Marked by an iron pendant light, the tiled area would only fit our round kitchen table.

Nana's walnut dining room table, the antique armoire, and the spare bedroom set had all sold with the house. I knew it pained Mama to part with those things when Nana had treasured them for years, but the apartment overflowed with the bare minimum. Nana hadn't pointed out the missing furniture during our first night in the apartment. I doubted she ever would.

Light footsteps creaked on the carpeted floor while shadows darkened the gap beneath her bedroom door. Nana must have woken up sometime during my last trip up the stairs. I hoped that she would sleep longer after falling asleep around midnight.

I unpacked three mugs and the tea kettle and placed them on the beige Formica countertop. The stovetop sparked after a few tries, emitting gas into the air. Like the other appliances, rusted scratches marked the fading white enamel exterior and reminded me of the kitchen we had when I was little. I poured the tea and placed one cup on the breakfast bar for Mama, carrying the other two toward the distressed mumbling from behind the door. The hallway stretched for three steps before separating into two doorways. One led to Nana's room, the master bedroom, and the other to my room. I had chosen the second bedroom because Mama insisted on using the living room sofa despite my offers to switch. Though Mama compromised on the closet arrangement and agreed to take half of mine. Back at home—our old home—Nana had spent most of the time in her room, so we agreed she should have the largest space.

I knocked on the door twice while balancing one mug on my palm and the other by the handle. I pushed open the door before the mug could burn a ring into my skin.

"Nana?" I slowly entered the room.

She faced the window, her outline darkened by the shadow of early morning, a gray hue cast over her thin arms, all the way to her bare feet, which shifted in the carpet. Light radiated from behind her. The last streaks of red bled into purple and blue at the edges of the sky. Her arms folded tighter into a light pink wrap dotted with tiny, embroidered daisies. I set the steaming cups on the nightstand before going to Nana and placing a hand on her shoulder.

She startled and blinked at me while emerging from a trance.

I gave her shoulder a light squeeze. "Good morning, Nana. When did you wake up?"

"Just a little while ago, I think." She rubbed her hands over her face before turning toward me, her eyes stilling on my face. "When are we going home?"

"This is home."

"No, when are we going *home*?" Her words came out louder the second time but cracked with hoarseness.

She asked that question repeatedly since we had arrived here yesterday. Sometimes she said it with quiet helplessness, sometimes it was an angry demand, other times, the worst times, it was a panicked cry, shrill with fear. I hoped she would soon adjust to the change. Until then, I would do the only thing I could. I took Nana by the hands and drew her toward her favorite beige armchair. Nana resisted at first with a light tug of her hands and a sour expression, but she swayed on her feet and gave in to my guidance. After settling into the chair, she took the mug from me, which had cooled enough that it wouldn't burn her if she spilled.

Tea seemed to be the only thing that calmed her. She started every day with a cup of tea and a book for as long as I could remember. Maybe something about that routine still comforted her. Nana's doctors warned of possible consequences after a move and suggested we preserve everything familiar to her. So, we planned to set up her room first. Clinging to her favorite things with an anxious possessiveness, she might notice if they had been moved or dusted. The books went next to her armchair, the jewelry box on her nightstand, the trinkets lined up on one row of the bookshelf. She loved her ceramic mug the most, so I unpacked that first. Next, I would search the boxes for her other belongings and try to make her room feel like home.

While Mama drove to and from the house with boxes to unload, I looked for more of Nana's items in unlabeled boxes. At first, we had tried sticking to an organizational system by packing and labeling the boxes by room, but when the house sale closed on August first, we threw everything together without a moment to spare. I slid a pair of scissors across the top of a box labeled kitchen, but based on how we had packed in the final days, I didn't know what to expect. I peeled back the top layer of aprons, oven mitts, and dish rags to find a stack of papers at the bottom. I figured they were Mama's old office files. While flipping through a few folders, one spilled its contents onto the floor. Papers floated to the ground like fallen autumn leaves and I scrambled to gather them.

A familiar blue paper peaked out from the mess on the floor. The paper was folded into thirds, only the blank sides visible. Deep creases showed where Mama had grasped the paper, shriveled patches sprouted where her tears had fallen, the surface faded where she had held it to her chest, eyes sealed shut. Like a secret ritual, she had read it for months. Sometimes in the morning, sometimes in the evening, always when she thought I wouldn't notice, but her glossy eyes and reddened nose were hard to miss. I always noticed.

I hadn't read the blue paper once, whatever it was. The death certificate maybe? To warrant such a reaction from Mama, it could only be that. I knew Mama just wanted to protect me from whatever the file said, and I agreed. I didn't want to read the file. Part of me still clung to the idea that ignoring the words would make them less true. I doubted the blue paper contained anything I wanted to hear, only reminding me of the resolution I would never have. Just holding the thin slip of paper made a deep knot form in my stomach.

My phone rang. Startled, I set down the papers and answered the call. Mama beckoned me to join her in the parking lot outside to unload a truck full of boxes. Her voice was high and stringy. I didn't want her to discover me with the blue paper while she was already overwhelmed. I searched for the folder in the mess on the floor as a knot traveled its way up my throat. I shoved the blue paper, still unopened, into the folder and snapped it shut. After burying the folder back in the box, I headed outside.

Mama stood at the back of the van, deconstructing the wall of boxes.

She tried to lift a box, but it would not budge. Her expression soured, and she sat on the curb, huffing and out of breath. Her gasps turned to sobs, and I rushed to sit by her side.

"I can't do this anymore. Everything hurts and there's too many boxes to move. I don't know how we're going to get this done in time," she said.

Mama could push through just about anything if something needed to be done. Through the years of raising Grace and me alone, she braved illness, exhaustion, and multiple jobs without a dent in her level-headed composure, until losing Grace hit her with a force she had yet to recover from. She kept fighting because she had to, but the toll showed in the sharp cliffs of her collarbone and the resigned dullness in her eyes.

My heart clenched as Mama rested her head in her hands, utterly defeated. I wanted to see her free of the pain and guilt that drove her to exhaustion. She hadn't been happy in such a long time, and her only moments of leisure were spent feeling unwell. I remembered Leonard's business card with the information on group therapy. I hadn't mentioned it to her yet, but maybe I could finally talk with her about it. After saying goodbye to the house this morning, I felt as if she had let down her barricades for the first time in a while. Maybe I had lowered my walls as well.

I grabbed her hand. "There's something I've been wanting to talk to you about."

She looked at me with bloodshot eyes.

"I met with the Center's social worker, Leonard, a few weeks ago about a resident. She was struggling after losing her husband, and he thought a grief support group would help. There's one at the recreation center every Saturday. He said we could come, and I think maybe we should."

She furrowed her brows. "When would I have the time for that? No. I just need to get caught up with everything. I'm just overwhelmed, that's it."

"Mama, you need help. We can't keep going on like this, pretending everything is okay when we both know it's not."

"You can go if you want."

"I want you to come with me. Please? I need you to be there."

She looked up at the sky as if the clouds held her answer. "Okay."

A slow smile spread across my face. "Okay?"

"Yes, okay. We'll go to the support group." Mama grimaced as she stood. She turned to me and held out her hand. "Now, up you go. Time's a-wasting."

For a long time, I felt fragile, like I would blow away with the slightest breeze, and no one would notice. I didn't want anyone to notice. I wanted to hide and let myself retreat inward, away from the threatening world. Life became frightening as I discovered it does not abide by justice, logic, or the comforts of fairness. Our relationship wasn't perfect, and we never said goodbye. I had so much left to say to her, and now I never could. Maybe there was no one to blame for that. I had to stop looking for her death to make sense, because it never would.

A friend once told me fairness does not apply to matters as important as life and death. And he was right. All I can do is learn from my regrets. I took that lesson with me as my relationships began to change. However, the problem with letting people in and enjoying life is the fear of losing it all. I clung to my grandma, who slowly began to slip away. I wanted to spend every possible moment with her because we didn't know how much time she had left. Everything changed around me while I stood still, recovering from our devastating loss. I grieved more than I realized. More than just Grace, I lost holiday traditions, financial stability, and the future I envisioned. But I couldn't stop my life from changing or prevent loss from happening. Though I certainly tried. I found a job, took another semester off from school, and did anything to protect my predetermined path. But plans do not coincide with loss. For a while, I had a difficult time adjusting because I relied only on myself. I was taught to keep my misfortune a secret, like it was somehow shameful to ask for help. People think they need to suffer alone and figure out everything by themselves. Or maybe that was just me—and Mama. It took me a long time to let go of the shame that I was not strong enough to face it by myself, but you can't heal until you do. Loss isn't meant to be carried alone. No one objects that love is meant to be shared, you don't keep it to yourself. Loss is the other side of that coin, and so it, too, must be shared. All you can hope for is someone kind enough to share the burden with you. Maybe you find that person in a friend, or through counseling. But what matters is that you try. The decision to live your life again starts with the willingness to learn how to grieve. It's a skill to be practiced like anything else. You can't stop loss from happening or live isolated from the world in fear of the next tragedy, but you can learn how to deal with them.

Looking back, you see these interruptions are not a diversion from your life—they are your life. If I had not taken the time to experience my diversions, I would have missed out on meeting a dear friend of mine. He shared my burden and taught me how to accept help. It started with Mama and me. We stopped avoiding one another and took our first step helping each other through our shared grief. For once, we were honest.

Finally, we stopped pretending everything was fine when we both knew it was not.

PART THREE

SIXTEEN

Since moving to our new apartment three months ago, I've had to take two buses to work each morning instead of one. Unlike our old house, which lay at the boundaries of the city outskirts, the bus routes near the apartment came once every hour. In order to make it to work on time this morning, I rode the six o'clock bus, half asleep, to the corner of Madison and Taylor. Every time I pushed through the bus doors, my feet itched to carry me three blocks left, all the way to the old house. I wanted to see the people who inhabited Nana's home of fifty years. Did they change out the wallpaper for something modern and plain? Would they paint over the red front door that reminded me of blooms of holly? Maybe they would redo the landscaping. What would become of Nana's rose bushes? I doubted the answers would bring me comfort.

I turned right, headed one block down, and caught the next bus, which dropped me right outside the Center's long entryway at six forty-five, an hour and fifteen minutes early. My keycard opened the front door, but the break room stayed locked until normal hours, and the custodians had not yet turned on the overhead lights, leaving me to wait in the dimly lit library, fighting to stay awake in the comfortable armchair.

Squeaking footsteps and merry whistling approached from down the hall. I sat up, straightening in my seat, and gripped the book that almost slipped from my lap. Not many employees arrived this early, so I wasn't used to people passing through, disturbing the quiet. I recognized the middle-aged man with quick, bouncing steps as he passed my chair.

"Leonard," I called.

He stopped midstride and walked over, spotting me. "Emma, you're here awfully early."

"My bus drops me off at this time. You're here early, too." It was strange seeing the Center's social worker outside of the grief groups that Mama and I had been going to for the past three months. I assumed he hardly left the confines of his small office at the Center because I hadn't run into him at work until now.

He pushed his glasses farther up his nose and adjusted the stack of files that he carried. "Yes, well, I have to get through all these files, and I have an even larger stack of paperwork waiting for me on my desk. But that can wait a few moments. How have you been? I know last Saturday was challenging for you and your mother." Last Saturday was Grace's birthday. Mama had wanted to stay in and observe a day of silence, but that was the last thing we needed. We had spent the last nine months since Grace's death unable to connect with each other. After befriending Ken, I realized sometimes what helps most is talking to someone outside the situation. With that in mind, I convinced her to come with me to the weekly grief group that Leonard ran.

"Saturday was difficult, but we were glad to have the group's support. It helped a lot."

"Good." He gave a quick nod. "I look forward to hearing your update next week."

"I'll see you then," I said as he turned to head down the hallway.

As I sat alone again, waiting for my shift to start, I remembered how difficult last week's update had been to give. Everyone in the group shared updates on how they were feeling during the week. Though, I found myself wanting to give the group good news, restraining the truth of my sadness for what would have been Grace's twenty-eighth birthday. Leonard didn't force members to share if they didn't want to, and I took advantage of that for the first couple of weeks. Tempted, I almost skipped my turn last week, but my fellow group members had become familiar faces, and I learned that they would understand my feelings. Not one of them were strangers to grief, pain, or hardship. Each person in the group of fifteen experienced loss. A young married couple had lost a newborn, a few widows had lost spouses and siblings, one middle-aged woman grieved a divorce, and a young mother of three came with her family to grieve her cancer diagnosis.

In the recreation center gymnasium, sitting in a circle on foldable chairs, loss felt universal. But everyone's story was different, and each loss was unique. We all processed our losses differently and at our own pace. Leonard said that healing depended on a multitude of factors, and we shouldn't get discouraged if it didn't happen as quickly as we would like. Until last week, I wasn't sure if Mama had processed at all.

Mama and I had sat side by side in the circle, wearing black in remembrance of Grace's birthday. Mama's face had appeared stoic and flat, her eyes focused, her movements tight and controlled, as if trying to convince me that she would not fall apart.

The woman next to me finished sharing how she began enjoying her hobbies again, and even went to a line dancing group alone for the first time since her husband died. We echoed support for her as she beamed. Then, it was my turn. During the car ride, I had mentally rehearsed what I would say. I knew if I arrived unprepared, with all those eyes staring at me, I would falter and end up telling everyone that I had a splendid week and nothing important happened. But that would be a lie. My reflection of the day sat bittersweet on my tongue.

"This morning I woke up and realized my sister is no longer seven years older than me. For my entire life, we were seven years apart. Today is her birthday, but she will forever remain twenty-seven. I thought a lot about what that means to me. Like how wrong it will feel when I pass her in age, or how I will never know what she looks like with gray hair. I questioned why she had to die and agonized that I would never know the details of how it happened or make sense of it all. I spent hours consumed by this indignance, until I reminded myself that I would never know how, why, or what if. Now when I think of Grace, I want to carry with me the good memories, instead of pondering things I cannot change. I remembered a friend told me that it may never feel like the right time, but at some point, I have to focus on how things are now, because I deserve to enjoy my life. At first, today seemed like the worst day to start enjoying my life, but I had a feeling that Grace would want me to celebrate. After all, she loved birthdays." The circle murmured in agreement as they often did after I shared Ken's wisdom. Frequently, I shared his advice with the group. It was easier to explain my feelings through Ken's words. Somehow, he perceived what I couldn't express.

I looked over, and saw Mama tearing up, breaking her expressionless mask.

Leonard spoke up. "Thank you for sharing that, Emma. I think we all commend your strength on such a difficult day."

I smiled, flattered by the group's support.

Leonard inclined his head toward Mama. "Gina, how are you doing with all of this?"

"Well—" Her voice broke and she looked down, clearing her throat. "I'm not sure. As well as can be expected, I suppose."

Leonard leaned forward, removing his notepad and pen from his breast pocket. "You said 'As well as can be expected.' What is it that you expect from yourself today?" He clicked his pen in anticipation of her answer.

"Life goes on. My responsibilities don't go away just because I'm grieving. I still have to take care of Emma and my mother, and I'm still looking for work."

"So, you're taking care of all these responsibilities. Who is taking care of you?"

Mama blinked. "I am."

"Are you?" One thing I liked about Leonard is that he didn't let people lie to themselves.

Mama exhaled a ragged breath, and I studied her conflicted face, awaiting her answer. That was the reason I came and dragged her with me. I needed her to admit to herself that surviving was not enough anymore.

"I could do better," she said.

Leonard gave Mama an affirming nod. "Don't be too hard on yourself. Getting out of bed was an accomplishment today." The group nodded in agreement. "But it's important to ask for help when you need it. Lean on your family or whoever you can. Let them be there for you. You didn't choose this outcome, but you now have to choose how you are going to respond to it."

"Acknowledging these feelings is like acknowledging that Grace is gone. It's too much for me," Mama said. I had felt the same way for a long time. Though, I didn't know Mama still did.

"Making the choice to avoid those feelings discourages actual healing. You are too focused on numbing the pain to heal what is causing it," he said, his voice firm. He thumbed through his notepad until finding a particular page and squinting at it. "That brings me to the point of today's meeting. The avoidance of feelings becomes a cycle of pain that will only progress until you make a choice to face it. The way to stop the cycle is to take an honest look inward," he pointed to his chest, "and ask what we need to do to heal ourselves. Sometimes that means asking others for what we need."

"I don't want to burden anyone," Mama said.

"What makes you think you're a burden?"

"Because it's my fault." She began to cry, and I reached for her hand.

Leonard's brows pinched together. "Would you blame Lisa and Bill for the death of their son?"

Mama looked across the circle at the young couple and shook her head.

He pointed his pen at Mama. "Exactly. Have that same compassion for yourself."

The circle passed a box of tissues until it reached Mama and she blew her nose before nodding in understanding.

"Perhaps you could give yourself some credit for the effort you are making to process your grief," he said. Mama relaxed into her chair, and I breathed a sigh of relief at seeing calm wash over her face. He flipped to a new page and jotted down some notes before looking up, assessing the group. "For this week's assignment, I would like to draw from Emma's wise words. It is important to take steps toward focusing on self-care and simple comforts as you work toward enjoying your current life. Take some time to think about what you need, and how you are going to get it. Imagine what enjoying your life would look like. Then acknowledge what you must do to help yourself get there while addressing the obstacles that stand in your way."

Group concluded, and I left while thinking over the homework Leonard gave us for the week. For Mama, acknowledging obstacles led her to a new doctor the following day to figure out the aches, pains, and fatigue that had ailed her for several months. It turned out she had fibromyalgia, likely caused by stress. When she returned home from the appointment with a diagnosis and treatment plan, her steps seemed lighter, as if a weight had been lifted.

I wondered what it would mean to enjoy my life again. I enjoyed my life now—in a way. My simple routine brought me comfort in a time when I had none, but perhaps I had become too comfortable. I knew things would change again, and I felt the overwhelming pressure to decide what lay ahead. The Center had become a haven, apart from the rest of the world, where I didn't have to worry about what I wanted to do with my life or how to tackle the plans and goals I had set for myself. But without the financial strain of trying to keep the house, Nana's social security and our rationed savings covered the apartment's cheap rent. So, I began to question: What excuse did I have for continuing to work at the Center? What would come next?

The whirring of electricity swelled as the fluorescent lights switched on overhead, chasing away my thoughts of the past few days. I squinted my eyes, blocking out the flash of brightness overhead. The Center's library came back into focus, as did the distant jangling of the custodian's keys. The first sounds of activity signaled me to pack up my things and head to Mrs. Hubert's office to start my day. Despite receiving a simple schedule, I had a difficult time focusing on my tasks, consumed by Leonard's assignment. I dwelled on the uncertainty of my future until lunchtime, as I waited to meet with Ken.

Ken arrived a few minutes late, leaning on his cane with more force than usual. "Hi there, Emma." A breathless wheeze clipped his words. It was unusual to see him this strained. The elevator to his apartment was only around the corner, but it appeared like he had traveled much farther than that. Maybe he hadn't come from his apartment; it would explain his apparent exertion.

"Hi, Ken. What have you been up to?" I observed him closely while we stood at the side of the walkway. Ken didn't move to take our usual seat in the corner, so we stood sandwiched by the resident traffic that moved around us like molasses.

"Oh, just this and that." He waved his hand dismissively. After a moment, he took a deep breath and then headed over to our spot, the sofa near the fireplace. My concern soon faded as Ken talked and joked as usual.

"And how is your physical therapy going?" I asked. He still went twice a week and, according to his doctor, would continue to do so for the foreseeable future despite the initial three-month plan. Ken had joked that they didn't want to lose their best patient. Though I could tell he was disappointed. I had also hoped we would return to our normal daily lunches.

"I did a quarter mile yesterday. I would've gone farther, too, if they hadn't stopped me," he said.

"You've come a long way since we met. How long has it been now…over four months? It can't be." It was difficult to remember a time before knowing Ken, but it also felt like a brief flash of a moment. Time seemed to work differently here.

"Yep, over four months." He raised his brows in disbelief. "And you've been working here for how long?"

I thought for a moment. "Almost ten months."

"How long are you planning on sticking around?"

His question caught me off guard. I hadn't given it much thought until the grief group last weekend. It was difficult enough trying to get through each day. Predicting what my future would look like seemed impossible.

I shrugged, coming up short for an answer. "Your guess is as good as mine."

"My guess is you won't be here for much longer."

"Why would you think that?"

"A smart young woman like yourself needs to get out into the world and try new things. Besides, you clearly wouldn't be happy staying here forever."

Was it that obvious? My recent thoughts of the future had awakened a restlessness and longing to return to school.

"I haven't figured everything out yet. There's a lot to think about, and Mama still hasn't found a job. Though she did start sending out her résumé again. For a while there, I thought she gave up. In the meantime, I'm not unhappy here."

He scoffed. "The highlight of your day is talking to me." He wasn't wrong.

I crossed my arms. "What's wrong with that?"

"Nothing, for now, but I think you should look into returning to school. It's time to start thinking about what your future goals might be." He sounded how I imagined a father would. Even so, sometimes it bothered me when he spoke the difficult truths. I hesitated to further the discussion, but his persistence on the topic also brought me indescribable hope.

It was nice to have someone who cared about my future and wanted to help me figure out my next steps. I was reluctant to talk to Mama about my future. She vowed to help support me through school, worsening the pressure she felt to find a job. With her recent diagnosis, I didn't want to add to her stress and guilt.

"It's hard to imagine the next step. When I left school, my major was undecided, though I leaned toward business or finance. I thought a career in that field would be practical and dependable, even if I wouldn't enjoy it. But now, I'm different from when I left, and I have no clue if that's what I should do."

"You should stick to your strengths and what you like to do. You know what I think?" he said, shaking a finger before leaving it to rest on his shaven chin. "You would make an excellent doctor."

I laughed. "I don't know about that. I'm much too squeamish. Besides, I've been in doctor's offices enough for one lifetime with all my grandma's appointments."

"You're good with people, and you've got the brains for it."

I ducked my head and looked down.

"I mean it—not many people can beat me at checkers fair and square," he said.

"Even if I was smart enough, I wouldn't consider myself a people person. I'm far too shy."

"True, but you're a great people person when you're not shy," he said.

"If I limit my work to times when I'm not being shy, I'll be a doctor who can only see one patient. That's you."

He shook his head. "Nah, you'll get there. You're made of tougher stuff than you think. You just have to figure out what you're hiding from and find the courage to go on the journey, wherever it takes you. Remember, you are what you decide to be." He picked up his napkin, holding it in the air. "A square is only a square if you call it so."

I frowned. "What else would you call it?"

He turned the napkin forty-five degrees and smirked. "A diamond."

SEVENTEEN

After a few more weeks of meeting for lunch in the library, I longed for a change of scenery. "Do you want to go outside today? It was warm when I arrived here this morning," I asked Ken. We hadn't visited the spot by the lake in a while. Even on days when the late fall chill subsided, Ken still declined to meet anywhere but the library.

He hesitated, and for a moment I thought he hadn't heard me. He lifted his nose, mouth parting slightly as he gazed outside a nearby window, as if he could smell the fresh air through the concrete walls. "No, we better stay here." His answer was clipped, telling me not to argue.

His pale and drawn pallor made me think he could use time outside. It reminded me of how he had looked when we first met; his skin had looked like paper, thin enough to show the map of veins running underneath. Bruises and dark blotches had dotted along the exposed skin of his hands and under his eyes like spilled ink. He had resisted my help then. He was both stubborn and routine-driven, a combination that didn't agree with illness.

A similar discontentment now grated his stiff features as he took his seat by the fireplace. Even so, Ken insisted the doctors had cleared him with a clean bill of health. While his self-proclaimed title of "favorite physical therapy patient" might be a stretch, he did seem to be improving.

He didn't share his troubles, and his distant gaze lingered over to the window. Recently, when our conversations reached a lull, his attention would wander outside, just over my shoulder. What did he think about, in those moments he seemed so far away? I wasn't sure it was my place to ask. Instead, I turned the conversation to work.

"Can you believe all the Thanksgiving decorations around here? Mrs. Hubert made us caregivers put these up in the past week." I pointed to the wall decorations. "I had no idea decorating would be part of my job description." We had adorned the common areas with fall leaf garlands and crimson tablecloths that made me feel underdressed as I passed the expensive displays.

He inspected one of the new decorations, a candle holder placed on the side table, and turned it in his fingers, letting the light reflect off the baroque mirrored sides. "They take Thanksgiving and Christmas to the extreme around here. I'm sure half of my room and board fee goes to party supplies stores." The holidays had passed just before I started working at the Center, but now I had a chance to experience the full effect of retirement home celebrations.

"There's never a dull moment, that's for sure. Next week we're going to be paired in teams to start working on the winter wonderland. Hopefully, that group project will go better than the last." I recalled the events on the Fourth of July.

"Yes, I hope so, too. Don't worry, I'm sure you'll find a good group of friends here soon."

"I'm not worried about it." I brushed off his assurance as if it were a speck of lint.

"It's important to surround yourself with good people, especially given the extent of your support system."

I looked away, his observation striking a nerve. I didn't take offense since Ken volunteered to be half of my support system, but it reminded me of how isolated I still felt. "I do have good people; I have you." I kept my tone light, trying to hide how the truth of his comment affected me.

A frown cut harsh lines into his face, but his eyes remained soft. "I won't be around forever, Emma."

It was my turn to scowl. "Don't say things like that." I wished his joyful and humorous nature would return.

"It's true. And I'm not doing you any favors by letting you sit around with me all the time."

My eyes widened. "What do you mean? Are you saying we can't have lunch anymore?" My voice shook. A long-buried panic struck me with such force that I felt confused. I waited for his answer like I had waited for my father's postcards long ago.

"Of course we'll still have lunch. That's not what I meant."

I nodded, relieved that my assumption wasn't true.

"I just think it would be good for you to branch out more," he said.

"What's the point? Most other people don't understand what I'm going through. If I wanted to, I could make some superficial friends and fill my time talking about things that don't interest me anymore, but I don't want to pretend."

"Maybe if you express how you truly feel and share part of your story with others, you'll find people understand a lot more than you think. Has it ever occurred to you that other people are also pretending to be okay?"

I shrank back in my seat, feeling ashamed that I hadn't arrived at that realization before. Of course, people experienced losses all the time, but in the midst of my own grief, I hadn't paid much attention to others. It was difficult to imagine that my aloof and carefree coworkers might be going through their own difficulties. Isolated by the suffocating world of my grief, I always felt different from the others. But Ken was right. More than likely, there was someone else with me on the outside, looking in at a life they no longer recognized. Whoever they were, I hoped they had someone like Ken. Not that long ago, I was alone. If not for Ken, I didn't know what my life would look like now.

"I wouldn't know how to find those people," I said.

He smiled. "It's all people. At some point, you will begin to feel your loss connecting you to others, rather than isolating you from them."

"That's how I feel about the support group my mom and I go to."

"Right, here's another example." He straightened his posture like a professor before a lecture. "This one year I taught a group of students who had seen a record amount of gang activity the summer before. Three students were killed in just two short months. I didn't know what to expect going into that year, or if I'd have to break up fights and check people for guns. For the first time, I was frightened to teach there, not for myself, but for the students. You see, I had students from opposing gangs in one classroom. I knew this unofficially, of course, and the pain of those deaths was still fresh. But when I arrived there on the first day, nobody so much as looked each other in the eye. They weren't hardened criminals looking for vengeance, they were just kids being eaten alive by losses they didn't know how to deal with. By the end of the year, we had forged a community. Of course, not everyone went along with the program, but those who could make positive choices and work through their suffering were able to move forward with hope."

"How were you able to do all that?" I asked with wide eyes.

"Their outside community lacked structure, support, and resources. They were forced to grow up fast or sink. They weren't allowed to grieve. So, I showed them something different. Their first assignment was to research the mourning rituals in non-westernized cultures. I showed them that not everyone has the same 'tough it out and move on' attitude toward mourning. I asked them what they thought the point of the assignment was. They had no clue, so I told them to keep digging. And can you guess what they found?"

I shook my head, feeling just as confused as those students must have while hearing Ken's unconventional assignment.

"They found community. They saw how the people in cultures who practiced involved grieving processes helped one another and stuck together when one of their own passed on. My students presented research that showed those individuals have better mental and physical outcomes after loss. But I told them to dig deeper."

"Of course you told them that." I laughed. He would have been a tough grader. Tough, but fair.

He lifted his chin. "Useless is the lesson that is heard, but not applied." He paused and took a sip from his thermos before choking on a dry cough. I handed him a napkin as his face went from pale to red and back to pale again. He waved off my concern and tried to start again, only to delve into another coughing fit. The cause must have been whatever steamed out of his thermos; coffee by the smell of it. But his voice was hoarse, and my break was almost over.

"Why don't we finish the story on Monday?" I asked.

"No," He planted a hand on my forearm, preventing me from packing up. The force of his tone took me by surprise, as did his eyes, which widened to saucers and darkened with fear.

In a fluid motion, he relaxed back into his seat and molded his face to appear unreadable, apart from a dimple that dotted his left cheek. "I'm perfectly fine, you know I could talk for ages, and we still have some time." He frowned at his bare wrist as if checking a watch.

"If that's how you keep track of time, I can see why you're always late to physical therapy," I said before sliding back against the leather armrest.

He snorted a laugh. "Where was I? That's right, apply the lesson. So, I had them pick key aspects of the mourning rituals and implement them as a class. Over the year, I guided them to recognize vulnerability, channel emotional expression appropriately, reframe their relationship with the deceased, and perform culturally specific tasks to confront the losses. Sometimes they wrote essays, sometimes they read articles, sometimes we just gathered in a circle and talked. But in the end, I felt comfortable saying goodbye to them because they were prepared for what lay ahead, and they had each other." His gaze lingered over to the window again. His thoughts were lost to me as he looked outside, lips sealed shut and turned down. Had the memory of parting with his students upset him?

"I have a question. Which subject was that class supposed to be?" I asked, hoping to restore our equilibrium with a touch of humor.

His attention snapped back to me, and he wore an expression of disbelief. "Why, it was English of course." He smiled as he began gathering his discarded napkins and wrappers. "So you see my point, Emma, is that it's time for you to *apply*. There's a world outside of your grief, and you have to go find it. Your sister would not want you to become trapped in a continual cycle of mourning. Great is the power of pain when it is faced alone, but strong is the heart that beats with another, echoing one after the other. So where one beat ends the other begins, with never a moment of uncertainty about whether it will start again."

He had given the topic much thought, more than the average person gathering wisdom from life experiences. Perhaps it was for the benefit of his students, or something he had studied in school, but his knowledge of grief was much more intricate than one would gather from a textbook.

With his constant support and wisdom, I navigated through the last several months, struggling to accept my new normal. After all he taught me during our conversations about my life and my loss, he never tired from discussing my grief. But why? Why did he know exactly what to say, and why did he want to say it to me? Maybe it was a habit for him after all he did for his school, but I couldn't be sure.

These questions played on my mind often, but I never asked. Ken told me what he wanted me to know about himself. He never pushed me for answers, so I didn't want to push him. I knew him through his words, guidance, kindness, and generous understanding. Those were the gifts I would learn to accept. Maybe that was all I needed to know.

"That was your lesson for the day," he said. I smiled and started to pack up, but he hadn't moved. "Promise me you'll apply the lesson."

Not a trace of humor sparkled in his eyes. A cloud passed over his sunny exterior like it did on the Fourth of July. Once again, I sat wondering at his sudden mood shift. But I agreed, knowing my answer was important to him.

"I promise."

EIGHTEEN

———

Sunday morning smelled of black coffee and mothballs as I sat at the edge of Mama's bed. I stifled a yawn. In a panic, Mama had woken me in the early morning while mumbling about a missing interview suit and an entire stack of boxes to search through.

"I have absolutely nothing to wear," Mama said, her voice muffled as she dug through the last of the moving boxes tucked in the back of her closet. We moved in months ago, but still hadn't fully unpacked. Nana kept us both busy as we juggled her care. So, we often rummaged through closets and boxes to find what hadn't been put away. "I hope my good suit is in here. I can't afford to make a poor impression during my interview."

"I'm sure it's in there. Where else could it be? Besides, you still have time to find it. Your interview isn't until tomorrow." It was the first interview she had booked in over a month, so she had started preparing early.

"Tomorrow *morning*," Mama said as she emptied the box on the floor.

I set down my coffee mug on the bedside table and bent down to help dig through the pile of clothes. "Are you waiting to hear back from any other places that you sent job applications to?" I hoped she had something lined up in case this interview didn't work out.

"I applied to a few other places, but the opportunities aren't ideal. It's not like I could work at the grocery store; the hours are terrible, and it would cost more to have someone care for your grandma than I would earn. That's why I'm counting on this interview. It's with that bank down the street. I'm applying to be a teller. If I get it, I'd work convenient hours, and be home early enough to take care of her. They offer good pay and as a bonus I'd have Sundays off. I might even have an opportunity for advancement in the future if I go back to business school part time for an associate's degree." A small smile crossed her face. "Maybe one day, I'll have a small office, or at least a desk."

I looked up in surprise. "Would you go back to school?"

Mama shrugged. "I don't see why not, especially if they pay for the tuition as a part of their training program." After all this time, I couldn't imagine Mama having hopes of returning to school. I thought she had long forgotten those dreams as she pushed them aside for her family.

She focused on the pile of clothes in front of her, pretending not to notice my stunned expression. Beneath the surface, I knew she hid a glimmer of hope for the first time in a while. Maybe if the bank hired her, I could return to school without worrying about how she and Nana would fare on their own. The thought of leaving them wouldn't seem as bad if Mama had a job to go to.

"I really hope you get the job," I said softly.

"Here it is," Mama exclaimed, holding up her prized interview jacket and cream dress shirt. She slipped the jacket over her long nightgown to test the fit. When she smoothed out the wrinkles of the thick wool material, I noticed specks of white on the sleeve. I tried to brush them off, and when the dots turned out to be Mama's pale skin, I realized moths had eaten holes in the jacket.

"Just my luck," Mama said.

"Why don't we go buy a new one. I think it's about time. Obviously, this one isn't very lucky, anyway."

Mama considered the holes in the sleeve. "I suppose that would be all right. We can't get home too late, though. I have some house cleaning to do, and Nana shouldn't be left alone for long. Two hours tops. If we can't find anything by then, I'll have to sew this one."

I bounced on my toes. It had been a long time since we last went shopping. "I just checked on Nana and she's still sleeping. If we leave now, she might not notice we're gone."

We slipped out of the apartment and hurried to the car. The bright and sunny morning had an unexpected warmth for late November, and I shed my warmer jacket when I hopped in the car. Stalled by the morning traffic, we slowly made our way to the shopping center.

When we arrived, Mama suggested we visit the department stores first. We sifted through the discount racks of three different stores with no luck. Mama said we should go back home, but I convinced her to venture into one last store. Glass display cases lined the walls, and a large chandelier shone like a cluster of fireflies.

Mama tried to turn and walk out, but I dragged her to a rack and insisted she try on a tweed jacket. It was gray with a satin black trim. Silver buttons engraved with small anchors lined the front and cuffed the sleeves. I slid it over Mama's shoulders, and it shaped to her form. The color reflected gray flecks in her eyes and brought out the copper tones in her chestnut hair. Her eyes lit up as she appraised her appearance

in the jacket. I hadn't seen that look in a while. I twirled Mama
in front of the mirror as the sales associate eyed us from the
side. The saleswoman, dressed in a crisp business suit, took
one look at my worn sneakers and resigned to recline against
the counter while casting glances over her magazine.

"That's the one, you have to get it," I said.

Mama looked at the price and scoffed. "No way." She
slid it off and placed it back on the rack. "We shouldn't have
come here. We can't afford it."

Snatching the jacket from the rack, I said, "Remember
what Leonard said in group last week? Self-care is important.
You have to invest in yourself. I consider this an investment."

She put her hands on her hips, scowling.

"I'm not leaving without it. I deposited my paycheck yesterday, so let me buy it for you. Call it an early birthday present." Mama's birthday wasn't for another few months, but I
needed to convince her somehow. This was the first time we
did anything fun, anything for ourselves, in a long time. I
wouldn't let it end without Mama going home with that jacket.

Sensing a potential purchase, the sales associate
approached while Mama and I debated over the garment in
hushed voices. The woman's owl-like eyes cast back and forth
between us. She wore a forced smile, drawn between dimples.
"How are you ladies doing?" she asked, looming between me
and Mama as we tugged on each shoulder of the jacket.

"Just fine, thank you," Mama said in a calm tone, attempting to conceal our disagreement.

"We'll take this, please," I spoke over Mama as I won the
tug of war and handed the sales associate the jacket.

"Wonderful," the bird-like woman said. She snatched up
the jacket and turned on her heels without a moment's pause
to hear Mama's protest.

Mama colored beet red and fumed as I handed over my card and took the garment bag from the cashier. Because of her strong sense of decorum, she allowed the purchase, refusing to cause a scene in such an upscale place.

"I can't believe you did that," Mama said as we strapped ourselves into the car. "That jacket costs more than two weeks' worth of groceries."

I shrugged. "I told you, call it an early birthday present and a good luck charm. If it works like it's supposed to, it will pay for itself."

"Fine," she grumbled. "But that's my birthday, Christmas, and Mother's Day presents all wrapped into one." Her eyes glimmered and I thought a small part of her still dreamed of the finer things, delighting in the experience.

"Deal," I said as I turned on the radio. We listened to a throwback station playing our favorite hits from when I was little. We smiled and laughed as we rode home, and it all felt perfectly normal.

NINETEEN

"We must have forgotten to lock the door," I said, standing outside the apartment, pushing on the door handle. I reversed the direction of the key, which seemed to have locked rather than unlocked the door.

"No, I definitely remember locking it on our way out," Mama said.

I shrugged. The metal could have stuck because of the dropping temperatures. I walked down the hall to check on Nana and saw her door wide open. She must have woken up while we were shopping. The trip took longer than expected and we had returned an hour late. I headed toward the kitchen. Maybe Nana had gone to look for a snack. She wasn't there. I searched Mama's bedroom, then the bathroom, the closets, the living room, and the kitchen again.

She wasn't here.

Then Mama checked again with me. I shook with the uncertainty of what to do.

"The door," I said, realizing it had been unlocked after all. "Nana must have left on her own."

Mama raked her hands over her face and through her hair, blinking rapidly as she ran to the window. "She couldn't have gone far. I'll go check the common areas outside. You go check all the floors. If you can't find her, then start knocking on doors and ask if anybody's seen her."

I nodded, ran out the front door, and barreled down the steps. I checked the second floor, then, panting for air, checked the first floor. Panic coursed through my veins as I looked for Nana's familiar tufts of gray curls and round face. For hours, Mama and I trekked across the apartment complex parking lots and the surrounding blocks.

"Maybe we should call the police. We can't leave her out here all night." I sniffled as my nose ran from the cold and an afternoon of frightened tears.

Mama hadn't shed a single tear. Instead, she snapped into action, her eyes steeled with determination, and her focus sharpened with adrenaline that made her hands shake. "Let's keep looking a little longer. We'll call the police as a last resort."

We continued our search outside until the sun disappeared beneath the horizon. My feet ached from running, my lungs burned for air, and a chill had sunk into my bones. Nana must be terribly frightened, confused and alone. My heart clenched as I thought of Nana wandering and shivering in the cold. I felt just as lost as her; the area had become unrecognizable, transformed by a white blanket that sparkled like crystals under the blue light of the moon. I hurried down a dark street that stretched for miles.

A few paces away, I saw someone hunched over on a bench, resting their head in their hands. I rushed toward the concealed figure but became skeptical as I approached. Gym shoes protruded from the frayed ends of baggy jeans. I stopped in my tracks and thought I should turn back. But not before the person looked up. An unfamiliar angular face, with tired eyes and gaping lips stared at me. I hoped someone was looking for him.

Mama caught up and beckoned me to keep moving, searching farther down the street.

We came across a group of people huddled in a tunnel, covering themselves in newspapers to shield from the cold. We passed over their faces quickly. They shared Nana's far-away gaze, and I wanted to weep for them. But none of them were her, and we had to go on.

We mistook a surprising number of people for Nana, and I began to lose hope that we would find her. I lost track of where we were. Hopefully by the end of our search we could still find our way back home.

Under the orange glow of a streetlamp, I spotted a dark outline standing on the sidewalk. The figure stood still and unwavering. Could it be her, or was it just another shrub? I hurried forward to look further and called for Mama.

As I stepped closer, an outline of a person became clear in the shadowy figure. Mama trailed a few steps behind as we approached. The crunching sound of our footsteps on the ice-covered ground grew louder in the quiet stillness. Hands, feet, and legs appeared like carvings of stone illuminated by the streetlamp.

With a jarring movement, the figure turned to face my approaching footsteps. Light bounced off curly gray hair and a petite, sharp nose stuck out from shadows—it was Nana.

"Nana," I exclaimed as I ran to her. Mama and I reached her in a second.

Nana shrieked and lurched backward, almost causing her to slip on the ice.

I grabbed Nana's arm to stabilize her and looked into her widened eyes, as large and round as the moon that hung in the sky. Redness blotched her face, and her fingers colored a sickly blue, but darkness concealed the rest. "Nana, it's me."

As if I had said nothing, Nana tried to pull away, trembling. Her face contorted with confusion. With unfounded strength, she yanked her arm back, almost toppling to the ground. "Who are you?" she asked, her voice unsteady. She mumbled the words repeatedly while looking around the dark alley.

Mama grabbed Nana's other arm. "Mom, it's going to be okay, we're going to take you home now."

Nana's mouth turned down in a sorrowful arc. Tears pricked at her eyes, and small squeaks of fright escaped. As we walked back to find our car, which we had abandoned farther down the road, Nana resisted. Not even Mama's soothing voice and lavender perfume sparked recognition. Nana had mistaken me for other people plenty of times. Sometimes I was Gina, sometimes I was Grace, sometimes I was my deceased great aunt, but Nana always recognized me as someone important to her. But not this time. This time she didn't know who I was at all.

Mama and I held on to Nana's arms as we trod across the snow-slicked ground. Relief flooded through me, but Nana's confusion caused another round of worries to grow.

Nana winced and pulled back as I grabbed her hand. Dampness spread where my hand touched Nana's. Small puddles of red striped across my palm and I stopped in my tracks.

"Mama, wait for a second," I said.

Mama stopped and looked between my scarlet hand and Nana's arm. "There's blood. I see some on her hand and sleeve, she must have fallen."

We couldn't find a large gash or any obvious injuries. Mama inspected Nana, asking her if she had fallen and where it hurt. Nana had no answer, she could only ask questions. She tried to pull away again when Mama fingered through her hair, trying to look for any head injuries or signs of more blood.

I tried not to cry again at the thought of Nana falling and possibly hitting her head. Could that be why she didn't recognize either of us? How would a head injury affect her deteriorating memory?

When Nana refused to cooperate, Mama sighed, exhaling large puffs of visible air like smoke. "I think we're going to need to take her to the hospital. We have to make sure that she didn't hit her head."

I nodded, and we continued along the road with renewed urgency.

We turned the heat on full blast in the car, and eventually Nana stopped resisting our help, allowing me to slide in the back seat next to her. I wasn't sure if it was cold enough to get frostbite, but Nana had been outside for hours, and her teeth chattered so violently they might chip. Mama sped down the street and we reached the emergency room within a few minutes.

After searching through the pitch dark, my eyes winced at the blinding light coming from the entrance. My panic began to rise as doctors, patients, and wheelchairs buzzed around the small waiting room. The scene felt all too familiar—an unwelcome reminder of the last time we were at a hospital.

I sank into a seat and tried to make myself small in the chair while a grimacing man with large, fleshy arms leaned against our shared armrest.

Exhaustion weighed on my limbs, though my heart still raced with the final traces of adrenaline. Meanwhile, Nana turned and twisted in her seat, trying to get her bearings as her abundance of anxious energy swelled despite the exhausting day.

I wanted to hold Nana's hand to bring her comfort, but my proximity only frightened her. Like a cornered animal, she sneered and jumped if I leaned too close. Afraid that she would try to escape through the door, I didn't allow my attention to stray from her for even a second. After some time, she reclined into the seat with a glazed expression. Some color returned to her fingertips, but it drained from her eyes.

When thirty minutes had passed, Mama shot from her seat and strode to the front desk to complain about the long wait and explained the urgency of the situation to a receptionist who hadn't bothered to look up from her computer screen. And Mama, despite her manners, caused a scene in that waiting room. Once Mama turned that reddish hue, like sunburn scorching down her face and neck, the receptionist rose from her seat and fetched a doctor.

The doctor waived for us to follow and directed us to a back room.

Nana stopped at the threshold, unwilling to step into the room after me. Mama, the doctor, and the nurse urged her from behind. The nurse placed a hand on Nana's shoulder, causing her to shriek and protest as if the contact had shocked her.

The doctor spoke to her softly. "I'm only here to help. I'm going to need you to calm down." He planted his hands on her upper arms, but she only fought against his grasp. He spoke to the nurse over Nana's shoulder. "We're going to need backup."

Mama jumped in between the two. "Absolutely not," she said with a firmness that set the doctor back a few steps.

I wrapped my arms around myself while watching the scene unfold. If only Nana could remember who I was, I would pat her hand and hum a calming melody, as I had done countless times before. Now I couldn't get close enough for Nana to hear.

Another nurse appeared behind Nana in the hallway and stuck a syringe in her arm before anyone could register what was happening.

Nana's eyes went wide, a yelp escaped her parted lips, and her body stiffened. Then she wobbled on her feet and went limp as the nurse pushed on the lever, emptying the contents into her system.

I gasped as the doctor and both nurses helped lower Nana into a wheelchair.

Mama glared at the doctor, who avoided her eyes. The nurse wheeled Nana away, and the doctor stepped in front of Mama and me, preventing us from following.

The doctor's hard expression softened with sympathy. "You'll be together soon. We just have to take some scans and run tests to check for head injuries. Don't worry, she's in good hands," he said.

He directed us to a private sitting room where a nurse waited with a clipboard full of questions. Mama explained what happened earlier in the evening. I stared at my shaking hands, folded in my lap, while trying to hold myself together.

After some time, the doctor returned, his face like stone. "Ms. Rizzo, the good news is that your mother does not have a concussion. She has a scrape on her arm, and it looks like she might have fallen, but it's nothing serious. As for the confusion, it may be a progression of her condition. Does she have a specialist whom she currently sees?"

"Yes, she sees Dr. Webster from the dementia clinic across the street," Mama said.

"I would like her to follow up with Dr. Webster to discuss future options." He handed us a pamphlet on caring for people with dementia. "You might find some helpful resources in there. I would like to observe her overnight. You can either stay with her in her room tonight or come back in the morning."

"I'd like to stay with her. Thank you, Doctor."

The doctor left after reassuring us Nana would be just fine. I hoped I could believe him.

• • •

A while later, a nurse directed us to a room where Nana would be staying overnight. Nana lay in the bed asleep, looking peaceful from the sedative they had given her. The room had a tropical theme with paintings of boats and beaches hanging on the wall amid chalkboards listing the nurses' schedules. I expected to sleep in one of the two chairs that had been set up next to Nana's bed. The metal frame and light padding were far from comfortable, though sleep would be hard to come by, anyway. The whirring and beeping of Nana's machines and the smell of antiseptic alcohol overwhelmed any chance of rest for tonight.

Mama peered at the monitors as if she knew how to decipher their meaning, and then moved on to peruse the rest of the room. "Why don't I drive you home and I'll come back and stay with Nana?"

"No, I'm staying here with you guys," I said.

"You won't get a good night's rest here, and you have work early in the morning."

"I won't get a good night's rest at home, either. I'll just be up all night worrying."

"You know I'll call if something changes, but I think Nana will be okay." Nana probably would be all right, but Mama had been through a lot, too, and I wanted to stay if only to be a shoulder for her to rest her head on. I sat down in the chair and crossed my arms, unwilling to budge from the spot.

Mama didn't bother to argue further and sat down next to me. She picked up a magazine from the side table and handed me one on homes and gardening.

The words on the page were meaningless; I could only focus on the steady beeping of Nana's machines—a quiet reassurance that she would be okay. We stayed like that for hours until the exhaustion set in. I leaned against Mama's shoulder and closed my eyes. Sometime during the night, a nurse brought us a couple of blankets and pillows. I drifted in and out of a light sleep until streaks of light peeked through the curtains.

Realizing that I hadn't set an alarm for work, I stood up and stretched my aching limbs. Nana had slept through the night, still subdued from the sedative. Mama sat in the chair next to me with her head leaned back against the wall, only a light pillow cushioning the hard surface. Her face relaxed into a foreign look of calm as she slept, and I slipped out of the room for water, careful not to disturb either of them.

When I came back to the room, Mama awakened. She checked the time and guided me into the hallway to talk. "Why don't I drive you home now so you have enough time to get ready for work? I'll grab some clothes for Nana so she will have something to wear home and then I can drop you off on my way back here."

I agreed, and we headed out, stopping at the front desk to tell the receptionist we would be back soon. It was too early for visiting hours, but the receptionist made an exception and agreed to let Mama back in when she returned. We drove home in silence, both of us fighting to stay awake after our poor night's sleep. Fatigue made everything more difficult. I was out of breath after dragging myself up the three flights of stairs. Mama took a while to find her keys, which she swore she had put in the outer pocket of her bag, and by the time we made it inside, I needed to hurry to make it to work.

I showered and pulled on my light pink work outfit. My long-sleeve top wasn't washed since I didn't have time to do laundry yesterday, so I opted for my short sleeve uniform and went to Mama's closet to borrow a cardigan.

I went to open the closet door and froze. A white top and black blazer hung in a garment bag on the doorknob. In the chaos and worry, we had forgotten Mama's interview, which she needed to be at in a few hours.

"Mama, your interview," I said, my voice panicked.

Mama emerged from Nana's room with arms full of clothes. "Shoot." Her face fell. "I can't believe I forgot."

It almost seemed like the previous morning of shopping hadn't happened, like it was a good dream, and we woke up to a nightmare.

"I'll stay with Nana so you can go to the interview," I said.

"But what about your work?"

I shrugged. "I have plenty of sick days left. I'll just call in."

Mama shifted the clothes in her hand. "What if the doctor needs me to sign something, or what if something goes wrong while I'm away?"

"Then I'll call you. Your phone is charged, right?"

Mama nodded. "I suppose that could work. If you're sure you'll be okay waiting there alone."

"Nana and I will be okay, now go get ready."

I changed back into more comfortable clothes: sweatpants, a sweater, and my most reliable sneakers. While Mama ran around the house, gathering her résumé and briefcase, I packed some supplies for the day. I had a lot of experience packing a hospital bag. I grabbed a day's worth of snacks, my phone cord, and Nana's favorite book which I could read aloud if she woke. Then I helped Mama get ready for the interview, rushing to make a light breakfast while Mama brushed on concealer to hide the dark purple circling her eyes.

With Mama's expensive new suit jacket and some extra makeup, nobody would notice that she had spent the entire night sleeping in a hospital chair. It would be a tough interview to pull off given the current distractions, but if anyone could do it, Mama could. After shoveling down scrambled eggs and toast, we piled back into the car with our hospital bags and Mama's briefcase.

We neared the hospital, and Mama pestered me with questions. "Are you sure you brought enough food?" she asked.

"Yes, Mama. Don't worry, I'll be fine. Besides, you'll only be away for a few hours." I had stayed in hospitals equipped with far less for far longer during the days I had spent by my sister's side. This was much easier; Nana would be okay.

Mama dropped me back off at the hospital, leaving for the interview with a wary smile. I wished her good luck, and Mama replied she better not need it after how much we paid for the suit jacket. Although she joked, Mama's mouth gave a subtle twitch like it did whenever she felt nervous.

Sending up a silent wish, I waved as the car pulled away. I didn't want to see Mama rejected from another potential employer. Having achieved an equilibrium where Mama's sadness and functionality balanced, I feared anything that threatened to tip the scale. With Mama on the mend, and after talking with Ken about school plans, I wished not only for the job but also for the future I thought I had lost. The wish grew like a flower that bloomed and dared to face the sun, but it seemed too bright and warm to be true.

Now that I had a glimpse, the future was all I could ponder. But my hope remained tentative. If something had happened to Nana, I would have found myself back at square one, in a place of despairing loss. I climbed my way out of the darkness, grasping to small moments of joy as footholds. Ken reminded me how to laugh, how to dream, how to have goals and expectations. Day by day, I collected those moments until life became transformed. It was not shiny and new like it had been, but where my life lacked innocence, it emerged with the beauty of an ancient artifact that had survived upheaval, been buried for centuries, and was unearthed to wonder at with fascination. Ken taught me to appreciate the dents and scratches because they showed a history and taught a lesson that should be shared with others. And the lesson wasn't to stand guard, waiting for the next disaster.

I fell asleep waiting in Nana's room and woke to the sound of glass doors sliding open. Mama's head peeked through, and she slipped into the room, careful not to disturb Nana's sleep. The afternoon sun streamed in through the window, pooling on Nana's bed, so Mama went over to close the curtains.

Blinking my eyes, I looked to Mama's face, gauging how the interview went. I mouthed, "How did it go?"

Mama shrugged, her head tilting and eyebrows lifting in an expression that told me it went okay, but who really knows? She had come home from plenty of interviews thinking she had made a stellar impression, only to be rejected.

While we waited to sign Nana out of the hospital, Mama went over the bill with the receptionist. Based on the look on her face, I could tell it was costly. Now I understood Mama's reasons for selling the house. With the extra money from the sale, we could pay the bill and keep Nana out of the state care facilities. The forms took a while, and we headed for the car around five o'clock as a nurse wheeled Nana beside us.

Nana didn't talk during the drive home. Mama looked in the rearview mirror, peering into the back seat while asking how she felt. Nana gave a terse "fine" or "all right." Nothing more than that. Then it occurred to me that she might not remember the hospital, or why she had been there. When we reached the apartment, Nana headed straight for her room and closed the door as if nothing was amiss.

Mama collapsed on her futon and fell asleep before I finished throwing out the empty food wrappers from the bottom of my overnight bag. I hopped in the shower, wanting to scrub off the smell of hospital antiseptic. I could smell it on my skin and in my hair. It made my head ache and only brought reminders of painful things. Pulling back the curtains to Grace's room in the ICU. Her eyes closed, head slightly askew, tubes protruding everywhere, feeling Mama's hand shake under mine. My knees gave out, my body trembled. Just wash it away. Breathe; that was then, not now. Memories still came like tidal waves crashing over my thoughts. But they came less now, and when they did, I found a way to the surface.

TWENTY

On Tuesday, I fell back into my morning routine and slipped out of our apartment before everyone else woke up. I hadn't called in sick to work before yesterday, so I hoped Ken wasn't too worried when I didn't show up for our lunch. I would explain everything on Wednesday when we would meet again. Surely he would understand. I could stop by Ken's apartment before work started, though I had never stopped by unannounced before, and the main entrance to the residents' apartments would likely be locked.

When I arrived at the Center, I walked past the library where I sat each morning and headed to Mrs. Hubert's office. After missing the caregiver's weekly meeting, I needed to stop by early to pick up my schedule. A light glowed from her office among a hallway of darkened windows.

I knocked on her door before entering. "Hi Mrs. Hubert, I'm here for my assignment sheet."

She smiled and set down her coffee mug. "Yes, let me get that for you. Now, where did I put it?" While rummaging through the mess of papers on her desk, she asked, "How are you feeling?"

When I had called in sick on Monday, I had told her that I woke up with a cough and didn't want to risk getting any of the residents sick. I felt bad about lying, but the other option was to tell Mrs. Hubert the truth, and in the hospital room hallway, with nurses hurrying past with carts and wheelchairs, I couldn't find the words to explain.

"I'm feeling much better, thank you. I have allergies, so it was probably just the fallen leaves and seasonal mildew that bothered me."

"Well, good. I'm glad to hear it. Ah—here it is." She handed over my folder. "I had to modify your schedule for the week. Your original roster was split between the other caregivers. To lighten their workload, I gave you some of their temporary residents."

I was familiar with the procedure when a caregiver called in sick, but it made for a confusing day. I thanked her for the schedule and headed out. Intent on having a head start, I started my first task right away, trying to bring order to my difficult day.

• • •

My lunch break was a couple hours later than usual, and my stomach rumbled as I wheeled my temporary resident, Andrew, to physical therapy. As we turned the corner, entering the rehab and training facilities, I realized Ken should be there for his sessions. His physical therapy appointments prevented him from joining me for lunch on Tuesdays and Thursdays. I hoped to run into him so I might wave hello and promise to explain my absence later.

The training room was a concrete square with padded walls and scattered equipment. I took Andrew the long way around, navigating a maze of rubber exercise balls and stretching contraptions as I searched for Ken. He was nowhere to be found.

Andrew's physical therapist, Breanna, waited in a corner of the room, hands on her hips. "Hi, Andrew." Her face lit up with an animated smile as we approached. "Are you ready for your exercises today?"

He gave a shaky thumbs up.

"Excellent." She clapped her hands together. "Let's get you into the bouncer."

"Would you like me to help?" I asked. Perhaps if I waited I could spot Ken.

"That would be great, thanks," she said.

At a standing height, Andrew neared six feet tall, and my knees buckled as I supported half his weight. With some maneuvering, Breanna and I helped him into a piece of equipment that looked like a child's swing set attached to a web of stretchy bands and elastic pulleys.

Breanna tugged on her tight ponytail and straightened her elastic headband before starting a series of exercises. She had thanked me for my help at first, but now eyed me curiously as I stood along the side. I stuck around much longer than necessary, while scanning for a yellow hoodie that never appeared.

After about fifteen minutes Breanna said, "You know, I think another caregiver is scheduled to pick Andrew up, so you don't have to stay."

I couldn't think of an excuse to stay. "Oh. Okay, thanks." I headed for the door; my face flushed.

I almost made it to the hallway when I glimpsed Ken's physical therapist. I recognized her short hair and muscular build from when she had stopped us in the hall to admonish him for skipping sessions.

Hurrying toward her, I figured Ken would be there, too. But as I approached, I saw a frail-looking woman in his place.

The physical therapist recognized me before I could turn back. "Hi, I know you," she said, her voice raspy. "You were Ken's caregiver, right?"

"Yes, that's right. It's good to see you."

"Yeah, you too. It would be nice to see Ken sometime as well."

I sighed. "Has Ken been skipping his sessions again?"

"That's the strange thing. He was doing great with attendance, but he didn't show up today."

"I will have a talk with him when I see him tomorrow."

"Would you? That would be a big help." She pointed her finger. "Tell him if I don't see him here for his next appointment on Thursday, he's in trouble."

"Will do."

Ken held me accountable for the challenges I needed to work on and encouraged me to keep improving. We were friends, and that applied both ways. He didn't like his sessions, though he tried to hide it. It confronted him with weakness while he presented nothing short of stringent independence and a desire to help others rather than be helped. But he would have to learn to like it. He would be going to his physical therapy sessions, even if I had to drag him there myself.

I had just enough time left before my next task to check the library, just in case Ken had skipped his session to have lunch with me again.

The library bustled with activity, and I looked for the familiar yellow of his hoodie. I searched until I was sure he wasn't there. I hoped he had returned to his apartment.

• • •

For the rest of the day and the following morning, I couldn't focus on much else except figuring out Ken's unexplained absence during physical therapy. I would know soon enough, just a couple more minutes, and we would sit in our familiar spot for our Wednesday lunch, and we would be obliged to explain the absences of the previous few days to each other.

I waited by the elevator around noon and checked my watch. He was five minutes late. The light dinged and lit up above the doors as they slid open and closed, people shuffling in and out. I shifted farther away from the bustle of traffic that Ken often tried to avoid by arriving early. More than one person cast me a sideways look as I tried to avoid the stream of canes, wheelchairs, and shuffling feet that branched all around me.

Ten minutes late, I headed over to the library to find out if Ken had arrived there first. I found our seats by the fireplace empty but sat down anyway and placed my brown paper bag on my lap.

Twenty minutes passed, then thirty, and there was still no sign of him. I didn't take my eyes off the curved entryway. Craning my neck with each person who passed, I hoped Ken would appear, joking about the long lines at the first-floor restaurant. He would tease that it's about time I waited for him since I was always the one to run late. Except he couldn't do that because he never showed up. I didn't want to get up from the chair where I waited, but I had residents to attend to.

Throughout the day a familiar pit of despair formed in my stomach, and I wondered if I had upset him by missing Monday, and then yesterday, without explanation. Perhaps his feelings were hurt, or maybe he thought I was still out sick and decided to eat in his apartment until I let him know I was feeling better. I liked that explanation best and decided I would stop by his apartment right after my shift ended.

Except I forgot about the towering pile of paperwork that waited for me in Mrs. Hubert's office. At the end of each day, the caregivers handed in their residents' paperwork, and we all took turns filing. Today was my turn to file. Rushing into the office, I hoped to finish the task before the custodians locked the entrance to the residential areas. Or at least, while I was there, I could ask Mrs. Hubert where Ken had been.

I stopped short when I saw Jenna leaning over Mrs. Hubert's desk, jotting something down in a hurry. Except for us two, the office had emptied. My hope dwindled as I realized Mrs. Hubert had gone home for the day, her bright green coat missing from the hook.

I managed a small hello, but it sounded breathless from my speed walking. As I moved to take the files from Mrs. Hubert's desk, Jenna planted a palm on top of the stack.

"Could you maybe wait on filing those for a few minutes? I'm still finishing my forms," she said.

The paperwork was supposed to be filled out while we worked with each resident, not scribbled at the end of the day. She would get in a lot of trouble if I didn't agree. Though, she was not really asking for my permission. One hand still rested on the stack while she wrote with the other. I sat in silence while Jenna filled out page after page of forms. My chance of visiting Ken slipped away with each page she thumbed through.

I had enough. "You know Jenna, I have somewhere I really need to be. So I need to start—"

"Just one more second." Her harsh tone clipped my words.

"How about this? You can take all the time you need to finish your paperwork, and you can file it once you're done."

She looked at me as if I had said something absurd. "I filed yesterday."

"I can file for you next week."

"I actually have plans right after this so I can't stay, but thanks for offering. Anyway, I am just. About. Done," she said with each swish of her pen. She dropped her papers into the stack and strode out without so much as a smile. By the time I finished filing, the custodians had already locked the entryway to the residents' apartments. Only the residents, doctors, nurses, and custodians had keycard access to the locked doors. I would have to wait to talk with Ken.

• • •

The restless feeling and uneasy churning of my stomach that started on Wednesday had grown every moment since then, like upward *clicks* of roller coaster wheels on a track.

I couldn't concentrate on eating my breakfast the following morning, no matter how hard I tried; my mind flooded with thoughts of Ken's unexplained absence.

Yesterday, when I had realized at the end of my lunch break that Ken would not show up, I heard the first *click* of climbing wheels, approaching the drop. I felt the tides shift and a terrifying awareness filled every nerve of my being. But after Nana's episode, the entire week was tumultuous. So, I figured the anxious rumbling of something amiss came from the near disaster we had avoided with Nana a couple of days before.

Mama walked into the kitchen, interrupting my thoughts. Spilling over with worry, I told her about my concerns.

Mama sat across from me at the table, listening intently. "Don't worry," she said. "Maybe he didn't know how to get a hold of you since you were absent." Mama didn't know Ken very well, only from what I had told her. He was highly punctual and never missed the details.

"He wouldn't miss our lunch from a simple oversight."

"He could just be a little under the weather."

"Maybe," I said, my voice trailing.

"Will you see him today?"

"No, it's Thursday so he has physical therapy."

Mama tapped her chin. "Why don't you visit his apartment after work today?"

"That was my plan yesterday, but I had to file paperwork. Hopefully, I'll be done early enough today."

"How about I pick you up after work so you don't have to worry about missing the bus if you stay later."

"Thanks, Mama, I appreciate it." Touched by her kind offer, I was glad that I told her about my concerns. I went to work, bolstered by her support and comforted by my new plan.

• • •

After I finished my work, I hurried to the elevator and pressed the third-floor button. My plan depended on the apartment entryways still being unlocked. The elevator dinged, and I exited, approaching the large automatic door that guarded the apartment units. My anticipation drummed until the door slid open, still unlocked. I hurried over to Ken's door and knocked.

No answer.

Click.

I knocked again. Still no answer.

Click.

The nurses had finished the rounds for the day, so there was no one to ask.

Peering in his thin, gold mail slot, I could only see a pair of extra dress shoes, shined, and placed near the door. Maybe he was asleep, or maybe he was at a performance in the music hall that I didn't know about. I could think of plenty of reasons why he didn't answer the door. I stood outside while listening from the hallway for any sign of movement in the apartment.

Tears burned as I worked myself into a panic. Unsure of what to do, I looked around. If I didn't hurry out of there, the custodians would come around and ask me to leave before securing the doors. I grabbed a scratch piece of paper from my bag and scribbled a quick note. *Sorry, I was gone on Monday. I'll explain everything, but I'm back. Let's meet tomorrow. If you can't meet, give me a call on my cell phone.* I wrote down my number, folded up the paper, and slid it through the mail slot. I hadn't thought to give him my number before, I wasn't even sure if company policy allowed me to, but I didn't have any other options.

• • •

On Friday, I couldn't stay in the library, waiting for Ken to show up for lunch. Restless energy took full control of my feet as I fled the library fifteen minutes after waiting for him. He didn't even call to tell me he would be late.

Click.

Something possessed me as I opened the stairwell door and jogged up the stairs. My patience wore too thin to wait for the elevator, caged in by spearing canes and bulky wheelchairs. I reached the top of the third-floor stairs and charged toward Ken's apartment. After knocking on the door, I paced small circles on the doormat outside. When he didn't answer after the third set of knocks, I crouched down and peered through his mail slot.

Click.

My breath hitched and my heart and skipped a beat when I saw what lay on the other side: my note. I had left it there last night. There it lay folded on the doormat, just on the other side of the door, my black letters scrawled on the inside. He hadn't touched it.

I stood up, my legs sprung upward like tight coils, and I dashed from the door.

I ran right into Thomas and bounced back a few steps.

"Woah, sorry about that," he said, straightening the files that were almost knocked from his grasp. "Oh, hey, Emma. You would not believe how much paperwork I have to file before I can leave tonight." He looked up and narrowed his eyes on my face. "Hey, are you okay?"

I opened my mouth, but no words came out. I looked back toward Ken's door, and he followed my gaze. Blue, round eyes softened with sympathy, and his lips turned down.

Click.

No, not that look. I knew that look all too well. Almost a year ago, when I was at a hospital far away, I asked a doctor if my sister was ever going to wake up. The doctor made that same face.

I waited for Thomas to answer a question I hadn't asked.

"He had a heart attack. I'm sorry, I know you two were close. I checked in on him from time to time, and he always talked about you."

Click.

My stomach dropped. I had reached the freefall. I shook my head. No, I couldn't do this again. Not again. I looked at him, stunned. My eyes pleaded for him to change his answer.

"It happened so fast." His mouth pulled to the side, and he ran a hand through his hair, sending tufts of blond hair awry. "Someone paged me to go to his room on Monday, code blue. When I got there, another nurse had already found him." He gave me a half-smile and said softly, "He was in his favorite chair with a fresh cup of coffee and a newspaper. He looked peaceful."

I couldn't remember what had happened after receiving the shocking news, only that I had rushed to the parking lot, tears streaming down my face, and hopped in Mama's car. We stayed parked there until I could find the words to explain.

I called Mrs. Hubert from the car and told her that I needed to take tomorrow off, and maybe next week. Luckily I was sent to voicemail, and the shaking in my voice could have been from whatever illness I gave as an excuse.

Mama drove us home, then I crawled into bed. I hadn't moved far from it since.

Saturday morning, I lay on my bed with a book in one hand and the other sifting through my cat's long, fine hairs. My head pounded, but I read anyway. Despite how the words ran together, the alternative would be to lie there and do nothing. I had already taken far too many naps. The quiet would only make me more aware of all the aches and pains that converged in my chest, each breath requiring an exhausting effort. I had spent months feeling this way after Grace died, and I didn't know if I had the strength to climb my way out again.

Mama had urged me to get some fresh air and go for a walk with her outside. But then droplets of rain fell from the sky and ran down my windowpane. It fell faster and in thicker clumps until Mama stopped suggesting that we wait five more minutes for it to let up.

I traced the mix of snow and rain as it melted a path down my window. Mama kept bringing me warm tea, trying to ward off the chill that I couldn't get rid of. Utensils scraped and pots clinked together while Mama made pancakes like she had done every Saturday morning when I was little. Grace and I would gather around the table, waiting in anticipation, but now the thought of eating pancakes alone made me want to throw up.

Panic clawed up my throat, burning as it rose. Since Wednesday, I felt as if I were at the precipice of a roller coaster's descent, with the anticipation so frightening, building with every *click*, it seemed the sensation couldn't get any more terrifying. Then I fell. My stomach lodged in my throat, and I realized I was wrong. The way down was much, much worse.

TWENTY-ONE

A few days passed, and the future remained uncertain. My bones felt like lead, and I resigned to lie in my bed, close my eyes, and count the time ticking by, hoping it could heal me like everyone said it would. Tomorrow couldn't come soon enough, but a tomorrow without Ken was one I did not look forward to. So, I sat idly by, wishing for the people I had lost, settling for time to heal the void left by their absences.

But I couldn't remain in my room forever. Continuing to call in sick when I didn't know if I would ever return was not fair to Mrs. Hubert. I needed to decide. The pressure of returning to work loomed over my head. I didn't want to quit after Mrs. Hubert had given me a chance when I needed one, but I couldn't stand the thought of working there without Ken. Every inch of that place was a reminder that I had lost my friend. And I would not be able to carry on with my duties with that distraction. No, it was too soon.

"I can't go back," I said to Mama. She had hardly left my side the past few days. Doting and watching me from the corner of her eyes, she worried how I fared.

"You don't have to go back," Mama said. "We'll be okay for a while."

"But what will we do? I know I don't make much money, but I don't think we could afford to live on our savings and Nana's social security for much longer, especially with her recent hospital bills."

Mama shrugged without a trace of concern. "I'll find a job, any job. I'll work at a grocery store, or at night somewhere if I have to. I'll take care of us like I should have all along."

I wanted to be strong enough to go back. Strong like Ken told me I was. But I wasn't strong. I felt fragile and weak. The practical part of me said not to quit, we needed the income. It was a good job, an opportunity I would not get again. I needed to take time to figure out what my next steps would be. Maybe I should return to school, as I had discussed with Ken. Or should I take another semester off? Ken was supposed to help me decide. He always knew what to say to lead me down the right path.

Quitting without warning would not look good on my résumé. But I didn't want to be practical. I wanted to be comforted and taken care of. I wanted to stay at home in a ball of blankets, read a good book with my cat, and pretend the outside world didn't exist. I wanted to stay like that until my heart didn't hurt as much. And if Mama was offering that to me, then I could hardly refuse. I didn't want to be brave anymore. I just wanted to feel better.

I nodded to Mama. "All right, fine. If it's okay, I'm going to quit. And I'm going to go right now because I can't stand the thought of working there another day." I grabbed my keys and my bag, and paused at the door, realizing I hadn't changed out of my pajamas. I headed back to my room to dress.

Halfway down the hall, Mama called, "You can't go now."

I turned. "Why not?"

"It's eight o'clock at night. By the time you get there, everyone will be gone."

I whirled my head around to look out the window. Black peeked through the gaps in the curtain. I had been lying in bed for hours, though it felt like no time had passed.

"Oh." I deflated, dropped my keys back on the desk, and plopped myself on the couch. "First thing tomorrow, then. I'll talk to Mrs. Hubert, and it will be over."

Mama gave me a pat on the back and a warm smile. I felt guilty that my weakness was costing us the security we had fought so hard to earn. But my instincts told me to run, and they were too strong to fight.

• • •

Wednesday morning—I used to like Wednesday mornings. Halfway through the week, I usually woke up drained, but it used to be a good day because I would see Ken. I slipped on my sneakers and left the house in jeans and my heavy coat. Why bother to wear the uniform? I would be quitting, anyway. It felt odd to slip into my old routine. Waking up before everyone else, I grabbed a cup of tea and headed for my bus. I almost packed myself a lunch out of habit.

I looked out the bus windows, feeling disoriented and out of place. With the awareness it would be my last trip, my usual route seemed new. The route I used to enjoy, full of trees and vibrant greenery, became desolate in the early December frost. Browned and shriveled, the land braced for the barren winter ahead.

The bus screeched to a halt, sending me rocking back. I thanked the bus driver, giving him an extra-wide smile. He tipped his straw fedora as he did every day, and my heart tugged because it was our final goodbye, but only I knew. I shivered while descending the bus steps and turned toward the Center's long entryway. While everything around it looked dull, withered, and filled with the smog of nearby cars and factories, the Center remained tucked in its conifer-covered sanctuary.

I passed through the stone archway, the smell of pine and damp soil overcoming the gasoline. I started on the long trek toward the main entrance, down the path between tall trees that hid the Center from the outside world.

By the time I reached the front entrance, the cold had numbed my fingers. I looked down the hallway that would take me to Mrs. Hubert's office.

On an impulse, I turned right, diverted to the elevator, and pressed the button that glowed with the number three. I wanted to stand outside Ken's apartment one last time. I needed closure. Maybe just to prove to Ken that I could do it. "See Ken? I can be brave. I can be what you said I could. I can stand outside your door. I won't pace. I won't worry or fidget. I will stand there. And I will say goodbye."

I exited the elevator and ducked my head as I passed an elderly couple in the hallway. I didn't account for the possibility that other people might be around. Though it was still early, I hoped most of the residents would still be in their apartments.

I turned the corner and paused as I approached Ken's apartment. His door was open about a quarter way. From where I stood, I could see partly inside. Boxes were stacked everywhere. I considered turning around and leaving. Were people already there to pack up his belongings? Who could it be? He never mentioned any family members visiting, but he talked about them occasionally. He grew up with a lot of siblings, but only his younger sister remained. Then I remembered the photograph I once saw sitting on his side table: a picture of him with a wife and daughter. I never asked about it because he lived alone, and he hadn't brought it up. Maybe his daughter from the photograph had come to pick up his things.

I took a couple of steps forward and stiffened. A familiar yellow showed through the crack. I inched closer. Pale skin contrasted against the bright hue. It was impossible, but unmistakable.

Without another thought, I burst through the door. A woman with short white hair and a portly frame looked at me with startled, blue eyes. Glasses perched on the long bridge of her nose, framing her pale, oval face. The resemblance was clear. This had to be his younger sister, though her name didn't come to mind. Ken was considerably taller; his sister was about my height. We stared at each other, not knowing what to say.

I shifted on my feet. "I'm sorry, I mistook you for someone else." I said, blinking back tears of disappointment.

She followed my gaze to Ken's yellow hoodie which she had draped over her arm. "Did you know Ken?" she asked. Her voice was soft and sweet. It oozed kindness that made me want to stay.

I nodded, and a couple of tears escaped.

The woman shed a few as well. She looked so much like him. I edged farther into the room, drawn by the similarity of her mannerisms to Ken's. The way she postured and tilted her head—it was uncanny.

"You must be Ken's sister," I said after a long silence.

"Ah, yes. Where are my manners?" She set down the hoodie and turned to me, collecting herself. "I'm Ruth."

I shook her hand. "Emma. It's nice to meet you. Ken told me all about you."

She nodded and cast her eyes down. "I'm sure I would have heard about you as well, but Ken and I didn't talk as much as we should have. I moved to England, and Ken isn't—" she paused, "wasn't a fan of talking on the phone. I haven't been back to the States for almost a year."

I should have been polite and excused myself to let Ruth get back to sorting through Ken's belongings, but my curiosity brimmed. I had many questions about Ken, and Ruth would know so much about him. I already knew a lot, enough to fill in the blanks, but I needed to know for sure if I was right. I imagined he had been popular when he was younger, had a lot of friends, and played sports, given his judo training.

"What was he like when he was younger?" I asked.

Ruth smiled and looked up, as if her memories played on the ceiling. "Oh, he was a great big brother, very protective, of course. He always asked where I was going and who I was with. I liked to go out with my friends, but Ken stayed home. He was a loner, always preferred to be in his room studying or reading a book. He was quiet but very kind, the most thoughtful person you'll ever meet."

Her description shocked me. Maybe we had been more alike than I had thought.

"I could go on about him forever," Ruth said.

"I'd like to hear."

"All right, if I'm not keeping you from anything."

Ruth led me toward the sofa, and we sat across from each other.

"Ken was our mother's favorite," she said. "The rest of us were always a bit jealous of him. Our mother never admitted it, of course, but only his report cards made it on the refrigerator. She reserved a little extra space in her heart for him. Maybe he needed it more than the rest of us. He was very sensitive, and our two older brothers picked on him for it. They could be unkind, but their teasing didn't change Ken one bit. He was different from the rest of us. We were a rowdy bunch growing up, always running around outside all day. We would only come home when the sun went down and our shoes filled with mud. But Ken was quiet, well-mannered, and preferred to stay in his room to read books and learn something. Our brothers weren't mean on purpose, they just never understood what he was talking about. When I was little, we played school and he taught me from his books. Only our mother and I really understood him. He took after her more than any of us."

I smiled, picturing a younger Ken giving Ruth lectures as he often did with me.

"It was only fitting that he became a teacher in the end, with all that reading he did. Although he almost became a lawyer." Ruth's eyes lit up as if she dusted off a memory. "He changed his major about halfway through college after spending one summer interning at a firm downtown. He hated that job and trudged home every night looking the saddest I had ever seen him. He wanted to become a lawyer to do good. But he was certain all he'd ever do was paperwork for people defending criminals. He was so defeated. He was unsure of what to do after he quit, but nothing kept him down for long. I joined him at college the next fall. We ended up going to the same state school in Michigan. Since we're two years apart, he was already there when I arrived. It was quite an accomplishment at the time. Mind you, few women were going to universities back in that day. Though, I was only accepted for a two-year associate's degree. I was training to work in sales for a chemical company. The company I was working for helped pay my tuition; I wouldn't have been able to afford it otherwise. My parents had a lot of kids, and there wasn't enough money to go around. So, we all had to pay our way through college."

Ken had told me about his many siblings, though I didn't know their situation had been that difficult. Listening to Ruth's story, I had a newfound appreciation for Mama, who insisted on helping me through school despite our own financial troubles.

"Those years in college with Ken were some of the best. Out of all the siblings, I was always closest to him. I was the youngest, so most of them either picked on me or ignored me. Except Ken. He always looked out for me. He took care of me." Ruth's eyes misted, and she paused for a moment. "Oh, we had such fun. Occasionally, I could even drag Ken from his reading. We explored the local cafés and live music. Then I introduced him to my best friend, Meredith. It was love at first sight. For him at least." She laughed.

I turned to look at the picture set on the side table. A dark-haired woman with a delicate, heart-shaped face and almond eyes stared back. She looked around middle-aged in the picture, and she had aged gracefully.

"Yep, that's her," Ruth said. "Poor Ken was too shy to say more than three words when they first met." She pointed her thumb to her chest. "I talked some sense into him. I told him, 'If you don't ask her on a date, somebody else will.' One night he saw her dancing with Parker Kinsley." She smiled. "Every girl chased after him. He was the big man on campus and came from a wealthy family, too. Though Meredith saw through all that—she only agreed to dance with him to make Ken jealous. It worked, of course. He interrupted their dance and asked her out right then. She said yes, and the rest is history. He proposed right after their graduation two years later and they were married the minute he returned from serving in the national guard. They had their beautiful daughter, Mae, not long after that." She shook her head and squeezed her eyes shut. "It was such a tragedy what happened. They were a beautiful family."

"What happened?" I asked, leaning in.

She opened her eyes, focusing on me. "He didn't tell you?"

I shook my head.

"Well, whatever reasons he had don't matter now, so I might as well explain."

I edged forward on my seat in anticipation.

"It was the early nineties. Ken, Meredith, and Mae were taking a trip down to the beach. Ken drove his old 1975 Pontiac Grand Ville. It was a gorgeous baby blue convertible, and far too expensive for a teacher's salary. But it was the pride of his existence, second only to Mae. He bought it at a discount from someone who failed to mention that it broke down all the time. He worked on it constantly, always out there in the driveway, tinkering under the hood. One part fell off after the other, but he always tried to fix it up. Meredith told him he should just sell it for parts and buy a car they could use, but he refused. He would not give up on that car. He made sure to repair it so they could take it out on special occasions. It was the Fourth of July weekend, and they were celebrating Mae's high school graduation. They almost made it all the way there."

Her voice cracked, and I stiffened.

"They were on a long road that seemed to lead right into the ocean. Just one more stoplight and they would've reached the beach. The light turned red, but the brakes went out." She took a long breath. "Ken tried to stop but he couldn't. They were going downhill, right into traffic. He tried to stop the car by yanking the wheel, aiming for a field instead of an intersection. But the car flipped as he turned too quickly."

I gasped.

"The car was a hunk of steel and crushed Mae and Meredith underneath. They were gone in an instant. Ken was tossed from the car as it rolled, and by some miracle he walked away with a concussion and some broken ribs. Though, part of him died there with them. He blamed himself. For months he barely moved, or talked, or even left his house."

I wiped a few stray tears. How horrible for Ken. I had no idea.

"Ken refused to get rid of anything of theirs from his house. He was reserved before, but after, he became an absolute recluse, shutting himself in that house that looked more like a museum than a home. I tried to visit, but he never said much. All he could say was 'I should have gotten rid of that car like Meredith told me to.' He quit his job and just wasted away. It broke my heart to see him like that. Then he grew so angry that I had to stop visiting altogether. He said that I should hate him for what he did and that I should just leave him alone. Meredith was my best friend, and I loved Mae like she was my own. My husband and I were never blessed with kids. I couldn't get through to him. So, for a while, I gave him space, though I wouldn't have left him alone forever. I'm too much of a pest for that." A glimpse of Ken showed in the sparkle of her eyes as she joked.

"He wasn't angry and closed off when I met him," I said.

"It was that principal at the school he worked at. Leary, was it? He knocked on Ken's door one day and said he needed him to come back to work. Mr. Leary was about to retire, and he wanted Ken to take his place. It took some convincing, but Ken could never resist helping someone in need. At that point, I was at my wit's end trying to help him. I hadn't heard from him in months, and then he called me out of the blue, telling me he was going back to school to get a master's degree in education administration or something like that. I thought he'd lost it for good." She threw her hands up. "But he was completely serious. He graduated with his master's and became the principal of that school. Working with those kids changed him, and not just back to the kind person he used to be. He wasn't as timid anymore, and I was glad, because somehow he found a way to share his kind heart with others. Once he became principal, he stayed working at the school for years, long past the time he was supposed to retire."

I knew that part of the story. Ken had spoken of his students often.

"It wasn't until his first heart attack a few years ago that the doctor ordered him to retire."

My eyebrows shot up. "I didn't know he had a heart problem," I said. I couldn't believe the heart attack that killed him wasn't even his first. He knew he was sick with a heart condition all along and never said a thing. Part of me stewed with anger at him for keeping it a secret, and the other part knew that he probably didn't even worry about it himself. He always said, "I'll go when it's time to go."

Ruth nodded. "He was healthy as a horse for the longest time, but the accident broke his heart, and it never healed up quite right."

"Did he come to live here because of his health issues?" I asked.

"No, the last thing Ken wanted was a doctor telling him what to do. But after he retired, he couldn't stand the thought of spending the rest of his days in his home without a job to go to. He said the memories in the house began to suffocate him. He didn't get out much, with little else to do except reading and fishing. Years since his wife and daughter died, he still lived in that house, all their belongings untouched. He even moved into the spare room of his house, refusing to sleep in the same room that he had shared with his wife. It was long past time he cleared that place out. Finally, Ken agreed. So, he sold the house. I helped him pack it up, and he donated everything he could. That was a dreadful time for him. The things he absolutely couldn't part with he brought here." She glanced around the apartment. "That's why this place is packed to the brim with knickknacks and furniture. That armoire was inherited from Meredith's grandmother." Ruth pointed to the tall mahogany cabinet that housed all Ken's board games and the overflow of his books.

I imagined he had saved the worn board games inside as well. Maybe he had played on that same checkerboard with his daughter.

"Once he moved here, I didn't worry about him as much. Then I moved to England with my husband. We bought a place on the water where we always wanted to retire." She gave a rueful smile. "And now here we are."

I was too shocked by the story to respond.

Ruth filled the silence. "Well, anyway, I better get back to packing. But thank you for indulging an old woman in her ramblings."

I blinked, returning from my spinning thoughts. "No, it was my pleasure. I'm really glad I met you." I meant every word more than Ruth could know.

I stood up when Ruth said, "Wait. Let me give you my number." She dug in her purse for a piece of paper and pen. She scribbled on it and handed it over. "Call anytime."

I thanked her as we headed to the door, but my gaze lingered on the yellow hoodie that rested on the sofa.

Ruth picked it up and handed it to me. "Here, keep it."

"No, I couldn't," I said.

"I insist. He has an entire closet full of them, anyway."

I knew it.

"He said wearing yellow makes you happy. Though he probably made that up." Ruth chuckled. "It worked well enough for him."

I took the hoodie and held it to my chest.

"I wanted to thank you, for being his friend. I can tell you cared about him a lot." She paused. "You know, you remind me a lot of her, of Mae."

I smiled and blinked back more tears. I didn't know what to say. Maybe there was nothing else to say.

We hugged, and I looked back at his apartment one last time before leaving.

• • •

I walked through the halls in a daze. A few people in uniform passed me, giving me sideways glances as I wandered, clutching the yellow hoodie, lost in thought. Remembering where I was, I hurried to the side exit to avoid being seen by my residents, coworkers, or worse—Mrs. Hubert. Halfway down the path, I stopped short. The sight of two twin lakes reflected the grayness of the morning. My feet carried me in that direction. Deviating from the cobblestone path, I marched through the grass, which crunched under my feet with morning frost. I was pulled to the lake like a magnet. If only I could see it again in the glory of summer, sparkling and surrounded by the vibrant blooms. Not like this, patched with ice and still—too still.

The aching in my heart grew as I approached the towering willow tree and the bench where Ken and I had eaten countless lunches. It seemed absurd that our meeting place could still exist without him. In my memories, he was just as much a part of the scenery as the unmovable willow tree rooted into the ground.

I wanted to capture every detail, memorize every knot of the willow tree's trunk, observe every bird that landed on its branches, and every shadow it cast over the bench. The wind picked up, and I marveled as the tree stood tall, its long tendrils swinging in the breeze that whipped my hair and stung my eyes. The strong wood bent and swayed, but I felt the wind may snap me in half.

I thought about staying for a moment to sit on the bench. My breaking heart screamed not to, but something kept me there. Something in the breeze, in the lake, in the trees whispered to me, "Sit. Look down in the water, look at what stares back." My reflection showed tears streaming down my cheeks, my eyes soft and sparkling. My shoulders slumped and my hair tangled in places. This was not the same girl who arrived at the Center nearly a year ago, wearing a façade. My cool exterior was nowhere to be found, burned up by the grief I felt inside; it transformed me into someone else. Something inside me had been growing under the surface ever since Ken and I first spoke in the music hall. The wind sang a soothing melody as I hummed along with the tune, remembering how Ken had danced in the music hall that day without a care in the world.

How rare and precious it felt to be picked from a crowd. A room filled with people, but he looked over and saw me. A spark of recognition told me not to doubt. "He is like you," it said.

Yet, in some ways, we couldn't have been more different. When I was first assigned to work with Ken, his journey was nearing its end. Mine had just begun. His scars drew a map, showing me the way while I hid mine as they calloused. He set his sails and let the wind take him anywhere. I paddled against the current.

We shared three things in total, with only two in common at one time: A hope, a loss, and a simple breath that kept us alive.

When we met, I lacked the first. He gave it to me, and the ache of what we lost melted away. Neither could take the place of what had been there before, but we learned to live without it together. For a while, we shared a hope and a simple breath. Until Ken was relieved of the latter, and the sting of loss was returned to me.

Now I held all three. Because this time I had hope. He had left it as a gift, wrapped in a kindness that glowed. And I found the loss was something I could bear.

TWENTY-TWO

I returned home a few hours later to an empty house. Mama and Nana were at a doctor's appointment, but they would be home soon. I stood in front of the full-length mirror in my room while wearing the yellow hoodie that Ruth had given me. My hands ended near the elbows and the hem fell near my knees.

I hugged myself in it, thinking about all that time Ken had spent alone. I cried for him and the pain he must have felt. I knew what it was like to feel grief and loneliness. He not only lost his wife, but his daughter as well. In a split second, his life as he knew it was gone. He suffered for years trying to heal, and in the end, he succeeded.

Any doubt I had about how well I really knew him disappeared. He put his life back together because people needed his help. He went through the hard work of going back to school and returning to his job for the students he cared so much about. Was it the guilt that drove him forward at first? Perhaps. Did he try to find a way to even the score for something he blamed himself for? Maybe. But in time, he forgave himself. And from that point on, he no longer lived for himself, but for others.

For years, wherever he went, his pain and suffering went too, and he knew it as well as one knows their own shadow.

So, it made sense that he would recognize it in others and was drawn to help. That's why he befriended me and why he was intent on helping. I always suspected but I never knew.

My frustration simmered beneath guilt. I only found out about his tragic loss from his sister after he was gone. I could have helped him as he helped me, but I would never get a chance to hear from him what happened that day.

The front door opened, and I took off the hoodie, folded it, and placed it in a drawer where my cat couldn't shed all over it. I met Nana and Mama in the living room.

Nana drooped with fatigue, as she did after each doctor's appointment.

"How did it go?" I asked as Mama took off her jacket and hung it in the closet.

"Good, it was all good. They did another scan of her head, and there was no damage from the fall. Dr. Webster said they're going to look at increasing her dosage of medication."

At least it wasn't bad news.

"How about you?" Mama asked. "How did Mrs. Hubert take it? I'm sure she was devastated to lose her best worker."

I blinked, realization washing over me. Ruth's news had put me in such a state of shock, my original reason for going to the Center had completely slipped my mind. "I forgot to quit," I said in a daze.

Mama frowned, concern showing on her face. "What happened? Are you feeling okay? Maybe we should call Leonard."

I knew Mama worried about me since Ken died, so I hurried to explain. "I'm okay. I actually didn't make it to Mrs. Hubert's office. I decided to stop by Ken's room beforehand, just to see it one last time." I shifted on my feet, hoping the spontaneous decision didn't worry Mama further.

Her eyebrows shot up. "Oh, and how did that go?"

"Well, there was someone there, Ken's sister Ruth. She was packing up all his belongings. We talked for a while." I told her what Ruth shared with me. Mama listened, her eyes misting. "Then I came right home."

Ruth had answered the questions I never asked Ken. Questions I never asked him, or anyone else. Not even Mama. I thought distancing myself from the pain would make it better, but it only did the opposite. I never asked how Mama was doing or how she was feeling. Because to ask would be to acknowledge the pain. For a long time, I didn't believe I was strong enough. But if Ken taught me one thing, it was to ask.

"Mama, can I ask you a question?"

"Sure, Em. What is it?" Mama replied.

"How are you doing?"

She half smiled. "I should be asking you that."

"Really, I want to know."

She paused, contemplating the question, before looking at me with a firm gaze. "I am doing much better."

"How—how did you do it?"

Mama frowned. "Do what?"

I shifted on my feet, trying to find the words. "How did you move forward, you know, after Grace? You weren't well for a long time and suddenly you're getting better. How did you do it?"

"Well," she paused, searching for the answer, "besides our support group, I think what helped me was the letter we received in the mail. Reading that brought me hope."

"What letter? I asked.

"The letter on the blue paper that I have saved in Grace's file."

"Her death certificate?" I asked. I remembered when Mama began carrying it around. She looked at it all the time while weeping over the file Detective Sanders had given her.

Mama frowned and shook her head. "No, that's not her death certificate. That's a letter from one of Grace's organ recipients."

"What? I had no idea." I hadn't wanted to face Grace's death, so I never asked to see the blue paper, which I had assumed was her death certificate.

"I thought it would be upsetting to you if I showed you," she said.

I turned away, absorbing Mama's words.

She took a step toward me. "At first, it was really difficult for me to read. It wasn't until recently that it started to bring me comfort. I just didn't want to cause you any more pain by showing you. But I realize now it wasn't right to keep that hidden. I didn't know what to say or how to deal with Grace's death." All this time I thought Mama wept over a declaration of her death when really, she cried seeing the continued gifts of Grace's life.

I took her hand in mine. "It's okay, Mama. Can I see it?"

Mama disappeared into her room and came back with the letter a few minutes later. Together, we sat on the couch and read.

The blue paper was wrinkled and worn with use. The front was printed with an official letterhead. *Thank you for choosing organ donation.* I winced. My mind whirred like the helicopter blades that waited to take Grace away to the transplant hospital. The memory was enough to change my mind about reading the letter, and I shoved it back in Mama's hand.

Mama handed it back. "Trust me," she said.

After a moment's hesitation, I opened the letter and read.

I don't know where to begin or what to say. Thank you does not seem enough. I am sorry for your loss, and I wanted to let you know that because of you and your loved one's gift I am alive today. I was born with a birth defect, and I have been in and out of hospitals my whole life. My kidneys failed, and I was set to start dialysis when I received a call. They found a match for a kidney. My family and I were very grateful. They worried a lot when I felt sick. I read a saying through the organ transplant website that the worst day of one family's life is the best day of someone else's. Since the transplant, I have been recovering and I now have a chance at a normal life. I struggle at times knowing I have a chance at a normal life but your loved one has passed. If it's not asking too much of you, my family and I would love to know how your family is coping with your loss. I hope this letter brings your family some comfort and peace.

Sincerely,
Erin

The handwritten words looped and sloped as if penned by a younger person, though the message was carefully constructed. Erin seemed hopeful but had likely spent most of her years in fear of death. Erin lived, as she phrased it, because of Grace's gift. I wished to view it as Erin did. Something was not taken from Grace—it was given. Grace gave Erin one of her kidneys, which was a tremendous gift to bestow. But I received something better. I would always have Grace's love.

...

I brought some of Erin's courage with me as I attended Ken's funeral a few days later. People filled the pews. There must have been more than a hundred people there. Ruth and her husband greeted me and Mama with warm hugs. Ruth sat at the front with a small group of others who must have been Ken's relatives.

One man, in particular, stood out. A nurse followed behind him, guiding his wheelchair to the front row and fiddling with oxygen tubes that led from a tank to his nose. Spots and deep wrinkles covered his skin, and his left eye wandered, giving him an absent-minded look as if only his body was present. I overheard Ruth welcoming him. That man turned out to be Mr. Leary, who must have been in his upper nineties. I couldn't believe that Mr. Leary sat in front of me, putting a face to the man from Ken and Ruth's stories.

The ceremony began with a procession of songs, readings, and a tearful introduction from Ruth. Some of Ken's friends and family members spoke as well. One speech included a group of twelve middle-aged individuals who approached the stage. They were his past students from the first class he taught after returning as a teacher and principal. As one after the other spoke, I realized I was just one of many whose lives had changed after knowing Ken. Although the seats were filled with people who knew him, our friendship remained special in my heart. I realized he touched many lives but cared for each one of us personally, individually, and unconditionally.

The ceremony was short but poignant. Not an eye was dry by the end. We were led out by a procession of bagpipes that wailed and quivered a sorrowful tune. Groups gathered outside, and Ken's students consoled one another as they wiped away tears. Some were sad, others regretful, as they spoke in broken voices about how they wished they had come back to see him before. I also wished I could have been there at the very end to thank him for all he did for me. I prayed my thoughts could somehow reach him as I left for home with a heavy heart.

TWENTY-THREE

After a few somber days, Mama and I decided to have a movie night together. The movies ended around midnight, but we stayed up much later talking about everything we had avoided for months. Exhausted, I fell asleep on the couch.

Tired and achy the next morning, I stretched to smooth out the kinks in my neck. It was almost ten o'clock. I headed over to the kitchen for a late breakfast.

Mama stood in front of the stove. "Look who finally woke up." she yawned. "You're not allowed to keep me up that late ever again."

"I recall the second movie being your idea," I replied.

"Yeah, maybe you're right." She poured tea for us and went to sit at the table. "So, I have some news."

My eyes widened. "What's wrong?"

"You know that job that I interviewed for while you stayed with Nana in the hospital?"

I edged forward in my chair. "Yes, of course."

"I got it."

I jumped up. "You're kidding."

"They called this morning. I start next week."

I leaped into Mama's arms and squeezed her tightly. A few happy tears escaped, then I broke our embrace. My eyes widened. "I knew it. That blazer *was* lucky." I could hardly wipe the smile off my face as we made celebratory cupcakes.

After an hour, the oven dinged and we sat at the table, testing the cupcakes to see if they had cooled enough to ice.

"So, getting that job changes a lot," Mama said. "What do you think you're going to do next?"

I needed to decide about my job at the Center. I had chosen to be honest with Mrs. Hubert about why I called in sick. Mrs. Hubert understood completely and offered me some time off from work. I took the time to think over my options with a level head instead of rushing into a decision. It would be difficult to go back to school with my family not yet out of the woods financially, but it was something I had wanted for so long, and Ken reminded me not to give up. There was a lot to consider. But I felt, whatever I decided, everything would be okay. I didn't know which way to go. But as Ken said, any step forward would be the right direction. For the time being, there was only one step I felt I must take.

I grabbed the blue letter that lay on the kitchen ledge. "I'm going to write back. That's what I will do next."

• • •

A blue letter sat on my desk, next to pages of written words. They rested side by side. One held a question, the other, an answer. I filled the blank white pages until my hand cramped and my heart ached. The words burst forth like a flood until it slowed to a drip. Finally, I reached the end.

So you see, Erin, that is how I came to write back to you. Once my mom and I talked openly with one another, she showed me your letter. When I first found out, I wished I had read it the day it arrived, but now I am glad I did not. I would not have been able to answer your question. You asked how we dealt with Grace's death, and I hope our story has given you some answers. But in order to answer you fully, I would spend my entire life writing this letter. It's been a year since she passed away, and I think it is fitting to send this to you on the anniversary of Grace's passing. My mom and I still miss her every day. But it brings us comfort knowing she lives on in the gift she has given you and in all our hearts.

Sincerely,
Grace's family.

I wrote the letter five times over before concluding it would never be perfect. I took it to the post office, sending with it the hope that my letter would bring Erin comfort. I had been doing that a lot lately, hoping for things. Hoping for the future, for happiness, for the chance to help others, as Ken did for me.

I headed back home. The cold froze my fingers, but my heart felt warm and full, and I realized what Ken had tried to tell me all along.

Hope is a prayer, spoken through kindness. It does not grant wishes. It does not even promise tomorrow. It only vows to take the pain of yesterday. So all that's left behind is love.

EPILOGUE

Five years passed since I wrote that letter to Erin. We exchanged many letters since. Because of Grace's gift, Erin went back to school with her friends and graduated college around the same time I graduated with a master's in social work.

After Mama settled into her new job, I returned to school and my path became clear: I wanted to help others as Ken had helped me. Mama's job allowed her to earn an associate's in business management, and she put it to good use. We started our own practice in grief counseling last year. I did as I had promised to Ken all those years ago: I applied the lesson.

Nana's condition worsened. But Mama and I expected that. We grieved her slowly, over the course of many years, as she slipped through our fingers. A time came when our care wasn't enough for her, and we moved her into a full-time facility. We visited often, and she spent many years in a state of quiet contentment. After four years she passed away, surrounded by those who loved her. I liked to imagine that she's with Gramps, Grace, and Ken, relieved from the burden of her illness.

The loss hit me just as hard as the ones before it. Healing the pain of the past didn't make future losses hurt any less. I found happiness in my memories of Grace and Ken, and one day the memories of Nana would join them, in that corner of my heart where melancholy melts back into love.

But it would take time. As Ken said, endings such as this are not happy.

Happiness begins when you choose to start again.

Dear Erin,

It took me a long time to write these words, and this may not be easy to read. I understand the ache in your heart more than you know, and I hope this story brings you comfort. I have asked all the same questions that burden you; maybe this will give you some answers. Most of all, I want you to know that you are not alone in your grief. The journey forward was a long one for all of us. Mine started at a cemetery in the woods one year ago on a blustery day, not unlike the one during which I currently write. I only ask that you read with an open heart and remember the strength that I know already exists within you.

On December twelfth, I became an only child.

That was the moment my life became ruled by necessity. What they don't tell you is that grief is overwhelming in the way it strips everything bare. Silence becomes noise, noise becomes silence, routines become survival. First you forget breakfast, then you forget to sleep, soon you find yourself doing these things only when you collapse from exhaustion or shrink a clothing size. For a while, that was my every day. Stuck in the middle of an endless push and pull. I yearned for my old life, lulled by the memory of Grace's flaming red hair and smiling face, while the same memories prompted me to run as far from home as I could. But no matter how far you try to run, the truth catches up. Denial doesn't last forever. The sooner you turn and face the truth, the sooner you can accept it. I knew the clock ticked on my avoidance. With every reminder, like Mama shedding tears over that blue paper, family pictures hanging in their faded frames, and flashing ambulances racing down the street, reality chipped away at my wall of thin ice. Simmering just beneath the surface, a swirl of emotions threatened to erupt. I pushed them away, fearing they would sweep me under the current and I would drown in them. But I already floated beneath the water—and called it air.

Because she didn't say goodbye, and neither could I.

For a long time, I felt fragile, like I would blow away with the slightest breeze, and no one would notice. I didn't want anyone to notice. I wanted to hide and let myself retreat inward, away from the threatening world. Life became frightening as I discovered it does not abide by justice, logic, or the comforts of fairness. Our relationship wasn't perfect, and we never said goodbye. I had so much left to say to her, and now I never could. Maybe there was no one to blame for that. I had to stop looking for her death to make sense, because it never would.

A friend once told me fairness does not apply to matters as important as life and death. And he was right. All I can do is learn from my regrets. I took that lesson with me as my relationships began to change. However, the problem with letting people in and enjoying life is the fear of losing it all. I clung to my grandma, who slowly began to slip away. I wanted to spend every possible moment with her because we didn't know how much time she had left. Everything changed around me while I stood still, recovering from our devastating loss. I grieved more than I realized. More than just Grace, I lost holiday traditions, financial stability, and the future I envisioned. But I couldn't stop my life from changing or prevent loss from happening. Though I certainly tried. I found a job, took another semester off from school, and did anything to protect my predetermined path. But plans do not coincide with loss. For a while, I had a difficult time adjusting because I relied only on myself. I was taught to keep my misfortune a secret, like it was somehow shameful to ask for help. People think they need to suffer alone and figure out everything by themselves. Or maybe that was just me—and Mama. It took me a long time to let go of the shame that I was not strong enough to face it by myself, but you can't heal until you do. Loss isn't meant to be carried alone. No one objects that love is meant to be shared, you don't keep it to yourself. Loss is the other side of that coin, and so it, too, must be shared. All you can hope for is someone kind enough to share the burden with you. Maybe you find that person in a friend, or through counseling. But what matters is that you try. The decision to live your life again starts with the willingness to learn how to grieve. It's a skill to be practiced like anything else. You can't stop loss from happening or live isolated from the world in fear of the next tragedy, but you can learn how to deal with them.

Looking back, you see these interruptions are not a diversion from your life—they are your life. If I had not taken the time to experience my diversions, I would have missed out on meeting a dear friend of mine. He shared my burden and taught me how to accept help. It started with Mama and me. We stopped avoiding one another and took our first step helping each other through our shared grief. For once, we were honest.

Finally, we stopped pretending everything was fine when we both knew it was not.

So you see, Erin, that is how I came to write back to you. Once my mom and I talked openly with one another, she showed me your letter. When I first found out, I wished I had read it the day it arrived, but now I am glad I did not. I would not have been able to answer your question. You asked how we dealt with Grace's death, and I hope our story has given you some answers. But in order to answer you fully, I would spend my entire life writing this letter. It's been a year since she passed away, and I think it is fitting to send this to you on the anniversary of Grace's passing. My mom and I still miss her every day. But it brings us comfort knowing she lives on in the gift she has given you and in all our hearts.

Sincerely,
Grace's family.